Teach Yourself VISUALLY

Raspberry Pi®

Richard Wentk

Visual

A Wiley Brand

D0406716

Teach Yourself VISUALLY™ Raspberry Pi®

Published by
John Wiley & Sons, Inc.
10475 Crosspoint Boulevard
Indianapolis, IN 46256

www.wiley.com

Published simultaneously in Canada

Copyright © 2014 by John Wiley & Sons, Inc., Indianapolis, Indiana

No part of this publication may be reproduced, stored in a retrieval system or transmitted in any form or by any means, electronic, mechanical, photocopying, recording, scanning or otherwise, except as permitted under Sections 107 or 108 of the 1976 United States Copyright Act, without either the prior written permission of the Publisher, or authorization through payment of the appropriate per-copy fee to the Copyright Clearance Center, 222 Rosewood Drive, Danvers, MA 01923, 978-750-8400, fax 978-646-8600. Requests to the Publisher for permission should be addressed to the Permissions Department, John Wiley & Sons, Inc., 111 River Street, Hoboken, NJ 07030, 201-748-6011, fax 201-748-6008, or online at www.wiley.com/go/permissions.

Wiley publishes in a variety of print and electronic formats and by print-on-demand. Some material included with standard print versions of this book may not be included in e-books or in print-on-demand. If this book refers to media such as a CD or DVD that is not included in the version you purchased, you may download this material at http://booksupport.wiley.com. For more information about Wiley products, visit www.wiley.com.

Library of Congress Control Number: 2013954228

ISBN: 978-1-118-76819-8

Manufactured in the United States of America

10 9 8 7 6 5 4 3 2 1

Trademark Acknowledgments

Wiley, Visual, the Visual logo, Teach Yourself VISUALLY, Read Less - Learn More and related trade dress are trademarks or registered trademarks of John Wiley & Sons, Inc. and/or its affiliates. Raspberry Pi is a registered trademark of the Raspberry Pi Foundation in the United Kingdom and other countries. All other trademarks are the property of their respective owners. John Wiley & Sons, Inc. is not associated with any product or vendor mentioned in this book.

LIMIT OF LIABILITY/DISCLAIMER OF WARRANTY: THE PUBLISHER AND THE AUTHOR MAKE NO REPRESENTATIONS OR WARRANTIES WITH RESPECT TO THE ACCURACY OR COMPLETENESS OF THE CONTENTS OF THIS WORK AND SPECIFICALLY DISCLAIM ALL WARRANTIES, INCLUDING WITHOUT LIMITATION WARRANTIES OF FITNESS FOR A PARTICULAR PURPOSE. NO WARRANTY MAY BE CREATED OR EXTENDED BY SALES OR PROMOTIONAL MATERIALS. THE ADVICE AND STRATEGIES CONTAINED HEREIN MAY NOT BE SUITABLE FOR EVERY SITUATION. THIS WORK IS SOLD WITH THE UNDERSTANDING THAT THE PUBLISHER IS NOT ENGAGED IN RENDERING LEGAL, ACCOUNTING, OR OTHER PROFESSIONAL SERVICES. IF PROFESSIONAL ASSISTANCE IS REQUIRED, THE SERVICES OF A COMPETENT PROFESSIONAL PERSON SHOULD BE SOUGHT. NEITHER THE PUBLISHER NOR THE AUTHOR SHALL BE LIABLE FOR DAMAGES ARISING HEREFROM. THE FACT THAT AN ORGANIZATION OR WEBSITE IS REFERRED TO IN THIS WORK AS A CITATION AND/OR A POTENTIAL SOURCE OF FURTHER INFORMATION DOES NOT MEAN THAT THE AUTHOR OR THE PUBLISHER ENDORSES THE INFORMATION THE ORGANIZATION OR WEBSITE MAY PROVIDE OR RECOMMENDATIONS IT MAY MAKE. FURTHER, READERS SHOULD BE AWARE THAT INTERNET WEBSITES LISTED IN THIS WORK MAY HAVE CHANGED OR DISAPPEARED BETWEEN WHEN THIS WORK WAS WRITTEN AND WHEN IT IS READ.

FOR PURPOSES OF ILLUSTRATING THE CONCEPTS AND TECHNIQUES DESCRIBED IN THIS BOOK, THE AUTHOR HAS CREATED VARIOUS NAMES, COMPANY NAMES, MAILING, E-MAIL AND INTERNET ADDRESSES, PHONE AND FAX NUMBERS AND SIMILAR INFORMATION, ALL OF WHICH ARE FICTITIOUS. ANY RESEMBLANCE OF THESE FICTITIOUS NAMES, ADDRESSES, PHONE AND FAX NUMBERS AND SIMILAR INFORMATION TO ANY ACTUAL PERSON, COMPANY AND/OR ORGANIZATION IS UNINTENTIONAL AND PURELY COINCIDENTAL.

Contact Us

For general information on our other products and services please contact our Customer Care Department within the U.S. at 877-762-2974, outside the U.S. at 317-572-3993 or fax 317-572-4002.

For technical support please visit www.wiley.com/techsupport.

Sales | Contact Wiley at (877) 762-2974 or fax (317) 572-4002.

Credits

Acquisitions Editor
Aaron Black

Sr. Project Editor
Sarah Hellert

Technical Editor
Paul Hallett

Copy Editor
Kim Heusel

**Director, Content Development
& Assembly**
Robyn Siesky

**Vice President and Executive
Group Publisher**
Richard Swadley

About the Author

Richard Wentk has been building, working with, and writing about technology since the 1980s. He has had a lot of fun installing Raspberry Pi boards around his home for music storage, remote heating control and efficiency, and security. He is also an app developer and the author of a number of books for developers and Mac users. For the latest news and information, visit his site at www.zettaboom.com.

Author's Acknowledgments

All books are a collaboration, and this one is no exception. I'd like to thank Aaron Black for giving the green light to this project, Paul Hallet for checking code and facts, and Sarah Hellert for making the transition from copy to print as smooth as possible.

Extra special thanks are due to Annette Saunders for cake.

How to Use This Book

Who This Book Is For

This book is for the reader who has never used this particular technology or software application. It is also for readers who want to expand their knowledge.

The Conventions in This Book

❶ Steps

This book uses a step-by-step format to guide you easily through each task. Numbered steps are actions you must do; bulleted steps clarify a point, step, or optional feature; and indented steps give you the result.

❷ Notes

Notes give additional information — special conditions that may occur during an operation, a situation that you want to avoid, or a cross reference to a related area of the book.

❸ Icons and Buttons

Icons and buttons show you exactly what you need to click to perform a step.

❹ Tips

Tips offer additional information, including warnings and shortcuts.

❺ Bold

Bold type shows command names, options, and text or numbers you must type.

❻ Italics

Italic type introduces and defines a new term.

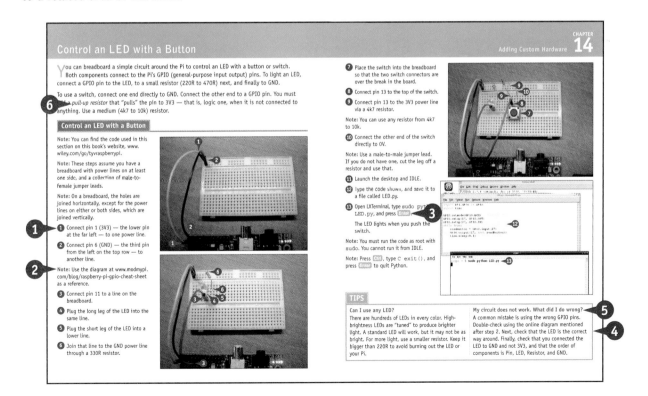

Table of Contents

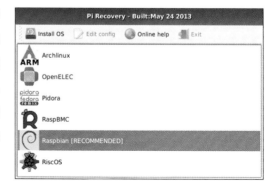

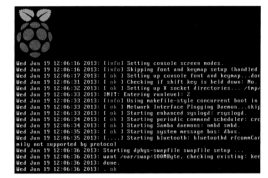

Table of Contents

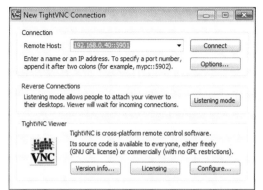

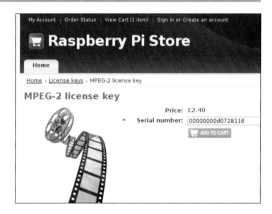

Table of Contents

Chapter 11 — Organizing Information with Python

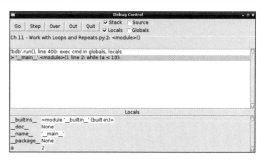

Chapter 12 — Getting Started with Pygame

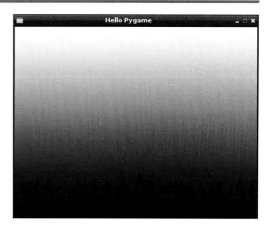

Table of Contents

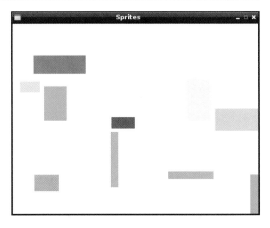

Chapter 14 Adding Custom Hardware

## CHAPTER 1

Getting Started with Raspberry Pi

To set up your Raspberry Pi, you must choose essential extras and connect them to your Pi. You can then power up your Pi for the first time and begin setting it up.

Introducing Raspberry Pi

The Raspberry Pi is a tiny computer designed in the United Kingdom and sold around the world at a very low price. The Pi ships as a bare circuit board with standard connections for a keyboard, mouse, monitor, and power supply. You must add these extras yourself. To keep costs down, the Pi uses an *SD card*, a small memory card, as a hard drive.

The Pi also includes extra connections you can use in your own electronic projects, and two software applications, Python and Scratch, for learning programming.

Compare the Pi and a PC/Mac

The Pi is much less powerful than a PC or Mac. You cannot run Microsoft Office on it. However, you can use it as a small media center and for programming games. You can also create network-based projects such as a web server, file server, or even a home automation system.

Understanding the Linux OS

As of summer 2013, some Pi kits ship with a tool called NOOBS (New Out of the Box Operating System) which gives users a choice of operating systems. This book describes the most popular and best-supported operating system — *Raspbian Wheezy*, a version of the popular free Linux operating system, often represented by a penguin mascot known as Tux. Linux is more challenging and hands-on than Windows and OS X, but is ideal for customization and for building hardware and software projects around the Pi. For information about getting started with NOOBS, see Chapter 2, and return to Chapter 1 after you use NOOBS to install Raspbian.

Compare the A and B Models

You can choose two models of the Pi board. The Model A has half the memory of the Model B (256MB versus 512MB), lacks the B's Ethernet network connector, and has a single USB socket instead of the B's stacked pair. It consumes a third less power. Many users develop a project with a Model B and build the finished version around a Model A.

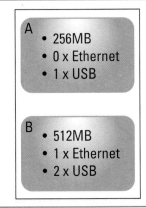

A
- 256MB
- 0 x Ethernet
- 1 x USB

B
- 512MB
- 1 x Ethernet
- 2 x USB

Take a Tour of Raspberry Pi

This tour shows the main connections and components of a Model B board.

A Micro USB Power

Connects your RPi to an external 5V power supply.

B Composite Video Jack

Connects your RPi to an old TV using a legacy composite video signal.

C HDMI Socket

Connects your RPi to a monitor or TV using a modern HDMI signal.

D 3.5mm Audio Jack

Connects your RPi to headphones, ear buds, or external speakers.

E Ethernet Socket

Connects your RPi to a network.

F Dual USB Socket

Two stacked sockets connect the RPi to a keyboard, mouse, or other accessories.

G Status LEDs

Light up to display the RPi's power, network, and disk status.

H GPIO Pins

Pins for general-purpose external connections, including optional add-ons and your own custom electronics.

I Camera Connector

Connects the RPi to an optional camera board.

J Display Connector

Connects the RPi to an optional external LCD display.

K SD Card Socket

The socket for the SD card, shown here in blue, is under the board at the right.

Choose Accessories

You must add a power supply, a keyboard, and a monitor or TV to your Pi. You can also add a mouse, a camera, a case, and Wi-Fi and/or Bluetooth *dongles* — small plastic USB aerials. With accessories, the total price of an RPi system is $50 to $105 (£35 to £80), excluding a monitor. You may be able to use an existing spare USB keyboard and mouse. But not all USB accessories are compatible. Check http://elinux.org/RPi_VerifiedPeripherals for user reports.

Select a Power Supply

Power your system with two 5V power supplies — one for the Pi, and one for an external USB hub. The Pi uses a special micro-USB connector for power, which is typically supplied by a power adapter plugged into a wall socket. A few phone chargers have compatible plugs, but most do not produce enough power. Do not power your Pi from a computer's spare USB socket.

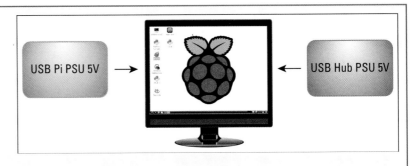

Add a USB Hub

Most accessories, including a keyboard, mouse, and Wi-Fi dongle, can connect directly to the Pi. But accessories sometimes draw so much power the Pi stops working. For reliable results, connect accessories through a USB hub — a box of extra USB sockets. Its power supply should be rated 2A or more.

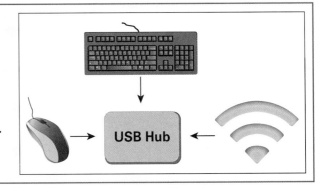

Select a Keyboard and Mouse

Most USB PC mice and keyboards work with the RPi. Wireless makes, such as Logitech, are likely to work. You can use a Bluetooth keyboard and mouse if you add a Bluetooth dongle, but you cannot set up Bluetooth without a working keyboard.

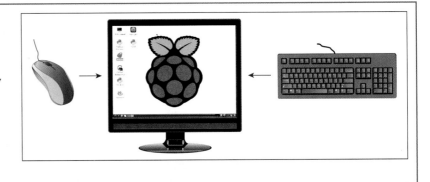

Select a Monitor

Although the RPi can connect to an old TV through its composite video jack, the HDMI (High-Definition Multimedia Interface) connector produces a cleaner and sharper digital signal. For good results, connect the HDMI output to any monitor or TV with an HDMI input. You can also use a monitor with a DVI-D or DVI-I input via an HDMI-DVI adapter cable. Older VGA sockets are not directly compatible.

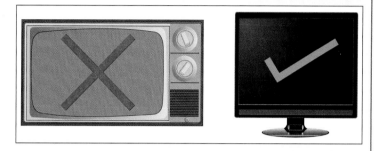

Buy an SD Card

The Pi is designed to work with an *SD card* — a small plastic memory card — instead of a hard drive. The card holds the Pi's operating system (OS) and software. Beginners should buy a card with the OS preinstalled. More experienced users can buy a blank card, which you can choose from the list at http://elinux.org/RPi_VerifiedPeripherals, and install the software using the instructions in Chapter 2.

Buy a Bundle

You can save time and money by buying an accessory bundle for your Pi. In the United States, Newark (www.newark.com) supplies a range of Model A and Model B bundles with prices from $45 to $105. In the United Kingdom, Maplin (www. maplin.co.uk) supplies a Pi with a set of guaranteed extras for £79.99.

Avoid Electronic Project Kits

Some Pi kits are collections of optional electronic components. Select a kit or bundle with the items listed on these pages. Ignore kits with breakout boxes, breadboards, jumper leads, switches, and LEDs. You can add these extras when you have more experience with your Pi.

Choose and Use a Case

You can enclose your Pi in a case to protect it from accidents and improve its looks. A case for your Pi is optional, but recommended. You can choose a case based on design and color, but for electronic projects pick a case with easy access to all connectors, including the GPIO pins. Standard cases are plastic boxes with connector holes. A more sophisticated option is a VESA mount case, with four screws and a plate for mounting your Pi on the back of a TV or monitor with prefitted VESA (Video Electronics Standards Organization) screw holes.

Choose and Use a Case

1 Open a web browser and visit http://elinux.org/RPi_Cases to view more than 50 case options.

2 Review the cases.

You can either build a case by following the linked instructions, or buy one from an online vendor.

Note: If you choose a prebuilt case, the elinux page includes links to vendors. You may have to search again to find vendors for a specific case in your country.

Note: This example uses a budget case with a VESA mount bought from Amazon.

3 Hold your Pi without touching the circuit board.

Note: You can avoid touching the board by holding the USB and Ethernet connectors, or the sides of the board. Do not squeeze too hard.

4 Slot your Pi into the case.

Ⓐ If you do not have a VESA case, position and tighten the rear screws to close the case.

Note: Some cases clip together from a number of plastic layers and do not use screws.

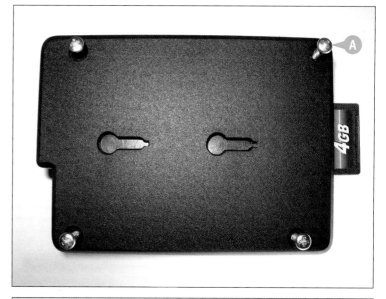

⑤ If you have a VESA case, secure the mounting plate to the rear of the case using the screws.

Note: The screw heads are behind the case in this photo. They fit between the VESA plate and the back of the monitor.

⑥ Position and tighten the four finger nuts to mount the case on the back of a monitor with a VESA mount.

Note: You can also use a VESA case to mount your Pi on a wall or fix it permanently to furniture.

The Pi is now enclosed in a case. If you used a VESA mount case, it is also mounted on the back of a monitor.

TIPS

Do I need a case?
Electronic circuits are very sensitive to static electricity. You can literally destroy your Pi by wearing synthetics or walking on synthetic carpet and touching the circuit board. A box helps protect your Pi from static and from other accidental damage.

What should I look for in a case?
Some cases are decorative, others are more practical. If you plan to use your Pi for electronic projects, look for a case with a slot for the GPIO, or general purpose IO, connector. Cases that support the optional Pi camera or an LCD screen are available but are not as popular or easy to find as plain cases.

Connect a Monitor

Although the Pi includes a composite video connector compatible with an old analog TV, this is a nostalgic option and gives poor output. For best results, use a modern monitor or TV with an HDMI connector. Most 19-inch or larger monitors capable of displaying a 1080p signal are compatible.

You can also use a slightly older monitor with a digital DVI connector if you use an optional cheap converter or special cable. Both are easy to find on Amazon or eBay by searching for "HDMI to DVI." Note that cheap converter cables are usually identical to much more expensive ones.

Connect a Monitor

1 If you are using an HDMI to HDMI cable, plug one end into the HDMI socket on the Pi.

2 Plug the other end into the HDMI socket on the rear of your monitor or TV.

Note: When you apply power to the Pi you may need to use the OSD, or on-screen display, on the monitor to select the HDMI input. See your monitor's manual for details.

3 If you are using an HDMI-to-DVI cable, plug the HDMI connector into the HDMI socket on your Pi.

4 Plug the DVI connector into the DVI socket on the rear of your monitor.

5 Tighten the thumb screws to secure the connection.

Your Pi is connected to a monitor, but is not yet powered up.

Note: When you apply power to the Pi you may need to use the OSD, or on-screen display, on the monitor to select the DVI input. See your monitor's manual for details.

TIPS

Can I use a monitor or projector with a VGA socket?
HDMI is not compatible with VGA. You must convert HDMI into VGA by passing it through an adapter box, which can cost from $50 to $200 (£30 to £150), depending on quality. Use HDMI or DVI if you can. The image quality is better, and the cost is much lower.

Can I use the composite video output to connect a monitor or projector?
Composite video has even lower quality than VGA. Use it as a last resort. You may need to experiment with the Overscan setting on the Setup Options screen to avoid black bars or missing lines on a projector or TV.

Connect USB Accessories

You can connect USB accessories in two ways. On a Model B, you can plug a keyboard and mouse into the two main USB connectors. This uses both free USB sockets, so you cannot connect other items. It may also make your Pi less reliable.

For better results, connect all accessories to a USB hub with an independent power supply, and then connect the hub to the main USB socket on your Pi. You can do this with both A and B models. Note that the micro-USB socket on the Pi is for power only; you cannot connect a hub to it.

Connect USB Accessories

1 Plug the hub's power adapter into a wall socket (mains socket).

Note: You may want to use a power strip with an optional surge protector for reliability.

Note: Do not connect the power from the adaptor to the hub yet.

2 Connect the keyboard to your hub.

3 Connect the mouse to your hub.

4 Plug the Wi-Fi dongle into the hub, if you have one.

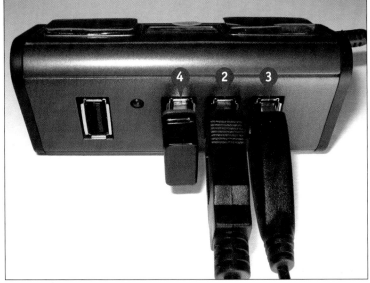

5 Connect the hub to the USB
socket on the Pi.

Note: Hubs typically have a cable
that ends in a flat, or A type,
USB connector. Plug this into the
Pi's USB socket.

6 Connect the hub to its power
supply to turn it on.

Note: The power connector and
socket on your hub may look
different.

The USB hub is powered up,
but the Pi is not yet running.

TIP

Can I use two hubs at the same time?
Yes. If you have an unusually complicated collection of accessories, you can use two different hubs, as long
as both have separate 2 amp power supplies. Plug each hub into a separate USB socket on the Pi. Note that
this is only possible on a Model B. Alternatively, you can buy hubs with eight or even more sockets, but two
separate hubs are more likely to work reliably and provide enough power.

Connect Power and Boot

The Pi does not have a power switch. You can power it up by turning on the power to its power supply and plugging the micro-USB cable into the corresponding socket on the Pi.

The Pi *boots*, or sets itself up so it is ready to work, within 30 seconds. It displays a stream of text on the screen as it works through its *boot sequence*, which is a list of steps it works through as it gets ready.

Connect Power and Boot

1 Plug the Pi's USB power supply into the wall socket (mains socket) or a power strip if you are using one.

Note: Some supplies include a built-in light to show that power is on.

2 Plug the other end of the power cable into the micro-USB socket on the Pi.

Note: The socket is tiny and slightly stiff. Insert the plug carefully, without forcing it.

Note: The Pi does not have a power switch. The micro-USB connector can be fragile. For extra reliability, choose a power supply with an A-type USB socket. You can then use a micro-USB to A-type cable to plug and unplug power at the socket, or via an optional A to A extender.

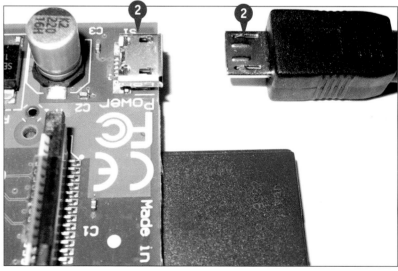

Ⓐ The Pi's power LED lights. The other LEDs may flash.

Note: For more information about the LEDs, open a web browser and visit www.raspberrypi.org/phpBB3/viewtopic.php?f=24&t=6952.

Ⓑ If you connected a monitor, it shows the Pi's *boot sequence*, a long list of messages displayed by the Pi as it launches its operating system.

TIPS

How do I know when boot has finished?
The first time you boot your Pi, it displays a configuration and setup screen. Thereafter, the Pi displays a *login prompt* that asks you to sign in with your username and password. When you log in correctly, it displays a *system prompt* — the computer name of the Pi, your username, a tilde (~), and a dollar sign ($). The system prompt shows your Pi is ready to respond to keyboard commands.

Can I unplug the power to power off?
Unplugging the power without shutting down can corrupt the data on the memory card, and your Pi may not boot again. Instead, follow the power down steps in Chapter 3.

## CHAPTER 2

Selecting an Operating System

Unlike a PC or a Mac, a Raspberry Pi can run many operating systems. The recommended OS, described in the rest of this book, is called Raspbian Wheezy. You can experiment with other OS options by installing them on an SD card.

Understanding OS Options

Before you can use your Pi, you must install an operating system, or OS, on an SD card. If you are assembling your own Pi system, you can use a free software application called NOOBS, or New Out of Box Software, to select an OS from a list and install it on a card. Older Pi kits included SD cards with Raspbian Wheezy preinstalled. Newer kits include cards with NOOBS preinstalled; you must use NOOBS to set up Raspbian Wheezy before you can use your Pi.

Understanding NOOBS

Because many users could not understand how to install an OS on a blank SD card, the creators of the Pi produced NOOBS to make the process simpler. NOOBS works in four steps. First, prepare an SD card. Next, download NOOBS, unzip it, and copy the files it holds to your card. Plug the card into your Pi, and apply power to start the Pi running, which is called *booting* the Pi. When NOOBS launches, select an operating system from a list built in to NOOBS and install it on the card. Finally, NOOBS restarts, or *reboots*, your Pi automatically, and the Pi launches the OS you installed on the card. You can then begin working with your operating system.

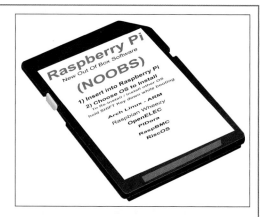

Understanding Linux Choices

You cannot install Windows or OS X on your Pi. Instead, the Pi works well with an alternative OS called Linux, which is free, highly customizable, and available in a number of different *distros*, or distributions. NOOBS includes three general Linux distros designed to work with your Pi called Raspbian Wheezy, Archilinux, and Pidora. This book is about Raspbian Wheezy. Archilinux and Pidora are more experimental and not recommended for beginners.

Understanding Media Center Choices

Most Linux distros are for general computing. But some are more specialized and designed to do one job well. A distro called XBMC turns any compatible computer into a media center and includes software for playing, downloading, streaming, and managing video and audio files. NOOBS includes two versions of XBMC created for the Pi — RaspBMC and OpenELEC. Either can turn your Pi into a powerful media player. XBMC is not covered in this book. You can find out more at http://xbmc.org/about.

Understanding Other OS Choices

As of summer 2013, NOOBS includes one OS that is not based on Linux. RiscOS is an
British desktop operating system developed during the late 80s and early 90s, and supports an optional
package of productivity software called NutPi, which sells for $50 (£35). RiscOS is not covered in this book.
You can find out more at www.riscosopen.org/content.

Understanding the Recovery Option

Because the Pi is designed for education, you can experiment freely with applications and settings. Some
mistakes can trash an operating system and stop it working. NOOBS includes a *recovery option* to rescue you
if you ever need to start from scratch: Boot while holding down **Shift** to relaunch NOOBS, wipe your SD
card, and reinstall an OS. Note this option wipes all the data and settings on the card.

Understanding Card Swapping

In theory you can use NOOBS to create a
collection of SD cards with different operating
systems. When you want to transform your Pi
into a different computer, you can power it
down, remove one SD card, plug in another,
and apply power again to reboot. In practice,
the Pi's SD card connector is not robust enough
for regular swapping, and it can become
unreliable after a few tens of swaps. You can

experiment with different OS options on different cards to a limited extent, but enthusiastic card swapping
is not recommended.

Understanding BerryBoot

BerryBoot is an alternative to NOOBS for more experienced
users. With BerryBoot you can install multiple operating
systems on a single card. You can pick a different OS
whenever you reboot, which makes your Pi more useful
and avoids physical card swapping. You can also use
BerryBoot to install operating systems on more robust
media, such as hard drives and USB flash drives. When you
gain more experience with Linux, you can customize the
list of operating systems available with BerryBoot.

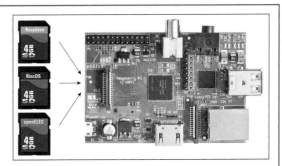

...an prepare an SD card for use with NOOBS by downloading and running a free application from ...he website of the SD Association. Different versions of the application are available for Macs and ...s, but they do the same job and are set up in a similar way.

Technically, you prepare a card by *formatting* it. This takes a few minutes and erases all the information on the card. You can format and reuse the same card more than once, but if you repeat the process many tens of times the card may become unreliable.

Prepare an SD Card

On a Mac

1 Connect a card reader and insert an SD card.

2 Open a web browser and visit www.sdcard.org/downloads/formatter_4/eula_mac.

Note: If you cannot find version 4 of the formatter, check www.sdcard.org/downloads to find the most recent version.

3 Click **I Accept**.

Your browser downloads the file.

4 Navigate to the PKG file in Finder, double-click it, and follow the steps to install the application.

5 Open your Applications folder and double-click **SDFormatter.app**.

6 If you have more than one card or USB stick connected, click the **Select Card** menu and select your SD card.

7 Click **Option**.

8 In the Logical Address Adjustment dialog, click **Yes** (○ changes to ◉)

9 Click **OK** to confirm.

10 Click **Format**.

The tool takes a few seconds to format the card.

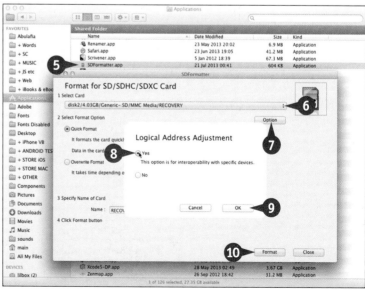

On a PC

1 Connect a card reader and insert an SD card.

2 Open a web browser and visit www.sdcard.org/downloads/formatter_4/eula_windows.

Note: If you cannot find version 4 of the formatter, check www.sdcard.org/downloads to find the most recent version.

3 Click **I Accept**.

Your browser downloads the file.

4 Navigate to the file, right-click it, and select **Extract All** to unzip it to a folder.

5 Open the folder, double-click **setup.exe**, and follow the steps to install the application.

6 Navigate to the SDA folder in Program Files and double-click **SDFormatter.exe**.

7 If you have more than one card or USB stick connected, click **Drive** and select the letter corresponding to your SD card.

8 Click **Option**.

9 Select **ON**.

10 Click **OK** to confirm.

11 Click **Format**.

The tool takes a few seconds to format the card.

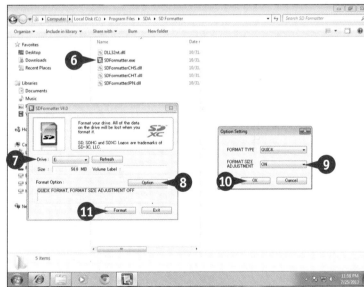

TIPS

Does the speed of the card matter?
SD cards come in four speeds, labeled 2, 4, 6, 10 and UHS (Ultra High Speed). Faster cards are more expensive and can be less reliable. All cards should work with the Pi, but the 6-speed is a good trade-off between cost, speed, and reliability. Because of hardware limitations, the Pi's card slot cannot make full use of faster speeds. Some users suggest always using 10-speed cards, but it is not clear if this genuinely improves reliability.

Do I have to give the card a name?
No. Leave the name field unchanged when you use the formatting application. NOOBS does not need a named card.

Copy NOOBS to an SD card

You can download NOOBS for free from the Raspberry Pi support site. Unzip it to reveal a collection of files. To install NOOBS on a card, use Windows Explorer or Finder to copy all files to the card.

Finder on the Mac and some unzip tools on a PC create a new folder when you unzip NOOBS. Do not copy the folder to your card. Copy the files in the folder.

Copy NOOBS to an SD Card

1 Follow the instructions in the previous section to prepare an SD card; leave it plugged in to your computer.

2 Open a web browser and visit http://downloads.raspberrypi.org/noobs.

Note: If you see a File Not Found message, repeat step **2**.

NOOBS should begin to download automatically.

Ⓐ If nothing happens, right-click **Direct Link** and select **Save link as**, **Download Linked File**.

3 On a Mac, open Finder.

Note: In Windows, skip to step **6**.

4 Navigate to the download location and find the NOOBS Zip file.

Note: The usual location is the Downloads folder. If you have customized your browser to save to a different folder, look there instead.

Note: The name of the NOOBS file includes the version number, for example, NOOBS_v1_2_1.zip.

5 Double-click the file to unzip it.

Ⓑ Finder unzips the contents of the file to a new folder.

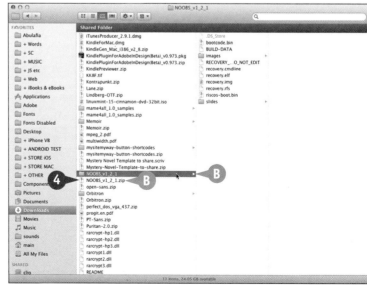

22

Note: On a Mac, skip steps **6** to **8**.

6 On a PC, open Windows Explorer and navigate to your Downloads folder.

7 Right-click the NOOBS file and select **Extract All**.

Ⓒ You can change the destination folder.

8 Click **Extract**.

9 Open a new window in either Finder or Windows Explorer.

Note: This example shows Finder on a Mac.

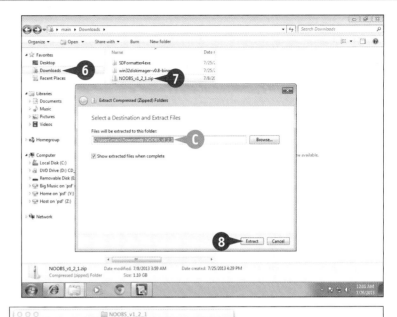

10 Navigate to the SD card.

Note: If you did not set a name for the card, the name appears as NO NAME.

11 Select all the files in the unzipped NOOBS folder and drag them to the empty SD card.

Note: Copy the files in the folder. Do not select and copy the folder itself.

12 Eject the card.

Note: On a Mac, click the eject triangle next to NO NAME in Finder. On a PC, open Computer or My Computer in Windows Explorer, right-click the drive, and select **Eject**.

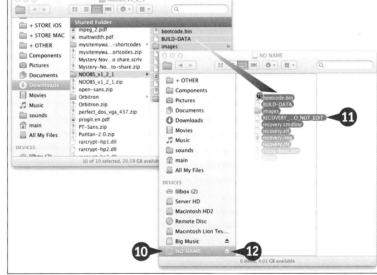

TIPS

Is there any difference between copying NOOBS on a PC or Mac?
There is no practical difference. Finder on the Mac creates a hidden file on the card, but NOOBS ignores this file.

What do I do if I have a card with Raspbian Wheezy preinstalled?
Ignore the instructions in this chapter. Simply plug the card in to your Pi and apply power. When Raspbian boots, see Chapter 3 to begin configuring it. Optionally, you can install NOOBS on a different card to experiment with the other OS choices. This book describes Raspbian only.

Select and Install Raspbian Wheezy

You can use NOOBS to select and install an OS on an SD card. NOOBS runs the first time you power up your Pi after preparing an SD card on your Mac or PC and inserting it into the Pi's card slot. In NOOBS, you can select an OS and install it on the card.

NOOBS does not run again unless you force it to. When you reboot, your Pi launches the OS you picked. But if you hold down $\boxed{\text{Shift}}$ on your keyboard while rebooting, NOOBS displays its recovery option. You can use this option to wipe the contents of your card and install another OS.

Select and Install Raspbian Wheezy

Note: NOOBS requires a USB hub, a mouse, and a power supply. Work through Chapter 1 if you have not yet bought these items and connected your Pi to them.

1 Plug the card you created in the previous sections in this chapter in to your Pi.

Note: The card slot is under the Pi. Plug the card in the slot so the label is visible from the bottom, as in the photo.

2 Connect your Pi to the power supply you selected in Chapter 1.

NOOBS launches automatically.

Note: You can select a different language in the menu at the bottom of the screen. The default British English option is also suitable for users in the United States.

A Raspbian is preselected.

3 Click **Install OS**.

Note: To install a different OS, select one of the other OS options before clicking Install OS.

4 When the alert box appears, click **Yes** to confirm.

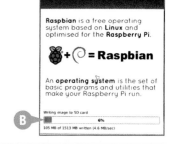

Raspbian is a free operating system based on **Linux** and optimised for the **Raspberry Pi**.

🍓 + ⌬ = Raspbian

An **operating system** is the set of basic programs and utilities that make your Raspberry Pi run.

ⓑ NOOBS begins copying Raspbian to the SD card.

Note: NOOBS displays a progress bar and various notes about Raspbian as it works.

When NOOBS finishes it reboots your Pi automatically. Initially, your Pi displays many lines of scrolling text. After a minute or so it displays the Raspbian configuration options. To use these options to configure your Pi, see Chapter 3.

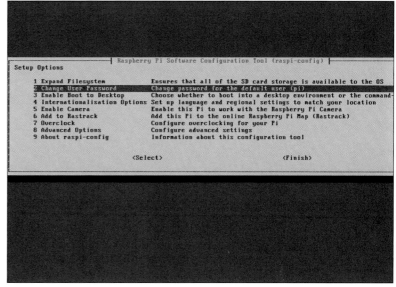

TIPS

What happens if I install a different OS?
Every OS launches in a different way. The many lines of scrolling text are common to Linux, but each distro displays different information as it boots. If you do not install Raspbian, you will not see the configuration options described in the Chapter 3.

Can I unplug the Pi to power it down?
No! You should always shut down your Pi first before unplugging the power. If you do not, the information on the SD card can become corrupted. See Chapter 3 for detailed instructions on shutting down the Pi.

Back Up an SD Card

Y ou can use a Mac or PC to back up the contents of an SD card. Backing up a card saves configuration options, installed applications, and other files. You can make multiple backups as you work. The backup process works with every Pi OS, including Raspbian Wheezy.

Note you cannot simply copy the files from a card to back it up. On a Mac, use the Disk Utility application. On a PC, use a free application called win32DiskImager.

Back Up an SD Card

Shut Down the Pi

1 Shut down your Pi using the instructions Chapter 3.

Note: Do not simply unplug the power lead.

On a Mac

1 Unplug the SD card from the Pi and insert it into a card reader connected to your Mac.

2 Navigate to the Utilities folder in Applications and double-click the **Disk Utility** application.

3 Click the card device to select it.

Note: Do not select the headings under the device. The correct item includes the words Generic and SD.

4 Click **New Image**.

A You can optionally change the filename and location of the backup in the Save As field.

5 Click **Save**.

The utility creates a DMG file that holds the contents of the card, and adds the file to the list of disk images in the area at the left.

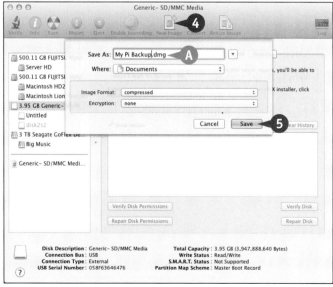

On a PC

1. Open a web browser and visit http://sourceforge.net/projects/win32diskimager. Click **Download**.

2. Double-click **Win32DiskImager-v0.8-binary.zip** and extract it to a folder.

Note: The version number may be greater than 0.8.

3. In Windows Explorer, create a file with an IMG extension, for example, by right-clicking, selecting **New** and then **Text Document**, and renaming the file extension to .img.

Note: Version 0.8 of Win32DiskImage has a bug. You must create an IMG file manually in Windows Explorer before Win32DiskImager allows you to write a backup file.

4. Double-click **Win32DiskImager.exe** to launch it.

5. Click the folder icon (📁).

6. Navigate to the file you created in step **1** and click it.

7. Click **Open**.

8. Click **Read**.

Win32DiskImager copies the contents of your card to an IMG file. This can take up to 20 minutes.

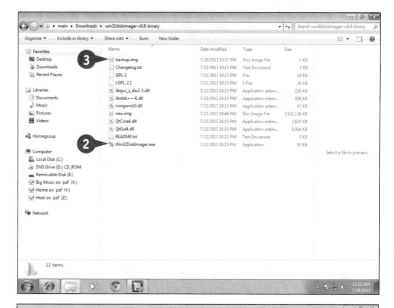

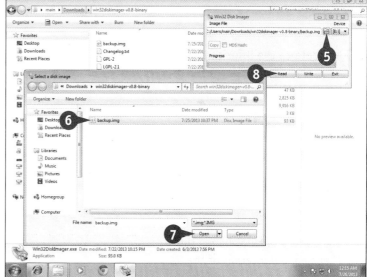

TIP

How do I restore a backup?

On the Mac, insert a card, run DiskUtility, click **Restore**, drag the backup file from the lower list at the left to the Source field, and the card you inserted to the Destination field. Click **Restore**. On a PC, run Win32DiskImager, click the file icon, select the backup file, click the device letter icon, select the card device, and then click **Write**.

Get Started with BerryBoot

You can use a free application called BerryBoot to install multiple operating systems. With BerryBoot, you can switch between a different OS every time you restart your Pi. You can also install OS files on other devices, including USB memory sticks and hard drives. Where a 4GB SD card has room for just one or two OS options, a 16GB or 32GB USB stick gives you room for many more.

BerryBoot is easy to use. Note that it downloads files from the Internet when you install a new OS. This can take an hour or two, and requires a good broadband connection.

Get Started with BerryBoot

1 Follow the instructions in the section "Prepare an SD Card" to prepare a blank SD card.

2 Open a web browser and visit www. berryterminal.com/doku.php/berryboot.

3 Download the latest version of the berryboot.zip file.

4 Follow the instructions in the section "Copy NOOBS to an SD Card" to copy the BerryBoot files to your card. Instead of downloading and copying the NOOBS files, copy the BerryBoot files you downloaded in step **3**.

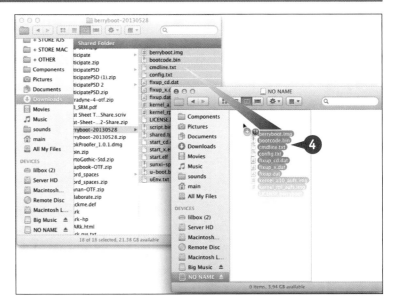

5 Place the SD card into your Pi and apply power.

BerryBoot displays a Welcome screen.

6 Click **Yes** (◯ changes to ◉).

7 Click a network option (◯ changes to ◉).

Note: You must connect your Pi to the Internet to use BerryBoot.

8 Select a time zone and a keyboard layout.

Note: You can skip step **8** if you do not customize BerryBoot or change any advanced settings.

9 Click **OK**.

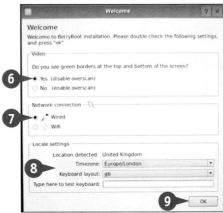

10 Select a storage device for your OS files.

Note: The SD card is labeled "device mmcblk0." If you connected your Pi to any other storage device, it appears automatically in the list.

11 Click **Format**.

BerryBoot reformats the card.

Note: This wipes all the information on your storage device. Be very careful, and double-check that you are not wiping useful information.

12 Select an operating system from the list.

13 Click **OK**.

BerryBoot downloads the files for the OS and installs them on the device you selected in step **10**.

Note: When you restart your Pi, BerryBoot loads a screen with a list of installed OS options. Click **Add OS** to add another OS to the list, **Delete** to remove an OS, and **Make Default** to choose the OS loaded by BerryBoot after a short wait.

Note: Experienced users can edit the boot options. See the BerryBoot web page for details.

TIPS

Can I extend the OS list?
Yes, but not easily. The Pi supports many alternative OS options. But BerryBoot is only compatible with those supplied in a special format known as SquashFS. Converting the files included in an OS to the SquashFS format and customizing the BerryBoot OS list is an advanced project. You can find out more at www.berryterminal.com/doku.php/berryboot/adding_custom_distributions.

Can I install an OS on a card without BerryBoot or NOOBS?
Yes. BerryBoot and NOOBS simplify installation, but you can install an OS on a card without them. For a detailed guide to manual installation, see http://elinux.org/RPi_Easy_SD_Card_Setup.

## CHAPTER 3

Setting Up Raspbian

Before you can use your Pi you must set it up. You can change the password, select a keyboard layout to match the keyboard you are using, set a time zone, and set up the memory card. Optionally, you can also overclock the Pi so it runs faster.

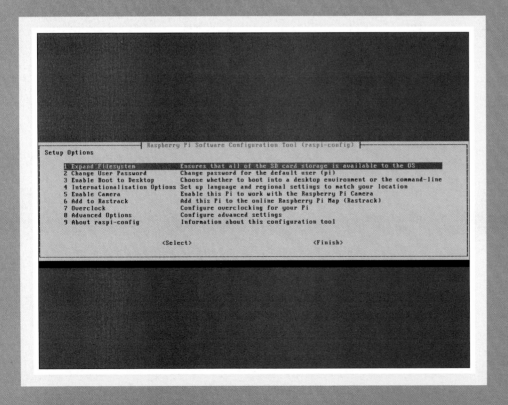

Set a Password

The first time the Pi boots, a Setup Options screen, also known as the Configuration tool, appears. On this screen, you can change your Pi's basic settings, including your user password. The default username is *pi*, and the default password is *raspberry*.

You can shorten the password to a single letter for convenience or choose a much longer password for security. You cannot set a blank password or disable the login prompt.

Select a Password

1 Boot up and wait until the Setup Options screen appears.

2 Press ⬇ to position the red highlight on the Change User Password option and press **Enter**.

Note: You can also press ➡ to highlight <Select> and press **Enter**.

Note: Because the Pi's software is always being updated, your Pi may not show the same setup options in the same order.

3 Press **Enter** again.

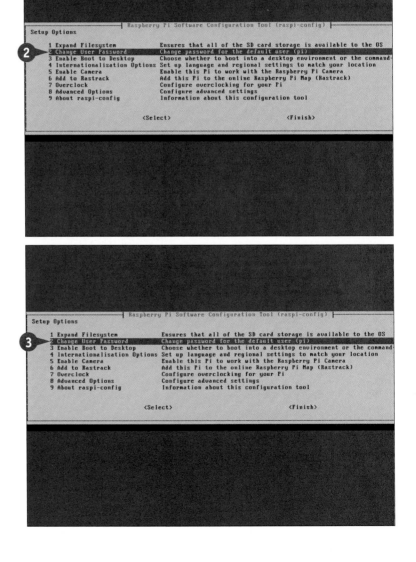

Ⓐ The Pi shows a prompt at the bottom of the screen.

④ Type your new password and press **Enter** at the prompt.

Note: The password does not appear on the screen as you type.

The Pi asks you to enter your password again.

⑤ Type your new password again and press **Enter**.

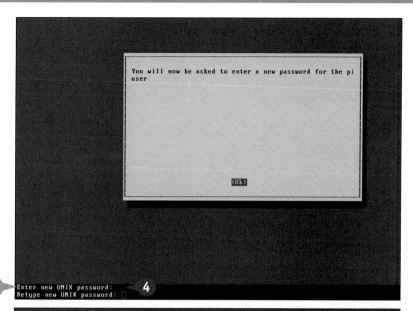

You will now be asked to enter a new password for the pi user

<Ok>

A message appears saying your password changed successfully.

⑥ Press **Enter** to return to the Setup Options screen.

Ⓐ Enter new UNIX password:
Retype new UNIX password: ▯ ④

Password changed successfully

<Ok> ⑥

TIPS

How do I quit the Setup Options?

On the main Setup Options screen, press ➡ to highlight <Finish> and press **Enter**. The Pi displays the *system prompt*, a short text message ending with a dollar sign ($), to show it is ready for commands. Note that the Setup Options text remains on the screen, but you cannot scroll up and down the options.

What should I do if I lose my password?

If you lose your password, you can buy a fresh copy of the operating system on an SD card or create your own fresh copy (see Chapter 2). You can then configure the Pi again from scratch. Experienced users can attempt hacks and workarounds to reset the password. For a list of suggestions see www.raspberrypi.org/phpBB3/viewtopic.php?f=28&t=44114.

Select a Keyboard Layout

Y ou can use the Setup Options to *localize* your Pi so it produces the letters and characters printed on the keys.

This step is recommended. If you do not understand a setting, leave it unchanged. If your keyboard produces incorrect characters, run Setup Options again (explained in the section "Revise the Configuration" later in this chapter) and check online for the correct settings for your hardware and local language. You may need to try various combinations until you find one that works.

Select a Keyboard Layout

1 On the Setup Options screen, press ⬆ and ⬇ to select Internationalisation Options and press Enter.

2 Press ⬆ and ⬇ to select Change Keyboard Layout and press Enter.

3 Wait until the Pi loads the keyboard configuration page.

Note: This screen appears after about 15 seconds. The Pi seems to be doing nothing while it loads.

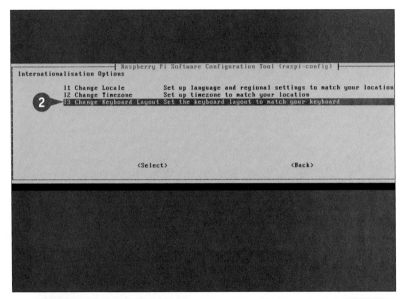

Ⓐ The Pi displays a list of keyboard makes and models.

4 Press ⬆ and ⬇ to select your keyboard model and press Enter.

Note: If you cannot see your keyboard or do not know which one to select, select **Generic Keyboard** for the United States or **Generic Keyboard (Intl)** for the United Kingdom.

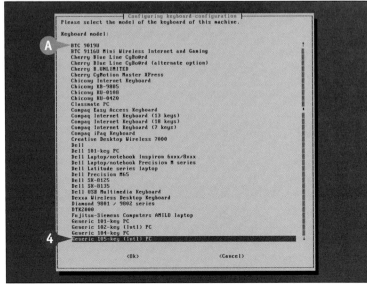

The Keyboard Layout screen appears.

5 Press ⬆ and ⬇ to select a keyboard subtype on the list and press Enter.

Note: The default option is usually correct. Select a Macintosh keyboard layout if you are using an Apple keyboard.

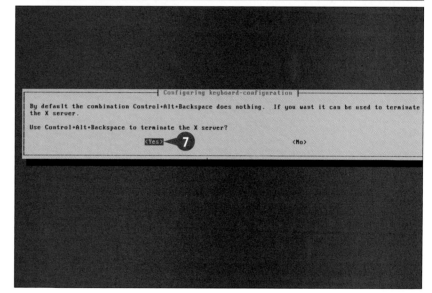

6 Press ➡ and Enter to skip the AltGR and Compose Key screens.

7 Press Enter to select the option to use Control+Alt+Backspace to quit the Pi's desktop if it is running.

After 10 seconds, the Pi returns you to the Setup Options screen. The new keyboard layout is now set.

TIP

How do I boot with numlock on?

If your keyboard has a numeric keypad, you may want to boot your Pi with the numbers enabled. Unfortunately this option is not included in the keyboard settings. Like many Linux options, numlock is controlled by a setting in a text file. Chapters 4 and 6 explain how to edit and save important text files. If you already know how, do the following: type `sudo nano /etc/kbd/config` at the command prompt. Delete the hash (#) character at the start of the LEDS=+num line. Save the file and reboot.

Select a Time Zone

You can use the Time Zone option to set how your Pi displays the time and date, and how it manages Daylight saving time (Summer time).

Note that the Pi does not have a full built-in clock. It uses a "fake" clock that loads the time from the Internet. If you do not connect your Pi to the Internet, the clock will be wrong. You cannot use the Time Zone setup option to set the time.

Select a Time Zone

1 On the Setup Options screen, press ⬆ and ⬇ to select Internationalisation Options and press **Enter**.

2 Press ⬆ and ⬇ to select Change Timezone and press **Enter**.

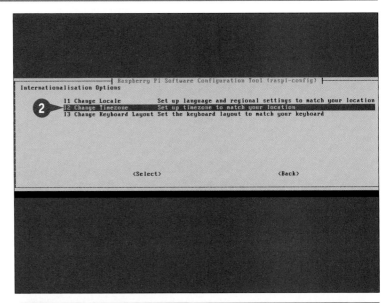

After a few seconds, the Pi displays the Geographic Area screen with a list of continents.

3 Press ⬆ and ⬇ to select your region and press **Enter**.

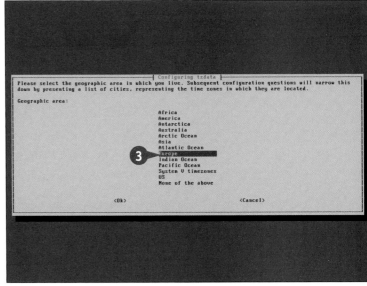

The Time Zone screen appears with a list of time zone regions.

4 Press ⬆ and ⬇ to select your nearest city or region and press Enter.

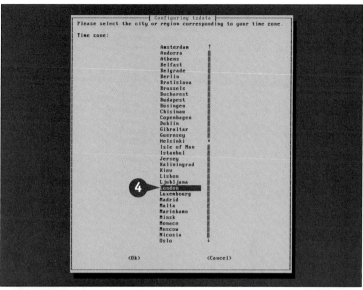

Ⓐ The Pi displays a message confirming that the Time Zone has changed, and then it returns you to the Setup Options screen.

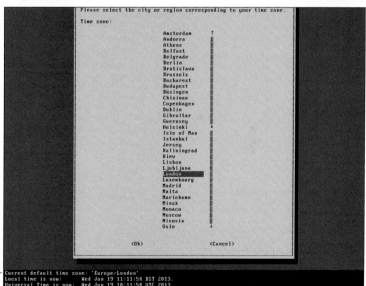

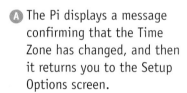

TIPS

Does the Pi always forget the time when powered down?
Because there is no clock, the Pi cannot remember the time. If you need a Pi that keeps time without a network connection even when powered down, you can select from a range of add-on clock boards. Search for "Raspberry Pi Clock" for details, or see Chapter 14. Most require some experience with the Linux command line.

Does having the wrong time matter?
If you create or edit files, the Pi tags them with the current time. If the current time is wrong the files do not show up if you search for recent files. Depending how you use your Pi, this may not cause problems, but you should avoid it if you can.

Manage Memory and SD Card Options

Memory is limited on the Pi. You can change two settings to make the most of the Pi's built-in memory and the free space on the SD card.

The Expand Filesystem option reformats your SD card to make all of its space available for storage. By default, storage is limited to 2GB, even on larger cards. This option expands it to make full use of the card. The Memory Split option in Advanced Options splits the Pi's memory between the built-in graphics and the operating system.

Manage Memory and SD Card Options

① On the Setup Options screen, press ⬆ and ⬇ to select the Expand Filesystem option and press Enter.

The Pi displays some text, which flashes past too quickly to read, and then displays a message saying the file system will be enlarged upon the next reboot.

② Press Enter again to return to the Setup Options screen.

③ Press ⬆ and ⬇ to select Advanced Options and press Enter.

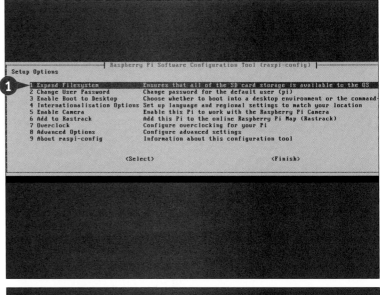

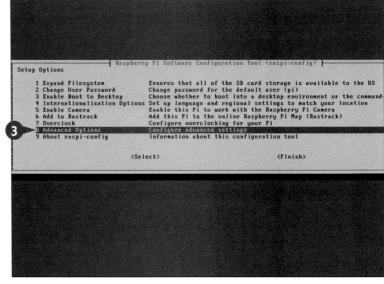

④ Press ⬆ and ⬇ to select Memory Split and press Enter.

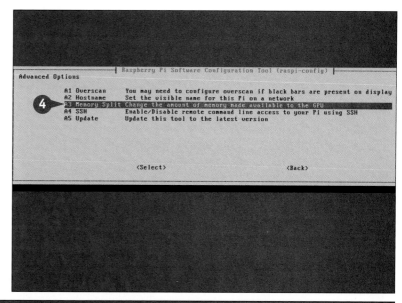

⑤ Type one of the numbers from the list at the top.

⑥ Press Enter to return to the Setup Options screen.

The Pi reorganizes its memory and gives more to the options you selected.

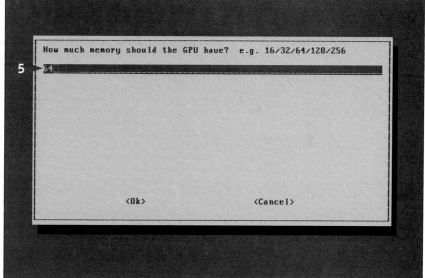

TIPS

Which number should I choose for the memory split?
On a Model B, 64 is a good compromise. It is enough to show the desktop without wasting memory. Select 128 or 256 if you use your Pi for very complex games or HD (high-definition) video playback. If you run your Pi from the command line without using the desktop, choose 16. On a Model A, select 64 or less unless you use your Pi solely for HD video.

Will reformatting the card destroy its contents?
No. The reformatting option is smart enough to reformat and repartition the card without losing information.

Set Up Overclocking

You can overclock your Pi to make it run faster. *Overclocking* modifies key system settings. It improves performance, but makes your Pi run hotter. Overclocking does not void the warranty, but it can make your Pi less reliable and shorten its working life.

To overclock your Pi, select the Overclock option in the Configuration tool. You can choose one of five speed presets. The faster a preset, the hotter your Pi runs and the more likely it is to stop working reliably. If you enclosed your Pi in a case it runs even hotter.

Set Up Overclocking

① On the Setup Options screen, press ⬆ and ⬇ to select Overclock and press Enter.

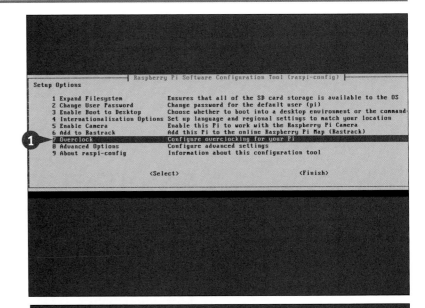

A warning screen appears.

② Press Enter to skip past the warning message.

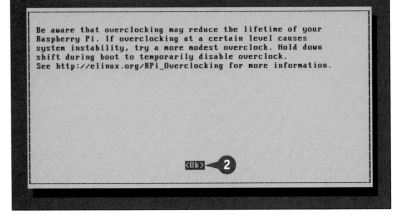

③ Press ⬆ and ⬇ to select an overclocking option and press `Enter`.

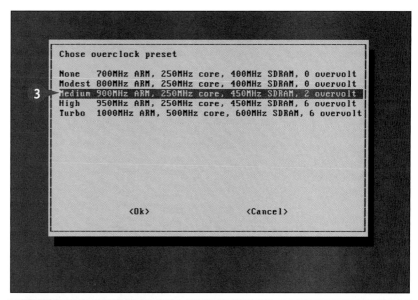

```
Chose overclock preset

None    700MHz ARM, 250MHz core, 400MHz SDRAM, 0 overvolt
Modest  800MHz ARM, 250MHz core, 400MHz SDRAM, 0 overvolt
Medium  900MHz ARM, 250MHz core, 450MHz SDRAM, 2 overvolt
High    950MHz ARM, 250MHz core, 450MHz SDRAM, 6 overvolt
Turbo   1000MHz ARM, 500MHz core, 600MHz SDRAM, 6 overvolt



              <Ok>                      <Cancel>
```

④ Press `Enter` again to return to the Setup Options screen.

Overclocking is set immediately. You do not need to reboot.

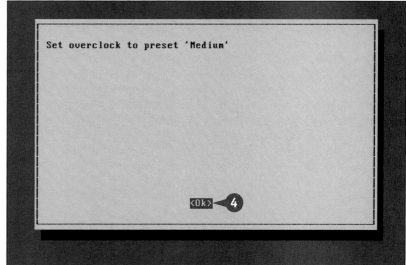

```
Set overclock to preset 'Medium'




                    <Ok>
```

TIPS

How much faster can my Pi go?
The Turbo overclocking preset boosts the speed by around 20 percent, which has a noticeable effect when viewing web pages or running games. The other presets offer a less obvious speed boost. The Medium option is a good compromise between speed and reliability. For many applications overclocking is not necessary.

How can I cool my Pi after overclocking?
Adventurous users have built complex cooling systems that use water or even liquefied gas. For more modest cooling, you can fit a *heatsink*, a small piece of metal with cooling fins, to the main chip on the board. Heatsinks cost a few dollars and are easy to fit. For more complex cooling, you may be able to improvise your own system from standard PC cooling components.

Connect to the Internet

You can link your Pi to the Internet by connecting it to a router or modem with a standard Ethernet cable. If your router is set up to provide local network addresses automatically, as consumer routers usually are, your Pi appears on your local network almost as soon as you connect it.

You can then load and view web pages, as described in Chapter 4. You can also begin to turn your Pi into a web server, file server, or home media player, as described in later chapters.

Connect to the Internet

1 Plug an Ethernet cable into your router.

2 Plug the other end of the cable into the Ethernet socket on your Pi.

After a few moments, your router automatically connects your Pi to your local network and the Internet.

Note: If you have an optional Wi-Fi dongle, you can connect the Pi over Wi-Fi. For details, see Chapter 4.

Note: Some applications require a static IP address. See Chapter 7 for details.

The Pi connects to the Internet. For information about using a web browser, see Chapter 4.

Revise the Configuration

When you finish configuring your Pi for the first time, the options you choose are saved to the memory card. You do not have to enter them again.

The Pi does not reload the Setup Options screen the next time it boots. But you can access the screen and change the options again — for example, if you decide to experiment with overclocking — by typing a simple text command.

Revise the Configuration

1 Power up the Pi, log in, and wait for the command-line prompt, indicated by the dollar sign ($).

2 Type sudo raspi-config and press **Enter**.

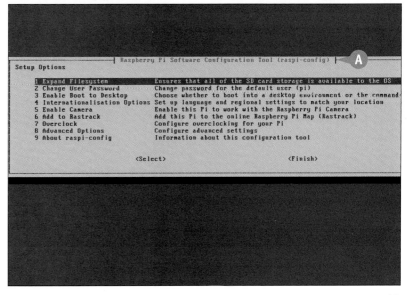

A The Setup Options screen appears. You can revise setup options here.

43

Update the Operating System

If you boot your Pi using an SD card with a preinstalled version of the OS, or *operating system*, the software that runs your Pi, it may be out of date. You can update the OS to the latest version by typing two simple commands at the command prompt. To do this, reboot your Pi and log in at the system prompt.

A full update can take a couple of hours, and you must connect your Pi to the Internet before you begin.

Update the Operating System

1 If you are starting from Setup Options, return to the main screen and press ➡ to select Finish and press Enter.

2 If you see a screen asking if you want to reboot now, press Enter again.

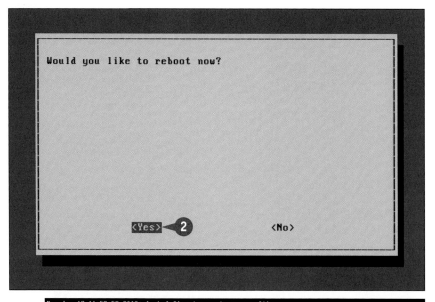

3 If you are starting from the login prompt, type pi and press Enter.

4 Type your password and press Enter.

Note: Remember to type your new password if you changed it in Setup Options.

5 When the dollar sign ($) prompt appears, type sudo apt-get update and press Enter.

Note: Include all spaces and punctuation. Make sure the spelling is correct.

Ⓐ The Pi starts displaying text to show that it is downloading and updating files.

6 Wait until the Done message appears, followed by the prompt.

7 When the dollar sign ($) prompt appears, type sudo apt-get upgrade and press Enter.

8 Press Y when the Pi asks if you want to continue.

Ⓑ The upgrade ends when the dollar sign ($) prompt reappears.

Note: The upgrade process can take a couple of minutes to a couple of hours.

Note: Linux does not tell you when updates are available. But you can update and upgrade at any time.

```
Debian GNU/Linux 7.0 pi tty1

pi login: pi
Password:

Last login: Mon Jun 17 11:52:33 BST 2013 on tty1
LINUX PI 3.6.11+ #456 PREEMPT Mon May 20 17:42:15 BST 2013 armv6l

The programs include with the Debian GNU/Linux system are free software:
the exact distribution terms for each program are described in the
individual files in /usr/share/doc/*/copyright

Debian GNU/Linux comes with ABSOLUTELY NO WARRANTY, to the extent
permitted by applicable law.
Mon Jun 17 12:24:04 BST 2013
pi@pi ~ $ sudo apt-get update
Get:1 http://archive.raspberrypi.org wheezy Release.gpg [490 B]
Get:2 http://mirrordirector.raspbian.org wheezy Release.gpg [490 B]
Get:3 http://archive.raspberrypi.org wheezy Release [7,200 B]
Get:4 http://mirrordirector.raspbian.org wheezy Release [14.4 kB]
Get:5 http://archive.raspberrypi.org wheezy/main armhf Packages [6,260 B]
Get:6 http://mirrordirector.raspbian.org wheezy/main armhf Packages [7,413 kB]
Ign http://archive.raspberrypi.org wheezy/main Translation-en_GB
Ign http://archive.raspberrypi.org wheezy/main Translation-en
Get:7 http://mirrordirector.raspbian.org wheezy/contrib armhf Packages [23.2 kB]
Get:8 http://mirrordirector.raspbian.org wheezy/non-free armhf Packages [48.0 kB]
Get:9 http://mirrordirector.raspbian.org wheezy/rpi armhf Packages [569 B]
Ign http://mirrordirector.raspbian.org wheezy/contrib Translation-en_GB
Ign http://mirrordirector.raspbian.org wheezy/contrib Translation-en
Ign http://mirrordirector.raspbian.org wheezy/main Translation-en_GB
Ign http://mirrordirector.raspbian.org wheezy/main Translation-en
Ign http://mirrordirector.raspbian.org wheezy/non-free Translation-en_GB
Ign http://mirrordirector.raspbian.org wheezy/non-free Translation-en
Ign http://mirrordirector.raspbian.org wheezy/rpi Translation-en_GB
Ign http://mirrordirector.raspbian.org wheezy/rpi Translation-en
Fetched 7,513 kB in 50s (148 kB/s)
Reading package lists... Done
pi@pi ~ $
```

```
Setting up libsasl2-modules:armhf (2.1.25.dfsg1-6+deb7u1) ...
Setting up alsa-base (1.0.25+3~deb7u1) ...
Setting up libpcsclite1:armhf (1.8.4-1+deb7u1) ...
Setting up php5-common (5.4.4-14+deb7u2) ...
Setting up php5-cgi (5.4.4-14+deb7u2) ...
Setting up libreadline5:armhf (5.2+dfsg-2~deb7u1) ...
Setting up isc-dhcp-common (4.2.2.dfsg.1-5+deb70u6) ...
Setting up isc-dhcp-client (4.2.2.dfsg.1-5+deb70u6) ...
Setting up nfs-common (1:1.2.6-4) ...
insserv: warning: current start runlevel(s) (empty) of script `nfs-common' overrides LSB defaults (
insserv: warning: current stop runlevel(s) (0 1 2 3 4 5 6 S) of script `nfs-common' overrides LSB d
.
Setting up liblapack3 (3.4.1+dfsg-1+deb70u1) ...
Setting up x11-common (1:7.7+3~deb7u1) ...
[ ok ] Setting up X socket directories... /tmp/.X11-unix /tmp/.ICE-unix.
Setting up xserver-xorg-input-all (1:7.7+3~deb7u1) ...
Setting up xserver-xorg (1:7.7+3~deb7u1) ...
Setting up raspberrypi-bootloader (1.20130617-1) ...
Memory split is now set in /boot/config.txt.
You may want to use raspi-config to set it
Removing 'diversion of /boot/bootcode.bin to /usr/share/rpikernelhack/bootcode.bin by rpikernelhack
Removing 'diversion of /boot/fixup.dat to /usr/share/rpikernelhack/fixup.dat by rpikernelhack'
Removing 'diversion of /boot/fixup_cd.dat to /usr/share/rpikernelhack/fixup_cd.dat by rpikernelhack
Removing 'diversion of /boot/fixup_x.dat to /usr/share/rpikernelhack/fixup_x.dat by rpikernelhack'
Removing 'diversion of /boot/kernel.img to /usr/share/rpikernelhack/kernel.img by rpikernelhack'
Removing 'diversion of /boot/kernel_cutdown.img to /usr/share/rpikernelhack/kernel_cutdown.img by r
Removing 'diversion of /boot/kernel_emergency.img to /usr/share/rpikernelhack/kernel_emergency.img
k'
Removing 'diversion of /boot/start.elf to /usr/share/rpikernelhack/start.elf by rpikernelhack'
Removing 'diversion of /boot/start_cd.elf to /usr/share/rpikernelhack/start_cd.elf by rpikernelhack
Removing 'diversion of /boot/start_x.elf to /usr/share/rpikernelhack/start_x.elf by rpikernelhack'
Setting up libraspberrypi0 (1.20130617-1) ...
Setting up libraspberrypi-dev (1.20130617-1) ...
Setting up libraspberrypi-doc (1.20130617-1) ...
Setting up libraspberrypi-bin (1.20130617-1) ...
Setting up tasksel-data (3.14.1) ...
Setting up tasksel (3.14.1) ...
Processing triggers for menu ...
pi@pi ~ $
```

TIPS

If I update, do I have to re-enter my setup options?

No. Updating the OS should leave your password, keyboard layout, and other settings unchanged. You do not have to reconfigure your Pi. Note that the options themselves change occasionally, especially if you upgrade as well as update. So you may see different options to those shown here.

Should I update if I made my own SD card?

If you used the instructions in Chapter 2 to make your own SD card, you can check the date of the most up-to-date version of Raspbian at www.raspberrypi.org/downloads. If there is a newer version, you can use the update and upgrade commands to update your OS. You do not need to make another card.

Launch the Desktop

You can launch the desktop on your Pi by typing the `startx` command at the system prompt. The Pi blanks the screen while the desktop loads — this can take awhile. After a few seconds the Pi displays a desktop with icons, a task bar, and official Raspberry Pi wallpaper.

Although some of the icons are unusual, the basic features of the desktop — clickable icons, a start menu, and a toolbar — should be familiar to users of Windows 7 and XP. Mac users may need to take some time to experiment with this environment.

Launch the Desktop

1 At the command prompt type `startx` and press **Enter**.

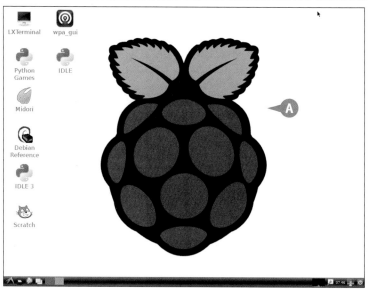

Ⓐ The Pi loads and displays the LXDE desktop.

Shut Down the Pi

Do not shut down your Pi by unplugging the power. You can corrupt the contents of the memory card, losing files and perhaps damaging the operating system and making it unstable or even unusable.

You can shut down the Pi from the command prompt. To get to the command prompt, you must quit the desktop. Note you can reboot your Pi by typing `sudo reboot`.

Shut Down the Pi

1 Click the power icon.

2 Click the **Logout** option on the floating menu.

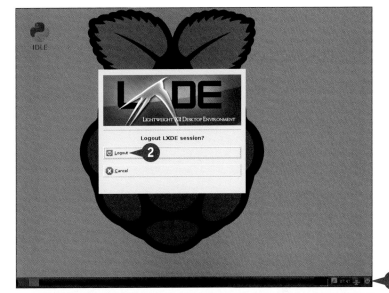

A The desktop quits and returns you to the command prompt.

3 Type `sudo poweroff` and press **Enter**.

The Pi runs a shutdown sequence.

Note: After your screen goes blank, wait until the ACT light on the Pi stops flashing before unplugging the power.

Note: If you launch the desktop as superuser/root — see Chapter 5 — the power button displays extra reboot and shutdown options when you click it.

## CHAPTER 4

Working with Applications

The Raspberry Pi comes with a basic set of preinstalled desktop applications. You can use them to finish setting up your Pi before you begin learning more about the Linux operating system.

Introducing Raspberry Pi Apps

The Raspberry Pi uses an operating system called Linux, which is popular with software developers. Linux comes in many different *distros*, or distributions. The official distro for the Pi is called called Raspbian Wheezy, a customized version of Debian, a distro known for its reliability. (The Pi includes a reference guide to Debian on the desktop, but the content is very technical.) In spite of the unusual name, Wheezy includes many familiar features. You can work with it by typing commands from the keyboard, or by launching applications from a desktop and using a mouse, keyboard, menus, and icons.

Understanding the Linux Desktop

In Linux, the desktop is a just another application. You can launch it manually after the Pi boots with the `startx` command. You can also select a Boot to Desktop option using `raspi-config`. Larger variants of Linux give you a choice of desktops. Because the Pi is a small computer with limited memory, Wheezy includes a single lightweight desktop application called LXDE.

Browse the Web

The default desktop on the Pi includes a web browser called Midori. Midori is designed for slow computers with limited memory but still provides advanced features such as tabs, page code inspection, and support for Mozilla plug-ins. On the Pi, Midori runs more slowly than the desktop browsers you may be used to.

Work with Commands

Because text commands are so widely used in Linux, LXDE includes a terminal application called LXTerminal. *Terminal* is an old computing word for a device that accepts text commands and displays text output.

Edit Text Files

Wheezy's text editor is called Leafpad. It is similar to Notepad on Windows and TextEdit on the Mac. However, Leafpad does not allow you to edit many important files. To fix this you must understand Linux security. For details, see the information about becoming a superuser in Chapter 5.

Work with Games and Software

Because the Pi is designed for education, it includes a "toy" programming language for kids called Scratch. It also includes two versions of the popular Python programming language and a set of extensions for Python called Pygame, which makes it easy to create simple animated games. Scratch, Python, and Pygame are described in later chapters.

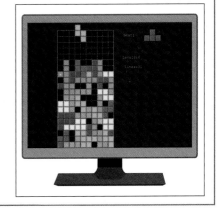

Check Your Speed

Because the Pi is slow, apps often take longer to respond than you may be used to. LXDE lacks an hourglass or a spinning beach ball to show when the operating system is busy. However, the bottom of the taskbar shows a miniature graph that tells you how hard the Pi is working. When the graph is solid green, the Pi is busy and may respond slowly.

Set Up Wi-Fi

You can connect your Pi to a network with Wi-Fi. To use Wi-Fi, plug an optional Wi-Fi *dongle* — a small aerial — into one of your Pi's USB ports. You can then configure a connection with the wpa_gui application on the desktop.

Always plug in a dongle with the power off. In theory, your Pi should be able to cope with live connection/disconnection. In practice, the power drained by a dongle may crash it, forcing it to reboot.

Set Up Wi-Fi

1 Plug a Wi-Fi dongle into one of the Pi's USB ports or into a connected USB hub.

2 Launch the desktop with `startx` if it is not already open.

3 Double-click **wpa_gui**.

The wpa_gui application dialog box opens.

4 Click **Scan**.

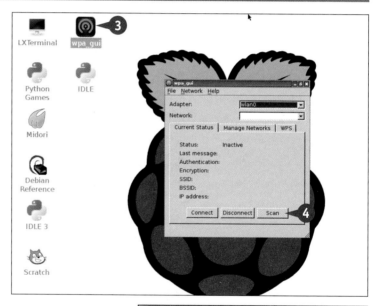

A dialog box opens and the Pi scans the available networks.

5 Double-click a network to set up a password.

Note: The signal column shows how strong the Wi-Fi signal is for each network. The smaller the number, the stronger the signal.

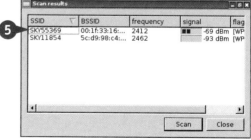

6 If the network uses WPA security, type the network password into the PSK box.

Note: If the network uses older and less secure WEP security, select **Static WEP (Shared Authentication)** from the Encryption menu and type the WEP key (or keys) into the WEP Keys box.

7 Click **Add**.

The Pi connects to the Wi-Fi network you selected.

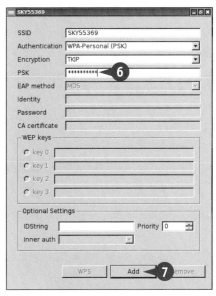

A You can click **Connect** if the wap_gui does not connect automatically.

TIP

Why does Wi-Fi not work for me?
Wi-Fi on the Pi is still somewhat experimental. You can improve your chances of a successful connection by making sure the Pi is close enough to your router or modem to pick up a strong signal. On some Wi-Fi products, you must push a button on them to confirm you are attempting to connect. Many common Wi-Fi dongles do not work reliably with the Pi. Some may work for a while and then stop. You may need to experiment with a few, powering down and rebooting between connection attempts, to get a reliable connection. As a last resort you can also type `sudo rm /etc/wpa_supplicant/wpa_supplicant.conf` at the command prompt to remove existing network information and run the steps in this section again.

View Web Pages

You can view web pages with the Midori browser. To open Midori, double-click its desktop icon. Midori includes support for tabs and for Mozilla-format plug-ins.

Midori on the Pi is not a speedy browser. Pages take a few seconds to load — noticeably longer than they take on a recent PC or Mac.

View Web Pages

1 Launch the desktop if it is not already open.

2 Double-click **Midori**.

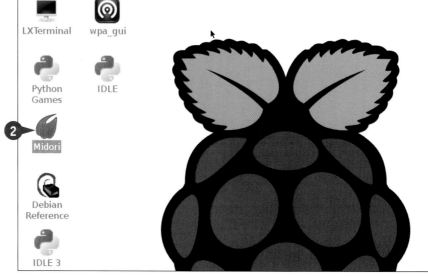

A Midori loads with a default page showing an introductory help file.

3 To view a different page, type its URL into the browser bar, just as you would when using a mainstream browser.

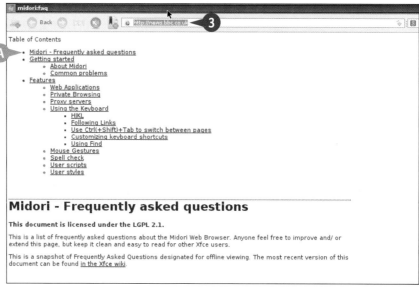

Midori goes to the new web page.

4 To perform a web search, type a phrase into the search bar.

5 To select a different search engine, click and hold the icon at the left of the search bar.

Note: By default, Midori uses the Duck Duck Go search engine.

6 To open another tab, click the **New Tab** icon ().

7 Click the gear icon () to view more options.

8 Click **Preferences**.

The Preferences opens.

9 Click any tab to select a set of preferences, such as Startup or Fonts.

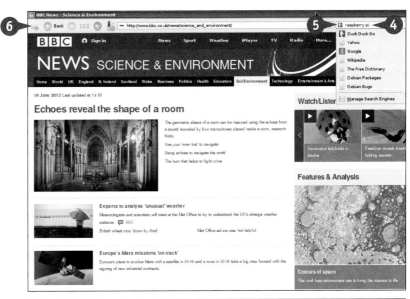

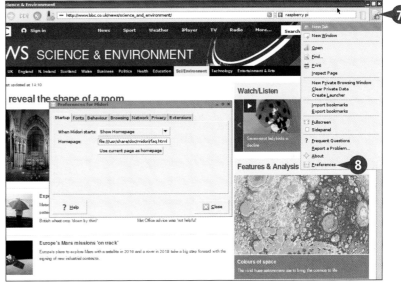

TIPS

Why does an application called Dillo sometimes appear?
Dillo is a very simple mini-browser that is ideal for browsing simple HTML help files. It is not useful for web browsing. By default, the taskbar at the lower left of the desktop launches Dillo from its web browser slot. To change this, follow the instructions for changing the taskbar in the section "Configure the Launch Panel."

Can I add Flash to Midori so I can watch videos?
Flash is no longer officially supported on Linux, but may still work if you are prepared to experiment with add-ons and extra downloads. For the most recent news, search the web for "Flash on Midori."

Work with Files in File Manager

You can navigate the file system using the File Manager tool on the desktop. To launch File Manager, click the icon to the right of the LXDE icon in the Application Launch bar. The Pi user can also double-click the File Manager icon.

Use the Forward, Back, and Home buttons to navigate through folders. A "level up" takes you to the containing folder one level up the directory tree. File Manager launches with a view of the /home/pi folder. To view the list of system folders, type **/** in the address bar. To open any folder, double-click it.

Work with Files in File Manager

1 Launch the desktop if it is not open.

2 Click the **File Manager** icon (■) in the Application Launch bar.

Ⓐ You can also click the **LXDE** icon (■), **Accessories**, and then **File Manager**.

Ⓑ LXDE launches File Manager in a window.

Note: Even if you are running as root, File Manager always displays the /home/pi folder.

3 To view the main system folder, drag the mouse over home/pi to highlight it, press Delete or Backspace, and press Enter.

Ⓒ File Manager displays the contents of /, the main system directory.

4 To open a folder, double-click it.

5 Repeat the double-click to drill down into a series of folders inside the / folder.

Note: This example shows the results of double-clicking **home**, **Pi**, and then **Desktop** to view /home/pi/Desktop.

6 Double-click **IDLE** to launch the Python editor application.

D The application launches in a new window.

Note: You can double-click any application to launch it.

Note: If a file is a text file or image, right-click it to view more options. For example, you can edit a text file with Leafpad.

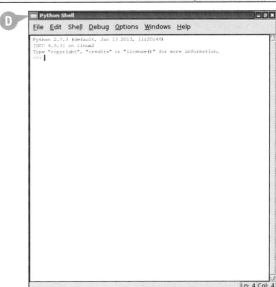

TIPS

How do I create a folder?

If you launch the desktop as the Pi user, many useful files and folders are security locked. You can close the desktop, promote yourself to superuser with the `sudo su` command, and then launch it again. Or you can click **Tools** and **Open Current Folder as Root** in the File Manager menu to give yourself temporary root privileges. You can then right-click to create a new folder or blank file.

Where can I find out more about the different system folders?

You can find a technical description at www.debianadmin.com/linux-directory-structure-overview.html. Search the web when you need to find the files for a specific application such as a web server.

Edit Text with Leafpad

You can use Leafpad to edit text files. Leafpad is a simple WYSIWYG (What You See Is What You Get) text editor with basic features. It is not a word processor, but you can use it to edit your Pi's configuration files.

Note that Leafpad does not allow you to edit critical files unless you have root superpowers. Use File Manager to promote yourself to root before you try to edit important files. For more about promoting yourself to root, see the previous section, "Work with Files in File Manager," and also Chapter 5.

Edit Text with Leafpad

1 Click the **LXDE** icon ( ).

2 Click **Accessories**.

3 Click **Leafpad**.

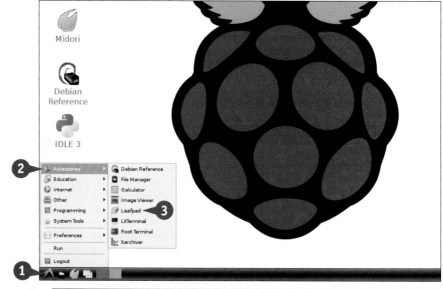

A Leafpad launches with an empty window.

4 Type some text.

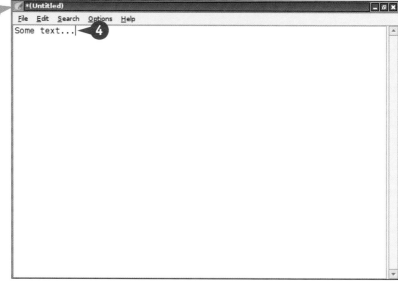

5 Click **File**.

6 Click **Save As**.

7 Click the **pi** icon to save the file to the /home/pi folder.

8 Type a name for the file.

9 Click **Save**.

Leafpad saves the file to your home folder.

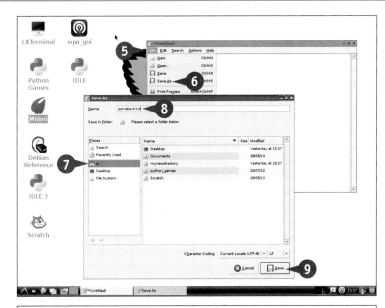

10 Click the **File Manager** icon (▣).

File Manager launches if it is not already open.

11 Double-click the file you saved.

Ⓑ Leafpad opens in a new window and loads the file into it.

TIP

Can I install a full word processor on the Pi?
You cannot install Microsoft Word, but you can download a free office suite called Libre Office from the Pi App Store. Because the Pi is a work in progress, Libre Office is not guaranteed to work. But you can still experiment with it. For more about using the Pi App Store, see Chapter 13.

Configure the Desktop

If you experiment with the desktop's many menus, you can find plenty of configuration options. With the most useful options you can customize the wallpaper, and add or remove icons on the desktop. Ignore the other options, which are not essential. Changing them may break the desktop.

Note there are two desktops. They show the same icons, but you can have different windows open on them. To switch desktops, click the blue/white rectangles in the bottom bar.

Configure the Desktop

1 Right-click the desktop.

2 Click **Desktop Preferences**.

3 In the Desktop Preferences, click the **Wallpaper** box.

4 Select a new file from the file selector.

5 Click **Open**.

The new wallpaper loads.

Note: The Pi does not include preinstalled wallpaper files. Use Midori to search for and save alternative wallpapers. Or you can leave the default Raspberry Pi wallpaper unchanged.

6 To change the font used for the desktop icons, click the **Label text font** box in the Desktop Preferences.

7 Select one of the alternative fonts.

Note: You can see a preview of the font in the Preview box.

8 Click **OK**.

Note: Do not access the Advanced tab in Desktop Preferences. You may accidentally remove the right-click menu.

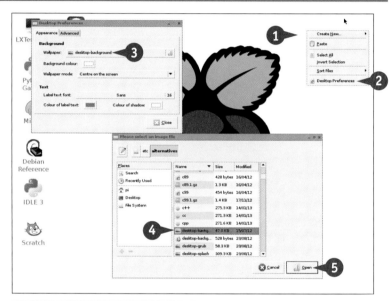

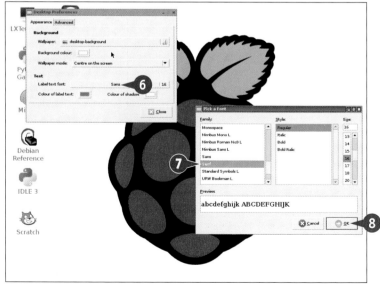

9 Click the **File Manager** icon (⬜).

File manager launches.

10 Type **/usr/share/application** into the address bar and press **Enter**.

Note: You can also type **/** to navigate to the root folder and then drill down by double-clicking the **usr**, **share**, and **applications** folders.

Ⓐ File Manager displays a list of installed applications.

11 Press and hold **Ctrl** and drag an application icon to the desktop to add it.

Note: You can keep adding applications until your desktop is full.

12 To remove an application from the desktop, right-click it.

13 Click **Delete**.

Note: Deleting an icon removes it from the desktop. It does not remove the application from your Pi.

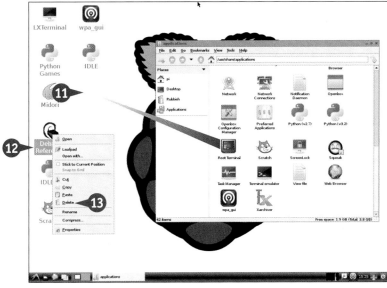

TIPS

Why does the Applications icon in File Manager show different applications?

The Applications item at the left of File Manager shows and controls the applications that appear in the desktop Start menu: /usr/share/applications shows applications installed on your Pi.

Can I customize the Applications in the Start menu?

Instead of dragging applications to the desktop, open two File Manager windows and drag applications from /usr/share/applications to the Applications directory. The top-level icons define the main launch menu headings. You can open them by double-clicking them.

Configure the Launch Panel

The Launch Panel is unique to LXDE. It is based on the Quick Launch apps that appear in the Windows XP taskbar. It looks like a single bar, but in fact it includes multiple items, including the main Start menu, quick links to File Manager and Web Browser, a CPU performance graph, and so on.

You can add and remove items and customize each item to control what it includes. You can also insert spacers between items to push them toward the left or right of the panel.

Configure the Launch Panel

1 Right-click the second or third icons from the left of the launch panel.

2 Click **"Application Launch Bar" Settings**.

The Application Launch Bar Preferences open.

3 Click **Web Browser**.

4 Click **Remove**.

Note: This removes the Dillo web browser that is preinstalled on the launch panel.

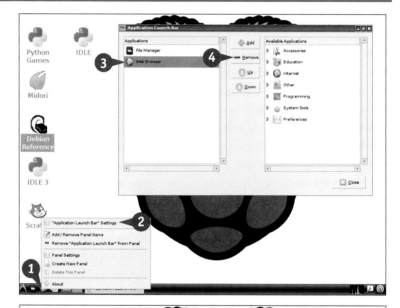

5 Click the triangle next to Internet.

6 Click **Midori**.

7 Click **Add**.

8 Click **Close**.

Ⓐ A Midori icon appears in the launch panel.

9 Right-click the launch panel.

10 Click **Panel Settings**.

The Panel Preferences open.

11 Click the **Panel Applets** tab.

12 Click **Add**.

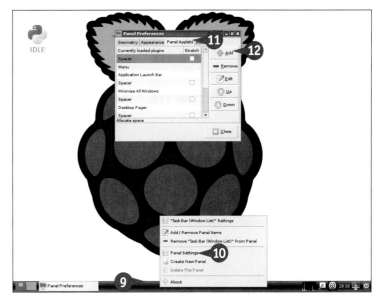

The Add Plugin to Panel pane appears.

13 Click **Temperature Monitor**.

14 Click **Add**.

B A temperature monitor appears on the panel.

15 Click **Up** or **Down** to move the monitor left or right on the panel.

Note: You can click **Remove** to remove an item from the launch panel.

TIPS

Why do I see different menus when I click in different locations?
The launch panel includes a selection of subpanels. When you click the LXDE icon you see a menu for the main panel and for the Menu panel. The panel next to it is called the Application Launch Bar panel. You can add and remove items from these subpanels, and also add and remove subpanels from the main panel.

Do I have to place items in subpanels?
No. You can add them directly to the main panel. Subpanels are useful for adding special features and for grouping applications.

## CHAPTER 5

Working with the Command Line

To get the most from your Pi you must learn about its Linux operating system. Linux is a powerful hands-on tool, but to use it you need technical knowledge and practice.

Introducing Linux

Chapter 4 introduces you to the Raspberry Pi's operating system, Raspbian Wheezy, which is a special version of Linux. In this chapter, you learn more about Linux and discover how you can use it to get under the hood of your Pi to work with files, change settings, install new applications, and set up other features.

Understanding the Command Line

Windows and OS X are designed around a desktop. On the Pi, you can learn basic programming without leaving the desktop. But some important features are only accessible through the command line. You control your Pi by typing short text commands and watching text responses on your monitor. Commands must be 100 percent accurate with no misspellings or other errors.

Understanding "Magic Word" Commands

Linux supports hundreds of commands and applications. Many have obscure names, so you cannot guess them. Most users only remember a handful. There is no easy way to view a complete list on the Pi, but you can — and should — find the "magic words" for each command by searching online. To save repeated searches, make a file with a list of useful commands as you learn them. You can type `help` for a basic list of commands or `man <command name>` to show a *man*, or Unix manual, page. Both are technical and not written for beginners.

Understanding Switches

In Linux, a command is a single lowercase word without spaces. Commands are modified with *switches* that provide extra options. To use switches, type the command and a space. Next, type a punctuation mark — usually a single or double minus sign (- or --). Finally, type the letter or word to select the switch. Repeat these steps to select additional switches. Most commands list their switches if you type man followed by the command name. The descriptions are cryptic and hard to understand. Search online for useful examples.

Understanding Root

For security reasons, critical commands and files can only be accessed by a special superuser called *root*, and not by the default Pi user account. You cannot log in as root, but you can give yourself *root privileges*, or the ability to impersonate root, in a variety of ways. In theory, this prevents disasters. As root, you can lose all your files or break critical applications if you make a mistake. In practice, you should back up your Pi regularly anyway; root security on a one-user system is an unavoidable distraction.

Get Hands On with Linux

If you are accustomed to Windows or OS X, learning Linux can be a challenge. Because the Pi is a hands-on computer, Linux teaches you to become a computer mechanic rather than a computer driver. Initially, many tasks seem unnecessarily difficult or complicated, and help can be hard to locate. With experience, some tasks become easier, and you can begin to imagine applications for your Pi that are not possible on other systems.

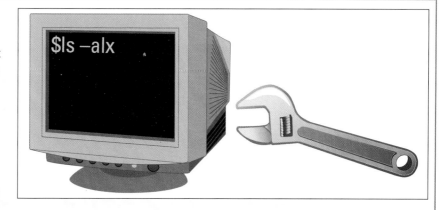

Using the Command Line

You can type commands at the main system prompt or in the LXTerminal application on the desktop. Note that on the Pi, some text output is colorized automatically. Commands must be 100 percent correct with the right command name, case, spacing, and switches. Capitalization is important.

Commands in LXTerminal work just like commands typed at the system prompt. Use whichever option is most convenient. There is one exception: If you promote yourself to root at the system prompt and launch the desktop with `startx`, you will see a blank desktop. Unlike the Pi user, the root superuser does not have any preinstalled desktop applications.

Using the Command Line

1 Power up Raspberry Pi and wait for it to boot.

2 Type `date` at the prompt and press **Enter**.

A Linux runs the date command and displays the result.

3 Type `startx` and press **Enter**.

B Linux launches the desktop.

4 Double-click **LXTerminal** to launch the desktop terminal app.

5 Type `date` and press **Enter** at the prompt.

C Linux runs the date command and displays the result.

The same command produces the same output at the command line and in LXTerminal.

Note: For clarity and detail, the rest of the illustrations in this book show LXTerminal running maximized with black-on-white text set in the preferences.

Become the Superuser

For security reasons, many commands only work if you are the root superuser. You cannot log in as root directly. However, you can use the sudo command, which is short for superuser do, to promote yourself temporarily to superuser. sudo superpowers last for one command. To promote yourself to root for as long as you stay logged in, use sudo su. This launches a special version of the command line with built-in superpowers. By default, this version does not display commands and their output in color.

Become the Superuser

1 Open LXTerminal.

2 Type apt-get install at the prompt and press Enter.

Ⓐ Linux displays a message telling you that you cannot run the command unless you are root.

Note: apt-get is a tool for installing software. You cannot run it as an ordinary user.

3 Type sudo apt-get install and press Enter.

Ⓑ You have superuser powers because of sudo, so Linux runs apt-get install.

Note: This example is a dummy run of apt-get install. It does not try to install any software.

4 Type sudo su and press Enter.

Note: Linux changes the prompt to show you are now root and have superuser powers.

5 Type apt-get install and press Enter.

Linux runs apt-get without needing sudo.

Note: To become the ordinary pi user again, type exit and press Enter or reboot your Pi.

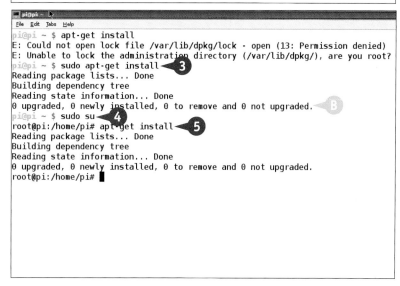

Understanding the File System

To get the most from your Pi, you must understand where to find important files and how to work with file security so you can change them. Because of Linux file security, you cannot change some files and directories without first becoming superuser, or root. If you try to, Linux displays an error message about permissions. You can get around security easily, but you must remember that you need to do it.

Understanding Linux Files

In Linux, everything is a file, including disk files and all other processes that produce or consume data. Even devices are treated as files. So your commands are treated as files created by the keyboard device, and you can play audio by copying a sound file to the audio device.

Understanding Users and Groups

Users are collected into groups. Users in a group can share files easily. Users outside a group cannot access the files.

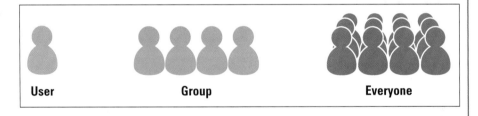

User   **Group**   **Everyone**

On a small computer like the Pi you are usually the only user, so this extra security may not be necessary. But it is built in to Linux, so you must work around it.

Understanding System Users

In addition to human users, Linux also includes a number of system users. For example, if you create a web server on your Pi,

Web Server   E-Mail Server   Media Server

the software that manages the web server is considered a user with its own special group. The root superuser is also a separate user with its own file group. This can cause security issues when you try to set up a web server or e-mail service on your Pi, so you must know how to manage file security for system users.

Understanding File Permissions

Every file has three permissions: read, write (that is, edit), and execute (that is, run as software).

These permissions are different for three user types: the file's owner, the file's group, and everyone else. Linux often keeps you from editing files, changing software settings, or running some applications until you give files the correct permissions. You can access most files as root, but for some applications you must work around the permissions system as the Pi user. Some applications only work if you set up the correct group permissions.

Understanding System Folders

With minor variations, critical folders and files are organized the same way on every Linux

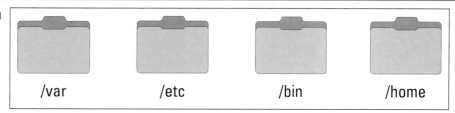

/var   /etc   /bin   /home

system. For example /bin holds system applications, /var holds application data that changes as Linux runs, and /etc holds configuration files and settings. To get the most from Linux, take some time to learn how key directories are organized. System folders are owned by root, and you cannot edit them as the default user.

Navigate and List Directories

File Manager gives you a convenient visual tool for navigating the file system of your Pi. But you can also navigate, find, create, edit, and delete files and folders from the command line. Use the `cd` command to change the current directory and `ls` to view directory contents. Useful switches for `ls` include `-l` for file details, `-a` to show hidden files, and `-R` to view files in subdirectories.

`cd` with no switches takes you to your /home/pi directory. As you navigate the file system, the command prompt always shows the current directory. Your user directory (/home/pi) is shortened to a tilde (~) to save space.

Navigate and List Directories

1 Launch LXTerminal if it is not already open.

2 Type `cd` and press **Enter**.

3 Type `ls` and press **Enter**.

A Linux lists the files in your /home/pi folder.

4 Type `ls -l` and press **Enter**.

B Linux lists the files with information about the owner, group, and creation date. (See Chapter 4 for more information about working with files.)

5 Type `cd Desktop` and press **Enter**.

Note: The `cd` command moves you to the Desktop folder in your home folder.

C Linux changes the command prompt to show you that you are now in /Desktop.

6 Type `ls` and press **Enter**.

D Linux lists the files in the Desktop folder.

7 Type `cd /` and press `Enter`.

E Linux changes the command prompt to show you that you are now in the / folder at the root of the folder tree.

8 Type `ls` and press `Enter`.

F Linux lists the files in the root folder.

Note: Folders are shown in blue letters.

9 Type `ls /home/pi` and press `Enter`.

G Linux lists the files in your /home/pi folder, even though you are currently in the root directory.

Note: You can specify a direct path to any directory or file in any command. You do not have to use `cd` first. (If you do, it often saves typing.)

Note: Linux hides certain housekeeping files. To see them, type `ls -a` and press `Enter`.

Note: To save typing, press `Tab`. Linux will often autocomplete a path.

```
pi@pi:/
File  Edit  Tabs  Help
pi@pi ~ $ cd
pi@pi ~ $ ls
Desktop  Documents  python_games  Scratch
pi@pi ~ $ ls -l
total 16
drwxr-xr-x 2 pi pi 4096 Jun 17 10:17 Desktop
drwxr-xr-x 3 pi pi 4096 May 28 20:34 Documents
drwxrwxr-x 2 pi pi 4096 Jul 20  2012 python_games
drwxr-xr-x 2 pi pi 4096 May 28 20:34 Scratch
pi@pi ~ $ cd Desktop
pi@pi ~/Desktop $ ls
anewfile.txt                         idle.desktop         python-games.desktop
debian-reference-common.desktop      lxterminal.desktop   scratch.desktop
idle3.desktop                        midori.desktop       wpa_gui.desktop
pi@pi ~/Desktop $ cd /
pi@pi / $ ls
bin    dev  home  lost+found  mnt  proc  run   selinux  sys  usr
boot   etc  lib   media       opt  root  sbin  srv      tmp  var
pi@pi / $
```

```
pi@pi:/
File  Edit  Tabs  Help
pi@pi ~ $ cd
pi@pi ~ $ ls
Desktop  Documents  python_games  Scratch
pi@pi ~ $ ls -l
total 16
drwxr-xr-x 2 pi pi 4096 Jun 17 10:17 Desktop
drwxr-xr-x 3 pi pi 4096 May 28 20:34 Documents
drwxrwxr-x 2 pi pi 4096 Jul 20  2012 python_games
drwxr-xr-x 2 pi pi 4096 May 28 20:34 Scratch
pi@pi ~ $ cd Desktop
pi@pi ~/Desktop $ ls
anewfile.txt                         idle.desktop         python-games.desktop
debian-reference-common.desktop      lxterminal.desktop   scratch.desktop
idle3.desktop                        midori.desktop       wpa_gui.desktop
pi@pi ~/Desktop $ cd /
pi@pi / $ ls
bin    dev  home  lost+found  mnt  proc  run   selinux  sys  usr
boot   etc  lib   media       opt  root  sbin  srv      tmp  var
pi@pi / $ ls /home/pi
Desktop  Documents  python_games  Scratch
pi@pi / $
```

TIPS

Can I move to any folder from any other?
The full address of any file or folder, including all the subfolders it is buried in, is called a *path*. If you know the path you can go to any item in the file system by typing `cd /` and pressing `Enter` and then typing `cd [full path]` and pressing `Enter`. You can also move up one directory by typing `cd ..` and pressing `Enter`. The space before the two periods is essential.

How can I remember where I am?
The current path always appears in the prompt. If you get lost, you can always return to your home user directory by typing `cd` and pressing `Enter` and to the root directory by typing `cd /` and pressing `Enter`.

Create a Directory

You can use the mkdir, or *make directory*, command to create a directory. Follow it with the name of your new directory. By default, Linux creates the directory at the current path, which is the Pi user path, unless you use cd [a path name] to select a different one.

You can use the touch command to create an empty file. Typically, you create files with a text editor called nano. But touch is occasionally useful when you want to create an empty file so Linux can work with it later.

Create a Directory

1 Type mkdir
mynewdirectory and
press Enter.

Linux creates the directory.

Note: Linux reports an error if it
cannot create the directory. It
does not display a message if the
command succeeds.

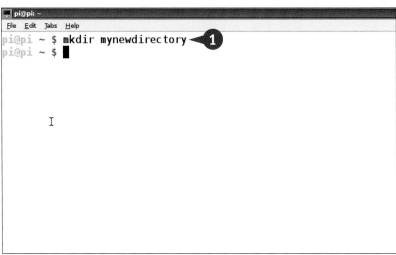

2 Type ls and press Enter to
list files and folders.

Ⓐ Your new directory appears in
the list.

3 Type cd
mynewdirectory and
press Enter to open the
directory.

Ⓑ Linux changes the prompt to
show the new path.

4 Type ls and press Enter to
list files.

Ⓒ Linux does not show any files
because you have not
created any yet.

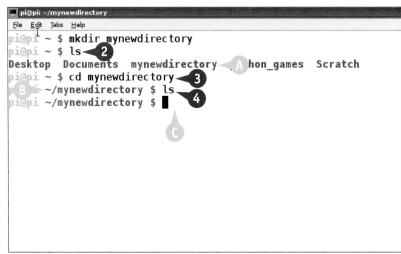

74

Delete Files and Directories

Y ou can use the rm command to delete a file, and rmdir, or *remove directory* command, to delete a directory. rrmdir only works on empty directories. To force deletion of a nonempty directory with its subdirectories, use rm -rf followed by the directory path.

Note that Linux has no trash feature and no undo options. Deletions are permanent, so use these commands with extreme care. Note that rm -rf * deletes all files in your Pi. Do not type it.

Delete Files and Directories

1 If you are not already in mynewdirectory, repeat the steps in the previous section, "Create a Directory," type cd mynewdirectory, and press **Enter**.

2 Type touch afile and press **Enter** to create an empty file called afile.

3 Type cd .. and press **Enter** to go up one directory level.

4 Type rmdir mynewdirectory and press **Enter** to delete the directory.

Ⓐ Linux displays an error message.

5 Type rm -rf mynewdirectory and press **Enter**.

Linux force-deletes the directory and any files inside it.

6 Type ls and press **Enter**.

Ⓑ The directory no longer exists.

75

View a File

You can use various commands to view the contents of a file. `cat` simply lists the file on the screen. `less` is a powerful file viewer with search options. You can select which lines appear on the screen and move around in the file while you view it. `less` is often used to slow down and split up the output from commands that generate too much text to fit on the screen, often with a Linux pipe. For details on Linux pipe see Chapter 6. This example displays a file with `cat` and `less`.

View a File

1 Type `cd` and press **Enter** to return to your home directory.

2 Type `cat Desktop/ midori.desktop` and press **Enter** to view the file that configures the Midori browser on the desktop.

A Linux displays the contents of the file. It scrolls off the screen.

Note: There are no files to view in the user directory, so this example displays a configuration file from the Desktop directory.

4 Type `less Desktop/ midori.desktop` and press **Enter**.

B Linux displays the file one screen at a time. Press **Spacebar** to show the next screen.

Note: To view the start of the file, press **G**. To view any line in the file, type the number of the line and press **G**.

Note: To exit `less`, or any other command line application while it is running, press **Ctrl**+**Z** or **Ctrl**+**C**.

Find a File or Command

You can use the `find` command to find a file by name. To avoid permission errors, run `find` as superuser by prefixing it with `sudo`. To use `find`, specify a starting directory for the search and the name switch to find a file by name. You can use wild cards. You can also search for files owned by a user or group, or with specific permissions. See the man page for details.

You can find the files that run a command with `whereis`. This is useful when you install a new application and have no idea where Linux put the files.

Find a File or Command

1 Type `sudo find / -name midori.desktop` and press Enter.

Note: `/` tells `find` to search all files, starting with the root directory.

Note: Searches are not instant on the Pi. Expect to wait at least a few seconds.

Ⓐ Linux shows the path to the midori.desktop file.

Note: There are two copies of the file — one set up for the default Pi user, and one with settings for all other users.

2 Type `whereis ls` and press Enter.

Ⓑ Linux shows the path to the file that holds the mini-application that runs the `ls` command.

Note: The second path is the location of the `ls` man page files.

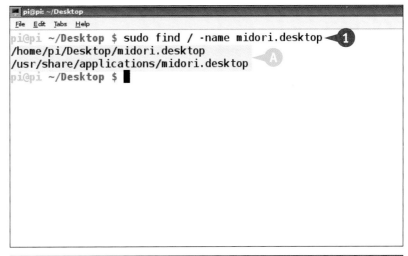

Copy, Move, and Rename Files

You can move files with the mv command. Linux does not have a rename command, but you can use mv to rename files. Effectively you move the files to a different name within the same directory. To copy files, use cp. Linux supports *wildcards* — a simple pattern-matching option that saves you typing. For example, * means all files, and *.txt means all files with the TXT extension.

Copy, Move, and Rename Files

1 Type cd and press **Enter** to return to your home directory.

2 Type touch afile.txt and press **Enter** to create an empty file named afile.txt.

3 Type cp afile.txt bfile.txt and press **Enter** to create a copy of the file.

4 Type ls and press **Enter** to confirm both files exist.

Linux shows both new files in the directory.

5 Type mv afile.txt cfile.txt and press **Enter**.

6 Type ls and press **Enter**.

Ⓐ Linux shows you have renamed afile.txt. It is now called cfile.txt.

Note: Because files are sorted alphabetically, cfile.txt is after bfile.txt in the list.

```
pi@pi: ~
File  Edit  Tabs  Help
pi@pi ~ $ cd       1
pi@pi ~ $ touch afile.txt    2
pi@pi ~ $ cp afile.txt bfile.txt   3
pi@pi ~ $ ls       4
afile.txt  bfile.txt  Desktop  Documents  python_games  Scratch
pi@pi ~ $ █
```

```
pi@pi: ~
File  Edit  Tabs  Help
pi@pi ~ $ cd
pi@pi ~ $ touch afile.txt
pi@pi ~ $ cp afile.txt bfile.txt
pi@pi ~ $ ls
afile.txt  bfile.txt  Desktop  Documents  python_games  Scratch
pi@pi ~ $ mv afile.txt cfile.txt   5
pi@pi ~ $ ls      6
bfile.txt  cfile.txt  Desktop  Documents  python_games  Scratch
pi@pi ~ $ █       Ⓐ
```

7 Type `cp bfile.txt /etc` and press Enter.

B Linux displays a permission error. /etc is a system directory and belongs to root. The pi user is not allowed to copy files to it.

8 Type `sudo cp bfile.txt /etc` and press Enter.

Note: As a shortcut, you can specify a directory for a copy or move without having to type the filename again. You can also specify a filename in full if you want the command to change it.

9 Type `ls /etc/*.txt` and press Enter to confirm the file has been copied.

Note: You can use wildcards with `ls` when you want to list certain files or file types.

10 Type `rm *.txt` and press Enter.

11 Type `ls` and press Enter.

C The output of `ls` confirms you have deleted both new .txt files.

12 Type `sudo rm /etc/bfile.txt` and press Enter.

The new file is removed from /etc.

```
pi@pi ~
File  Edit  Tabs  Help
pi@pi ~ $ cd
pi@pi ~ $ touch afile.txt
pi@pi ~ $ cp afile.txt bfile.txt
pi@pi ~ $ ls
afile.txt  bfile.txt  cfile.txt  Desktop  Documents  python_games  Scratch
pi@pi ~ $ mv afile.txt cfile.txt
pi@pi ~ $ ls
bfile.txt  cfile.txt  Desktop  Documents  python_games  Scratch
pi@pi ~ $ cp bfile.txt /etc
cp: cannot create regular file `/etc/bfile.txt': Permission denied
pi@pi ~ $ sudo cp bfile.txt /etc
pi@pi ~ $ ls /etc/*.txt
/etc/bfile.txt
pi@pi ~ $
```

```
pi@pi ~
File  Edit  Tabs  Help
pi@pi ~ $ cd
pi@pi ~ $ touch afile.txt
pi@pi ~ $ cp afile.txt bfile.txt
pi@pi ~ $ ls
afile.txt  bfile.txt  cfile.txt  Desktop  Documents  python_games  Scratch
pi@pi ~ $ mv afile.txt cfile.txt
pi@pi ~ $ ls
bfile.txt  cfile.txt  Desktop  Documents  python_games  Scratch
pi@pi ~ $ cp bfile.txt /etc
cp: cannot create regular file `/etc/bfile.txt': Permission denied
pi@pi ~ $ sudo cp bfile.txt /etc
pi@pi ~ $ ls /etc/*.txt
/etc/bfile.txt
pi@pi ~ $ rm *.txt
pi@pi ~ $ ls
Desktop  Documents  python_games  Scratch
pi@pi ~ $ sudo rm /etc/bfile.txt
pi@pi ~ $
```

TIP

Is there a way to do less typing?

Yes. If you press Tab, Linux attempts to complete the name of the current directory or file in the path for you. So, for example, /h Tab (with no space) expands to /home. If you then use /p Tab, Linux guesses the full path of /home/pi. This works with any directory and any file, in any command.

Work with File Permissions

Y ou can use the chmod command to change file permissions. You can specify permissions for root, the file owner, and the owner's group with three numeric codes, or as letter combinations. r, w, or x, specify read/write/execute permissions, and u, g, o, and a specify the user, group, and other (that is, everyone else). Use ls -l to review a file's current permissions before or after changing them.

chmod can be difficult to understand without examples and practice. You can find plenty online, for example, at www.tuxfiles.org/linuxhelp/filepermissions.html.

Work with File Permissions

1 If you are not already in the Desktop directory, type cd and press Enter; type cd Desktop and press Enter.

2 Type ls -l and press Enter to view detailed information about the files.

A Linux shows detailed information, with permissions at the left.

Note: Each permission is listed as rwx for user, group, and all, in that order. The first letter on the left is d if the file is a directory.

Note: a - indicates a permission is not available. For example, r— means a file can be read, but it cannot be edited or run executed as software.

3 Type chmod a = rwx midori.desktop and press Enter.

4 Type ls -l and press Enter.

B Linux shows that the permissions for midori. desktop have changed to rwx for user, group, and all.

```
pi@pi: ~/Desktop
File  Edit  Tabs  Help
pi@pi ~/Desktop $ cd
pi@pi ~ $ cd Desktop
pi@pi ~/Desktop $ ls -l          2
total 40
-rw-r--r-- 1 pi pi  634 Oct 29  2012 debian-reference-common.desktop
-rw-r--r-- 1 pi pi  224 May  6  2012 idle3.desktop
-rw-r--r-- 1 pi pi  238 Jun  6  2012 idle.desktop
-rw-r--r-- 1 pi pi 4953 Jun  1  2012 lxterminal.desktop
-rw-r--r-- 1 pi pi 5410 Jun 17 09:22 midori.desktop       A
-rw-r--r-- 1 pi pi  238 Oct 29  2012 python-games.desktop
-rw-r--r-- 1 pi pi  259 Jul  4  2012 scratch.desktop
-rw-r--r-- 1 pi pi  226 Nov 13  2012 wpa_gui.desktop
pi@pi ~/Desktop $
```

```
pi@pi: ~/Desktop
File  Edit  Tabs  Help
pi@pi ~/Desktop $ cd
pi@pi ~ $ cd Desktop
pi@pi ~/Desktop $ ls -l
total 40
-rw-r--r-- 1 pi pi  634 Oct 29  2012 debian-reference-common.desktop
-rw-r--r-- 1 pi pi  224 May  6  2012 idle3.desktop
-rw-r--r-- 1 pi pi  238 Jun  6  2012 idle.desktop
-rw-r--r-- 1 pi pi 4953 Jun  1  2012 lxterminal.desktop
-rw-r--r-- 1 pi pi 5410 Jun 17 09:22 midori.desktop
-rw-r--r-- 1 pi pi  238 Oct 29  2012 python-games.desktop
-rw-r--r-- 1 pi pi  259 Jul  4  2012 scratch.desktop
-rw-r--r-- 1 pi pi  226 Nov 13  2012 wpa_gui.desktop
pi@pi ~/Desktop $ chmod a=rwx midori.desktop       3
pi@pi ~/Desktop $ ls -l       4
total 40
-rw-r--r-- 1 pi pi  634 Oct 29  2012 debian-reference-common.desktop
-rw-r--r-- 1 pi pi  224 May  6  2012 idle3.desktop
-rw-r--r-- 1 pi pi  238 Jun  6  2012 idle.desktop
-rw-r--r-- 1 pi pi 4953 Jun  1  2012 lxterminal.desktop
-rwxrwxrwx 1 pi pi 5410 Jun 17 09:22 midori.desktop
-rw-r--r-- 1 pi pi  238 Oct 29  2012 python-games.desktop
-rw-r--r-- 1 pi pi  259 Jul  4  2012 scratch.desktop
-rw-r--r-- 1 pi pi  226 Nov 13  2012 wpa_gui.desktop
pi@pi ~/Desktop $
```

5 Type chmod o=r
midori.desktop and
press Enter.

6 Type ls -l and press
Enter.

Ⓒ Linux shows the other
(that is, all) permission
is now r.

Note: This means only the
file owner and file group can
edit it. Other users can read
it but they cannot change it.

```
pi@pi ~/Desktop $ chmod a=rwx midori.desktop
pi@pi ~/Desktop $ ls -l
total 40
-rw-r--r-- 1 pi pi  634 Oct 29  2012 debian-reference-common.desktop
-rw-r--r-- 1 pi pi  224 May  6  2012 idle3.desktop
-rw-r--r-- 1 pi pi  238 Jun  6  2012 idle.desktop
-rw-r--r-- 1 pi pi 4953 Jun  1  2012 lxterminal.desktop
-rwxrwxrwx 1 pi pi 5410 Jun 17 09:22 midori.desktop
-rw-r--r-- 1 pi pi  238 Oct 29  2012 python-games.desktop
-rw-r--r-- 1 pi pi  259 Jul  4  2012 scratch.desktop
-rw-r--r-- 1 pi pi  226 Nov 13  2012 wpa_gui.desktop
pi@pi ~/Desktop $ chmod o=r midori.desktop ◄━ 5
pi@pi ~/Desktop $ ls -l ◄━ 6
total 40
-rw-r--r-- 1 pi pi  634 Oct 29  2012 debian-reference-common.desktop
-rw-r--r-- 1 pi pi  224 May  6  2012 idle3.desktop
-rw-r--r-- 1 pi pi  238 Jun  6  2012 idle.desktop
-rw-r--r-- 1 pi pi 4953 Jun  1  2012 lxterminal.desktop
-rwxrwxr-- 1 pi pi 5410 Jun 17 09:22 midori.desktop
-rw-r--r-- 1 pi pi  238 Oct 29  2012 python-games.desktop
-rw-r--r-- 1 pi pi  259 Jul  4  2012 scratch.desktop
-rw-r--r-- 1 pi pi  226 Nov 13  2012 wpa_gui.desktop
pi@pi ~/Desktop $
```
pi@pi ~/Desktop

7 Type chmod 644
midori.desktop
and press Enter.

8 Type ls -l and press
Enter.

Ⓓ Linux shows the
permissions are now
rw- for the file owner,
and r- for the file
group and all other
users.

```
pi@pi ~/Desktop $ chmod o=r midori.desktop
pi@pi ~/Desktop $ ls -l
total 40
-rw-r--r-- 1 pi pi  634 Oct 29  2012 debian-reference-common.desktop
-rw-r--r-- 1 pi pi  224 May  6  2012 idle3.desktop
-rw-r--r-- 1 pi pi  238 Jun  6  2012 idle.desktop
-rw-r--r-- 1 pi pi 4953 Jun  1  2012 lxterminal.desktop
-rwxrwxr-- 1 pi pi 5410 Jun 17 09:22 midori.desktop
-rw-r--r-- 1 pi pi  238 Oct 29  2012 python-games.desktop
-rw-r--r-- 1 pi pi  259 Jul  4  2012 scratch.desktop
-rw-r--r-- 1 pi pi  226 Nov 13  2012 wpa_gui.desktop
pi@pi ~/Desktop $ chmod 644 midori.desktop ◄━ 7
pi@pi ~/Desktop $ ls -l ◄━ 8
total 40
-rw-r--r-- 1 pi pi  634 Oct 29  2012 debian-reference-common.desktop
-rw-r--r-- 1 pi pi  224 May  6  2012 idle3.desktop
-rw-r--r-- 1 pi pi  238 Jun  6  2012 idle.desktop
-rw-r--r-- 1 pi pi 4953 Jun  1  2012 lxterminal.desktop
-rw-r--r-- 1 pi pi 5410 Jun 17 09:22 midori.desktop
-rw-r--r-- 1 pi pi  238 Oct 29  2012 python-games.desktop
-rw-r--r-- 1 pi pi  259 Jul  4  2012 scratch.desktop
-rw-r--r-- 1 pi pi  226 Nov 13  2012 wpa_gui.desktop
pi@pi ~/Desktop $
```
pi@pi ~/Desktop

TIPS

Which numbers should I use with chmod?
The most useful numbers are 4, 5, 6, and 7. 4 is the
same as r--, 6 is rw-, and 7 is rwx. The numbers
are in the order of user, group, and other. 5 is a
popular way to make files that can be read but not
edited with r-x. 1 is --x and allows a file to be
executed but not copied, which may be appropriate
for secure applications.

How do I change a file's owner or group?
Some applications only work if the files they access
belong to a specific user or group. Use chown to
change a file's owner, and chgroup to change a
file's group. Changing a file's owner to root makes it
accessible to critical system software, but not to
casual access. Many Linux configuration files are
owned by root.

Using the Command Line History

Linux includes a *history* feature: You can use it to repeat commands without retyping them. You can also edit commands from the list. Editing a long command is quicker than typing it from scratch.

You can access the history in various ways. Pressing ⬆ repeatedly takes you back through your history list. You can also type ! ! to repeat the previous command. To view the history list, type `history`. To select commands by number type ! and the number.

Using the Command Line History

1 Press ⬆.

Ⓐ Linux automatically inserts your previous command after the prompt.

2 Press **Enter** to run the command. It works just as if you typed it in by hand.

Note: In this example the previous command was `ls -l`. You may see a different command.

Note: You can keep pressing ⬆ to scroll back through the history list.

3 Press ⬆ to load the previous command.

4 Press ◀ and ▶ to move the cursor on the command line.

5 Press **Delete** to remove text.

6 Type to insert text at the cursor position.

Note: To run the edited command, press **Enter**. You do not need to move the cursor to the end of the line.

```
pi@pi: ~/Desktop
File   Edit   Tabs   Help
pi@pi ~/Desktop $ ls -l ◀Ⓐ
total 40
-rw-r--r-- 1 pi pi  634 Oct 29  2012 debian-reference-common.desktop
-rw-r--r-- 1 pi pi  224 May  6  2012 idle3.desktop
-rw-r--r-- 1 pi pi  238 Jun  6  2012 idle.desktop
-rw-r--r-- 1 pi pi 4953 Jun  1  2012 lxterminal.desktop
-rw-r--r-- 1 pi pi 5410 Jun 17 09:22 midori.desktop
-rw-r--r-- 1 pi pi  238 Oct 29  2012 python-games.desktop
-rw-r--r-- 1 pi pi  259 Jul  4  2012 scratch.desktop
-rw-r--r-- 1 pi pi  226 Nov 13  2012 wpa_gui.desktop
pi@pi ~/Desktop $ █
```
2

```
pi@pi: ~/Desktop
File   Edit   Tabs   Help
pi@pi ~/Desktop $ ls -l
total 40
-rw-r--r-- 1 pi pi  634 Oct 29  2012 debian-reference-common.desktop
-rw-r--r-- 1 pi pi  224 May  6  2012 idle3.desktop
-rw-r--r-- 1 pi pi  238 Jun  6  2012 idle.desktop
-rw-r--r-- 1 pi pi 4953 Jun  1  2012 lxterminal.desktop
-rw-r--r-- 1 pi pi 5410 Jun 17 09:22 midori.desktop
-rw-r--r-- 1 pi pi  238 Oct 29  2012 python-games.desktop
-rw-r--r-- 1 pi pi  259 Jul  4  2012 scratch.desktop
-rw-r--r-- 1 pi pi  226 Nov 13  2012 wpa_gui.desktop
pi@pi ~/Desktop $ **6**▶ a█ ◀**4**
```
5

```
I
```

7 Type `history` and press
Enter.

B Linux displays a list of your
previous commands in order,
with an index.

8 Type ! followed by a number
with no space and press
Enter to use an index
number to select a command.

C Linux runs the command you
select.

Note: You can use any number.
This example runs `ls -l` at
index 1146. You will have a
different list with different
numbers.

Note: `history` includes many
timesaving features. For example,
you can search for previous
commands by pressing **Ctrl**+**R**
and typing part of the name. For
more information, search online
for "Linux history command."

```
1115  c
1116  cd
1117  touch afile.txt
1118  cp afile.txt bfile.txt
1119  ls
1120  mv afile.txt cfile.txt
1121  ls
1122  cp bfile.txt /etc
1123  sudo cp bfile.txt /etc
1124  ls /etc/*.txt
1125  rm *.txt
1126  ls
1127  sudo rm /etc/bfile.txt
1128  cd /Desktop
1129  cd Desktop
1130  c
1131  cd
1132  cd Desktop
1133  ls -l
1134  rm anewfile.txt
1135  c
1136  cd
1137  cd Desktop
1138  ls -l
1139  chmod a=rwx midori.desktop
1140  ls -l
1141  chmod o=r midori.desktop
1142  ls -l
1143  chmod 644 midori.desktop
1144  ls -l
1145  c
1146  ls -l
1147  ls -al
1148  history
pi@pi ~/Desktop $
```

```
1140  ls -l
1141  chmod o=r midori.desktop
1142  ls -l
1143  chmod 644 midori.desktop
1144  ls -l
1145  c
1146  ls -l
1147  ls -al
1148  history
pi@pi ~/Desktop $ !1146
ls -l
total 40
-rw-r--r-- 1 pi pi  634 Oct 29  2012 debian-reference-common.desktop
-rw-r--r-- 1 pi pi  224 May  6  2012 idle3.desktop
-rw-r--r-- 1 pi pi  238 Jun  6  2012 idle.desktop
-rw-r--r-- 1 pi pi 4953 Jun  1  2012 lxterminal.desktop
-rw-r--r-- 1 pi pi 5410 Jun 17 09:22 midori.desktop
-rw-r--r-- 1 pi pi  238 Oct 29  2012 python-games.desktop
-rw-r--r-- 1 pi pi  259 Jul  4  2012 scratch.desktop
-rw-r--r-- 1 pi pi  226 Nov 13  2012 wpa_gui.desktop
pi@pi ~/Desktop $
```

TIPS

Why does the history list change when I become root?
Linux keeps a separate history list for every user. When you promote yourself to root with `sudo su`, Linux automatically switches to the history it keeps for the root user.

How do I clear the history?
The simple but temporary option is `history -c`. For a more permanent solution, use `rm .bash_history`. This file is hidden, but if you include the dot prefix in the name you can view and edit it with `nano`. Logging out does not clear `.bash_history`. If you do not delete it, it literally remembers every command you have ever typed.

## CHAPTER 6

Understanding Advanced Commands

You can use the full power of Linux by learning how to work with files and commands in creative ways.

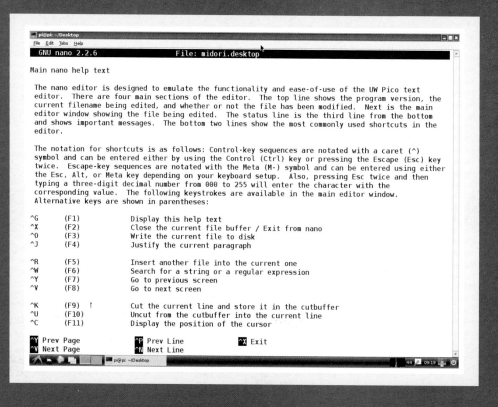

Understanding Advanced Linux

Compared to Windows or OS X, Linux can seem unnecessarily complex. The benefits become obvious when you discover how to combine commands into mini-applications, process text files and screen output in customizable ways, and make Linux perform commands automatically.

Understanding Aliases

Because commands are complex and hard to remember, you can

create *aliases*, which are short commands that perform longer commands. For example, if you type `alias l ="ls -Al"`, typing `l` as a command runs `ls -Al` and saves you some typing.

Understanding Pipes and Redirection

In Linux, everything is a file. The screen is a file called *stdout*, or standard output. It is often useful to redirect output from the screen to a file. In Linux, you simply press > after the command and add a filename. You can also *pipe*, or send, the output from one command straight to another by typing | between the commands.

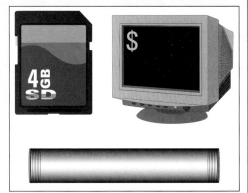

Combine Commands

Redirection and pipes add power to Linux. With pipes, you can create mini-applications by combining commands. For example, if a

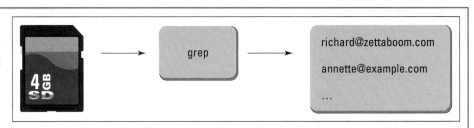

command produces too much text to fit on the screen, you can pipe it through a `less` command to split the text into pages that fit on the screen. With pipes, you can use Linux commands to improvise tiny applications to solve simple problems. For example, you can use a search command such as `grep` to find all the e-mail addresses or phone numbers in a file. With redirection, you can save the results of a pipe to a file.

Introducing grep and sed

The grep command searches a file for text. The sed command

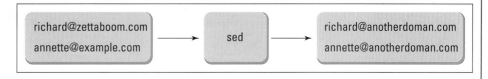

processes text on the fly, performing automatic editing and substitution. If you use pipes with grep and sed you can create your own search and replace tools, finding and changing complex text patterns and number ranges. grep and sed are far more powerful and open ended than the search-and-replace tools in most word processors.

Understanding Scripts, Shells, and Bash

With Linux, you can combine almost any number of commands to create *scripts* — custom applications that can repeat whole sequences of commands and make decisions as they work. Scripts are run by a *shell*, or a command processor. On the Pi, the shell is called Bash.

Understanding Scheduled Commands

You can schedule commands with crontab. A simple application might create an automatic backup daily. A more complex application might connect to your Twitter account every hour and send you an e-mail when you gain or lose followers.

Understanding Linux and Raspberry Pi

If you are new to Linux you may want to skip ahead to the Scratch and Python chapters (Chapters 9 and 10, respectively) to learn more about programming. You can then come back to this chapter and use what you learned about variables, loops, and conditional tests to start creating your own command scripts. If you want to build simple electronic projects, you need to know how to install and configure optional add-on applications. To get the most from your Pi, you can use a combination of timed Linux scripts, Python programming, and network commands to collect information from hardware sensors, online content,

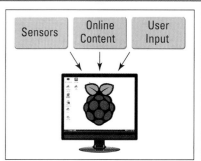

and live user input, and combine it to create unique and powerful custom applications.

Using the Nano Editor

Linux includes a selection of different text editors. An editor called nano is ideal for beginners. As a text editor, Linux does not support the mouse. You must use your keyboard to move around the file and make changes.

nano uses control-key commands. For example, to exit nano, press and hold Ctrl on your keyboard and type x. While running, nano shows a list of important control keys at the bottom of the screen. To view a complete list, press Ctrl+G, or press F1.

Using the Nano Editor

1 If you are running the desktop and LXTerminal is not already open, double-click it to open it.

Note: You can also run nano from the main system prompt without using the desktop.

2 Type cd Desktop and press Enter.

3 Type sudo nano midori. desktop and press Enter.

Linux launches nano and loads the midori.desktop file.

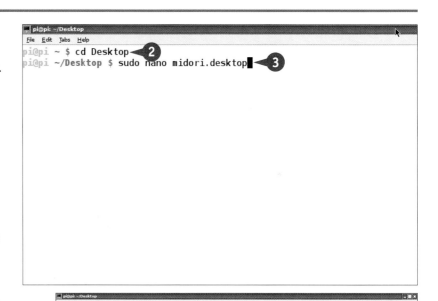

4 Press Ctrl+G or F1 to view a help file with a list of control-key commands.

Ⓐ nano shows the commands.

5 Use the control-key commands and ↑ ↓ keys to move through the help text.

Note: The help file is read-only.

6 To return to editing the file, press Ctrl+X.

Note: nano always ignores the mouse, even when the pointer is visible in LXTerminal.

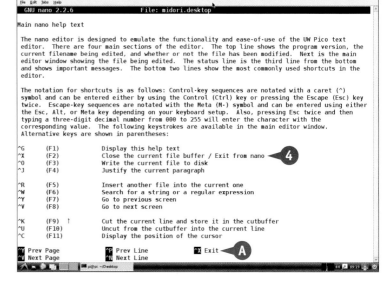

7 Using ⬆ and ⬇ and Ctrl+X and Ctrl+Y, scroll down to the first line marked GenericName.

8 Press ⬅ and ➡ to place the cursor just before Web Browser.

9 Type Lightweight and press Spacebar.

nano inserts the text you type at the cursor.

10 Press Ctrl+X and Enter.

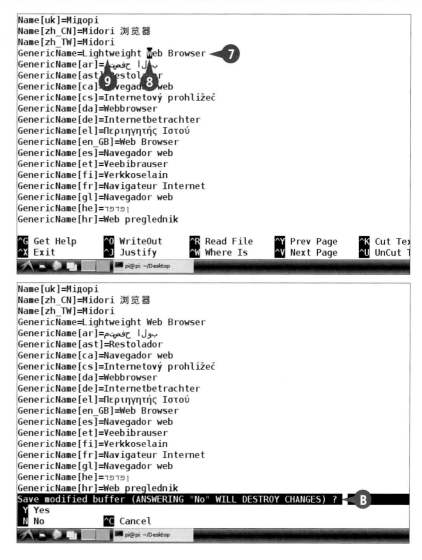

B nano displays a save confirmation question.

11 Type y to confirm you want to save the edited file, or n to cancel.

12 If you choose to confirm, press Enter to save the file.

Note: Before saving you can press Backspace and other keys to change the filename.

nano saves the file and exits to the command line.

Note: To check that you have changed the file, reload it in nano or list it with cat.

TIPS

Why should I use nano instead of Leafpad?
Leafpad is easier to use, especially if you are used to working with desktop applications. But Leafpad does not include a superuser option, and if you are not running the desktop as root you cannot use Leafpad to edit important files. At the command line, you can use sudo nano to edit any file.

What about other editors like vim and emacs?
Linux has many command-line text editors with different editing styles and features. vi and emacs are popular with programmers, but they are not aimed at beginners. To experiment with a version of vi called vim, type vi. emacs is not installed on the Pi, but you can use sudo apt-get install emacs to download it.

Set Up Autologin

Linux has many *boot options*, or settings that define what it does as it launches. You can customize these options by editing various system files. Many require intermediate or advanced experience levels. Autologin is a useful and relatively simple option. When you set up autologin, Linux logs you in as Pi automatically without asking for a username or password.

You can set up autologin by editing a file called /etc/inittab with nano. The commands in the file are very cryptic, but with care you can modify them successfully without understanding how they work, which is a good example of "magic word" programming.

Set Up Autologin

1 In LXTerminal or at the main command prompt type `sudo nano /etc/ inittab` and press Enter.

A nano launches and loads the /etc/inittab file, which sets up access to the Pi from the keyboard and screen.

2 Scroll down to the line shown in the figure, starting with `1:2345 respawn`.

3 Press Ctrl + A to start marking an area of text.

4 Press → to move the cursor to the end of the line.

5 Press Ctrl + K to cut the text into a buffer, and press Ctrl + U twice to paste two copies.

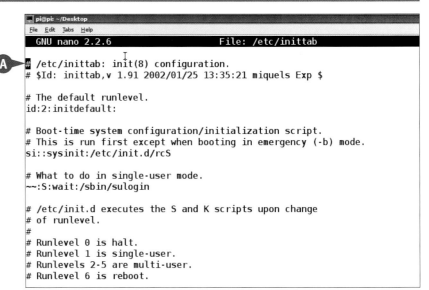

6 Add a hash (#) character at the start of the first copy to comment out the line so Linux ignores it.

7 Retype the second copy on a single line with no quotes:

```
1:2345:respawn:/
bin/login -f pi
tty1 <dev/tty1
>/dev/tty1 2>&1
```

Note: You must type this correctly, including all spaces and punctuation. Check it at least three times. Be sure to type /bin/ not /sbin/.

8 Press Ctrl+O and Ctrl+Y to save the file and Ctrl+X to quit.

9 Type sudo reboot and press Enter to restart your Pi.

The Pi restarts and logs you in without asking for your username or password.

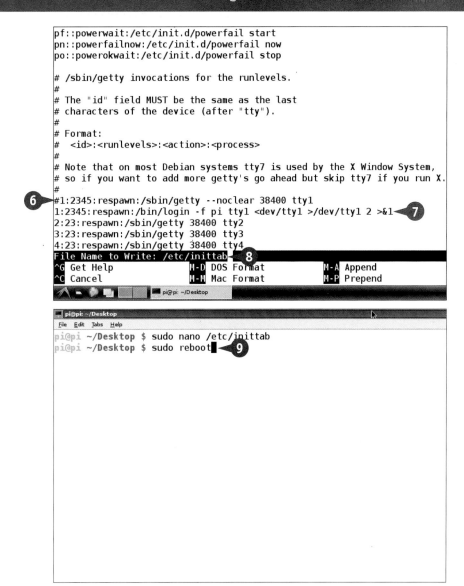

```
pf::powerwait:/etc/init.d/powerfail start
pn::powerfailnow:/etc/init.d/powerfail now
po::powerokwait:/etc/init.d/powerfail stop

# /sbin/getty invocations for the runlevels.
#
# The "id" field MUST be the same as the last
# characters of the device (after "tty").
#
# Format:
#   <id>:<runlevels>:<action>:<process>
#
# Note that on most Debian systems tty7 is used by the X Window System,
# so if you want to add more getty's go ahead but skip tty7 if you run X.
#
#1:2345:respawn:/sbin/getty --noclear 38400 tty1
1:2345:respawn:/bin/login -f pi tty1 <dev/tty1 >/dev/tty1 2 >&1
2:23:respawn:/sbin/getty 38400 tty2
3:23:respawn:/sbin/getty 38400 tty3
4:23:respawn:/sbin/getty 38400 tty4
File Name to Write: /etc/inittab
^G Get Help          M-D DOS Format        M-A Append
^C Cancel            M-M Mac Format        M-P Prepend
```

```
pi@pi: ~/Desktop
File  Edit  Tabs  Help
pi@pi ~/Desktop $ sudo nano /etc/inittab
pi@pi ~/Desktop $ sudo reboot
```

TIPS

Why do I get error messages and a locked screen after rebooting?

The edit works as long as you type it correctly. Remember, Linux commands must be 100 percent correct. If you forget to change sbin to bin or make some other mistake you will not be able to log in.

How can I fix this?

Although you cannot log in from your keyboard, Linux is still running on the Pi. If you have another computer on your network that can run a text terminal application you can still log in and edit files remotely. You can then use nano to correct the inittab file. For more about using your Pi remotely, see Chapter 7.

Download and Install Applications

You can install applications on your Pi with the `apt-get install` command. `apt` is short for Advanced Package Tools. Applications download as packages from an online collection known as the *repository*.

Although the technology used by `apt-get` is complicated, the command is easy to use — type `apt-get install` and the package name, and wait for installation to finish. Reinstalling an application automatically updates it to the latest version. You can remove applications with `apt-get autoremove --purge` and the package name. Note that some applications require the desktop, and you must run them from LXTerminal, not the system prompt.

Download and Install Applications

1 Launch the desktop and double-click **LXTerminal** to launch it.

2 When the prompt appears, type `sudo apt-get install geki2` and press Enter.

Note: `geki2` is a simple arcade game package.

Ⓐ `apt-get` runs a short preparation script and asks you to confirm installation.

3 Type `Y` (it must be uppercase) and press Enter at the prompt to confirm.

Note: You can cancel installation by typing `n` and pressing Enter.

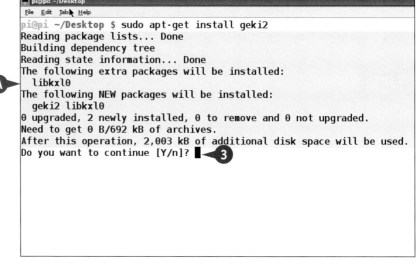

B apt-get generates a long list of messages as it downloads, unpacks, and installs the software.

Note: Installation can take anywhere from a minute to more than an hour, depending on the size of the package.

Note: If you see error messages, try restarting the process from step **1**.

C When the prompt reappears, installation is complete.

Note: apt-get does not display any further confirmation that a package installed successfully.

4 Type the name of the package and press Enter at the prompt to run it.

D The new application launches.

Note: geki2 launches in its own window. Some applications are text only and do not create a window.

Note: geki2 produces a text error message because audio is not yet set up correctly. To fix this, see Chapter 8.

TIPS

How do I know which package name to use?
Typically, you find the name online with a general web search, such as "Raspberry Pi web server" or "Raspberry Pi media center." You may find many different packages for each kind of applications — for example, you can run many different web servers on your Pi. But typically, only a couple of packages are popular and widely used. The rest are experimental, and you can ignore them.

How do I know which packages are available?
You can browse a list with categories at www.raspberryconnect.com/raspbian-packages-list or download the full current list (currently 32MB of text) from http://archive.raspbian.org/raspbian/dists/wheezy/main/binary-armhf/Packages.

Configure an Application

Linux applications use *configuration files* to manage settings. The /etc/inittab file in the section "Set Up Autologin" is a configuration file. Many configuration files live in /etc, but others can be anywhere in the file system. To configure an application you must find the right file, search online for suitable settings, and then use nano to edit the file.

Complex applications such as web servers often require "magic word" configuration settings. To save time, copy known working settings created by someone else.

Configure an Application

Note: This example makes a simple change to a Linux networking application to set the Pi's network name.

1. Launch the desktop.

2. Open LXTerminal.

3. Type cd /etc and press Enter.

4. Type ls and press Enter.

Ⓐ Linux shows a long list of configuration files and folders.

Note: Some applications are configured with a single file. Others keep a group of files in a directory.

Note: You may see a slightly different list of applications on your Pi. The top entries in this list have scrolled off the top of the screen.

4. Type sudo nano hostname and press Enter.

Ⓑ nano launches and loads the hostname file.

5. Change the first (and only) word in the file to a name of your choice.

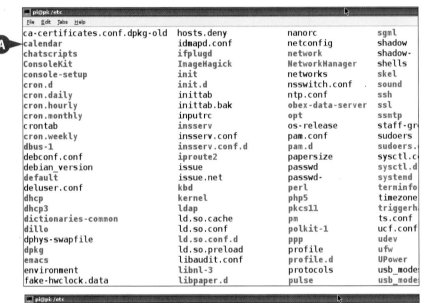

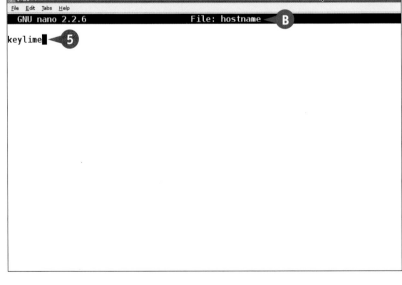

6 Press `Ctrl`+`O` and `Enter` to save the edited hostname file.

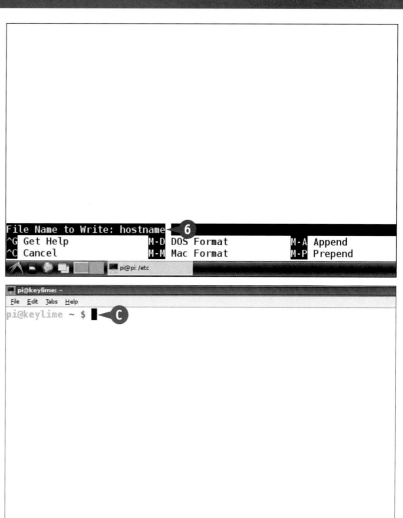

7 Press `Ctrl`+`X` to exit `nano`.

8 Type `sudo reboot` to reboot your Pi.

C After reboot the prompt shows the new hostname.

Note: If your Pi is connected to a network, you can access it using the new hostname.

TIPS

How do I know where to find the right file?

Many configuration files are in /etc. Some are in directories, and often have a .conf extension. For example, if you install a file server application called Samba — for details see Chapter 7 — it automatically creates a /etc/samba directory, and a file called samba.conf inside it. If you look in /etc and cannot find a file for your application, try searching online.

Can I break something by making a mistake?

Yes. Making a mistake in a configuration can have various effects, from breaking one application to breaking Linux. Always back up your system using the instructions in Chapter 2 before editing critical files.

Redirect Screen Output to a File

You can send output that usually appears on the screen to a file simply by typing > and a filename after the command. If the file does not exist, Linux creates it automatically. If it already contains text, Linux overwrites it.

Redirect Screen Output to a File

1 In LXTerminal or at the command prompt, type cd and press Enter to return to the Pi home directory.

2 Type ls > afile.txt and press Enter.

A Linux sends the output of the ls command to a file called afile.txt. The output does not appear on the screen.

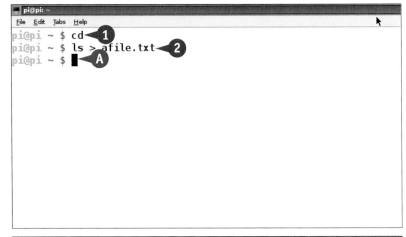

3 Type cat afile.txt and press Enter.

B Linux lists the file on the screen. It contains the output generated by the ls command.

Note: If you redirect a different command to the file its contents are overwritten.

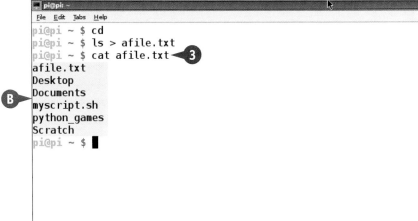

Combine Commands with a Pipe

You can send the output of one command to another command with a pipe. To set up a pipe, type the | character between the two commands. You can chain commands almost indefinitely.

Pipes have some very advanced uses. This section illustrates a very simple example, which pipes the output of ls -l through a command called less, which splits up long output so it fits into pages on the screen. You can use a command called tee to save the output to a command while also viewing the results on the screen.

Combine Commands with a Pipe

① Type cd /etc and press
Enter to move to the /etc
directory.

② Type ls -l | less
(spaces before and after the
| character) and press **Enter**.

Note: The | character is usually
on the lower left of your
keyboard. On a Mac, press
Option+**7**.

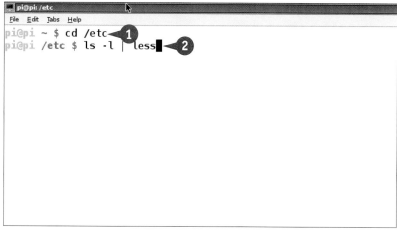

Ⓐ The bottom line of less
output is a mini command
prompt.

③ Press **Spacebar** to view pages
of output on the screen.

Note: To quit less and return
to the main command type q.

Note: Experiment with tee —
for example ls - l | tee
afile.txt — to confirm that
it writes to a file and displays
the output of a command at the
same time.

Note: You often need to prefix
tee with sudo to avoid
permission errors.

Process Text with grep and sed

$g$rep is a powerful text search command. sed is a powerful text manipulation command. You can use grep on its own to find words and phrases in files, or you can use it with sed to automatically replace words and phrases.

Both grep and sed have many options — too many to describe here. This example performs a simple search and replace on the contents of a file. You can find more complex examples and detailed user guides online.

Process Text with grep and sed

1 Type cd and press Enter to return to your home directory.

2 Type cd Desktop and press Enter to move to your /Desktop directory.

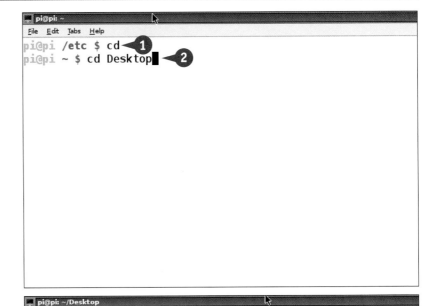

3 Type grep GNOME midori.desktop and press Enter.

Ⓐ grep lists all the lines in the midori.desktop file that include the word GNOME.

Note: When grep finds a word, it highlights it in red.

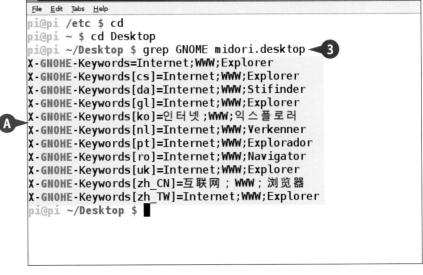

④ Type sed 's/GNOME/
ORC/g' midori.
desktop > anewfile.
txt and press Enter.

⑤ Type less
anewfile.txt and
press Enter to view the
contents of anewfile.

Ⓑ Linux changes all
occurrences of GNOME to
ORC and writes them to
a new file.

Note: GNOME is a family of
Linux desktop software.
Changing GNOME to ORC does
not do anything useful
except demonstrate how to
replace text.

TIPS

What else can I do with these commands?
These examples are very basic. Both `sed` and
`grep` support pattern matching using *regular
expressions* — a powerful but obscure set of
tools that can find almost any pattern of
letters, words, and numbers. Regular
expressions are often used in web design and
software development.

What are PERL and awk?
`awk` is a development of `sed`, and a simple programming
language in its own right. PERL is a further development of
`awk`, and is widely used to process text on web pages. `awk`
is preinstalled on the Pi, and you can find out more about
it online. A variant of PERL is also available as an optional
download. An even more powerful programming language
called Python is already installed (see Chapter 10).

Create a Simple Script

You can create more complex commands by combining simple ones in a *script*. Scripts can repeat commands, accept input from the user, and make decisions. Many Linux boot options run as scripts. This example creates a simple script that searches for a file given its name.

To make a script, write your commands into a file with nano. You must change the permissions on the file before the script can work and tell Linux to look in your home directory for the script; otherwise, it cannot run it. Note that nano adds cheerful colors to script files automatically.

Create a Simple Script

1 Type cd and press Enter to return to your home directory.

2 Type nano myscript.sh and press Enter.

3 Type the text shown in the figure exactly as shown, with all punctuation and spaces. The yellow word after echo is Searching....

Note: The first line loads the bash shell, the second types Searching... on the screen, the last line runs the find command. $1 reads the first word after the script name when you run the script.

4 Press Ctrl+O and Enter to save the file without changing its name, and press Ctrl+X to save the file and return to the command prompt.

5 Type chmod 755 myscript.sh and press Enter to change the permissions on the script so it can run correctly.

Note: Step 5 is essential. If you forget to do it, your script cannot run.

Note: You can also type chmod +x myscript.sh and press Enter.

6 Type `nano .bashrc` and press Enter.

Note: `.bashrc` is a configuration file for the Bash shell. Include the period in front of the name.

7 Add the following line to the end of the file and save it:

PATH=$PATH$HOME

8 Type `sudo reboot` and press Enter and wait while the Pi restarts.

Note: This line tells the Bash shell to look for scripts in your home directory.

9 Type `myscript.sh midori.desktop` and press Enter.

A The script runs and reports the path to the midori.desktop file in your Desktop directory.

Note: The script finds the filename you specify when you run it, and stops automatically.

Note: You can rename the script. Give scripts a distinctive name to avoid clashing with existing Linux commands.

```
GNU nano 2.2.6                         File: .bashrc

#alias ll='ls -l'
#alias la='ls -A'
#alias l='ls -CF'

# Alias definitions.
# You may want to put all your additions into a separate file like
# ~/.bash_aliases, instead of adding them here directly.
# See /usr/share/doc/bash-doc/examples in the bash-doc package.

if [ -f ~/.bash_aliases ]; then
    . ~/.bash_aliases
fi

# enable programmable completion features (you don't need to enable
# this, if it's already enabled in /etc/bash.bashrc and /etc/profile
# sources /etc/bash.bashrc).
if [ -f /etc/bash_completion ] && ! shopt -oq posix; then
    . /etc/bash_completion
fi

PATH=$PATH:$HOME          ◀━━ 7
```

```
pi@pi ~ $ cd
pi@pi ~ $ nano myscript.sh
pi@pi ~ $ chmod 755 myscript.sh
pi@pi ~ $ myscript.sh midori.desktop ◀━ 9
Searching...
/home/pi/Desktop/midori.desktop
/usr/share/applications/midori.desktop ◀━ A
pi@pi ~ $ ▮
```

TIPS

Why does my script say "command not found"?
Three mistakes can cause this. The first is mistyping the name of the script. The second happens if you edit a script file on a Windows PC and run it on the Pi. Windows adds junk characters to text. Strip them with a command called `dos2unix`. The third means you did not add the PATH command correctly.

Can other users run my script?
Other Pi users, including system processes, can run your script as long as they specify the full path of /home/pi/myscript.sh. If you make a subdirectory for your scripts, which many users do, you must specify the full path to the subdirectory and also update the PATH$ variable with the full path.

Run a Command at Set Times

Linux is designed to do many things at once. You can set it up to run scripts and commands automatically at any time of day or night at any interval from a minute to a decade.

To set up a timed script, use the `crontab -e` command. Linux runs a collection of timers behind the scenes. The `crontab` defines what the timers do, and when they do it. By default, the `crontab` reports command outputs with an automatic e-mail. This example redirects the output to the screen so you can see the command working.

Run a Command at Set Times

1 Type `crontab -e` and press **Enter** at the command prompt.

A The crontab command launches `nano` for you and loads the `crontab` configuration file ready for editing.

Note: By default, the file contains no active commands so the `crontab` does nothing.

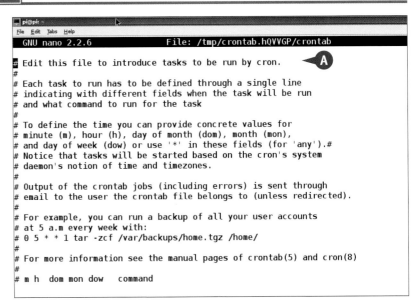

2 Type `*/1 * * * * date > /dev/tty1` on a line anywhere in the file and press **Enter**.

Note: Use `/tty1` if you are working on the Pi. If you are connected remotely, use the `tty` command to find the correct text.

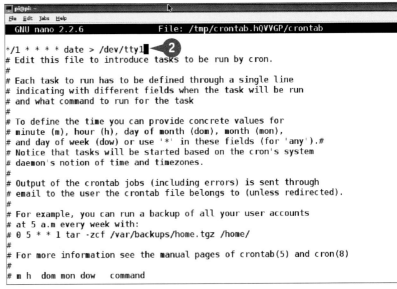

③ Press **Ctrl**+**X**, **Enter**, and **Ctrl**+**O** to save the file and exit nano.

ⓑ crontab quits and updates its task table.

Wait until the next whole minute.

ⓒ crontab shows the output of the date command — that is, the local time and date — on the screen.

ⓓ crontab repeats the command every minute.

Note: To stop the repetitions, type crontab -e, press **Enter**, and insert a hash (#) at the start of the first line. Save the file.

TIPS

What do the asterisks do?

crontab uses five input fields — minute, hour, day of month, month, and day of week. An asterisk means a field is ignored. An asterisk with a slash means "do this every (slash) multiples." */1 in the first position means "do this every minute." If you type a number without a slash, commands repeat whenever the time division matches the current time — "5 * * * *" means "do this five minutes past the hour."

What does /dev/tty1 do?

Linux is based on an older operating system called UNIX. When UNIX was invented, computers were connected to mechanical teletypewriters instead of electronic screens. /dev/tty1 means "teletypewriter device 1." The Pi uses a screen, but the screen file is still accessed with /dev/tty1 — the default virtual teletypewriter device on the Pi.

## CHAPTER 7

Networking Raspberry Pi

Your Pi works well on a network. You can control it remotely, share files, set up a web server, send e-mail, and even put your Pi on the Internet. Linux network tools provide a complete kit of software parts you can install and use as needed.

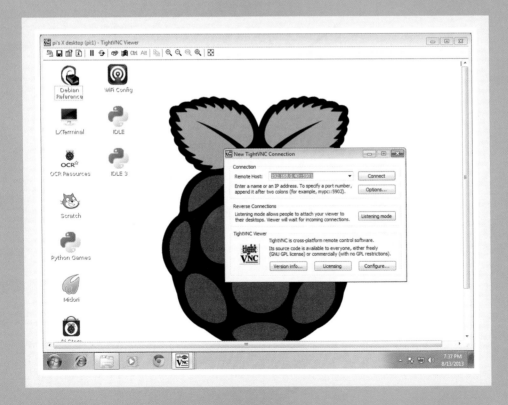

Understanding Networking

Your Pi works well on a network. You can control it remotely from another computer. You can set it up as a web server so you can create custom web pages to display useful information, such as readings from temperature sensors.

Understanding "Headless" Operation

"Headless" operation means remote control. Instead of typing on your Pi's keyboard and viewing its output on a monitor or TV, you can use the keyboard and screen of another computer on your network. You can also work with your Pi from any remote location over the Internet.

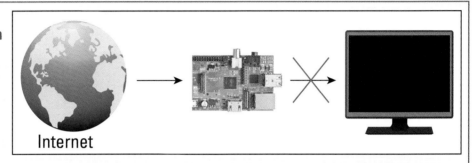

Understanding ssh

You can control your Pi in more than one way. `ssh` (secure shell) gives you remote access to the command line of your Pi. You can type commands and view the Pi's response on any remote computer with a *terminal client* — software for sending and viewing text. The `ssh` connection is *encrypted* — secured — so you can type passwords and other sensitive details safely.

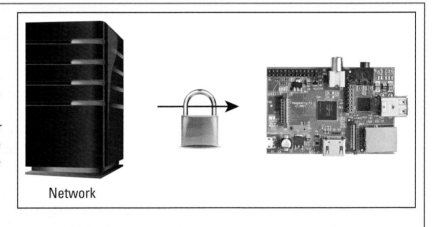

Understanding Virtual Network Computing

You can use VNC (Virtual Network Computing) for remote desktop access. VNC supports mouse actions and desktop graphics. You can view the Pi's desktop in a window on another computer and work remotely. To use VNC, you must install special VNC software on your Pi. You can use Safari on a Mac to access your Pi. On Windows, you can use free VNC client software.

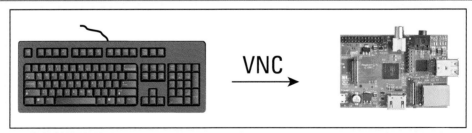

Understanding Samba

If you install a samba server on your Pi you can access its files using standard file viewers, such as Finder on the Mac and Windows Explorer on Windows systems. You do not need extra software. Although it is possible to set up Samba so you can use it over the Internet, Samba works best on your local network. It is

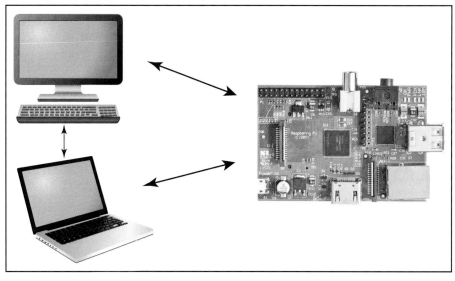

a good way to set up your Pi as a file server and to exchange files with other networked computers.

Understanding Web Servers

If you plan to use your Pi for software or hardware projects, you can install a web server to generate pages you can view in any web browser. Optionally, you can make the pages visible on the Internet. With a web server your Pi can display information generated by a script or small application. For example, your Pi can read information from hardware sensors, process the data, and use the web server to display results as text or graphics that can be viewed from any computer or smartphone with a web browser.

Understanding E-Mail Servers

You can use your Pi to send and receive e-mail. The Pi is not very fast. It is not a good replacement for e-mail on a desktop or laptop computer. But you can set up e-mail

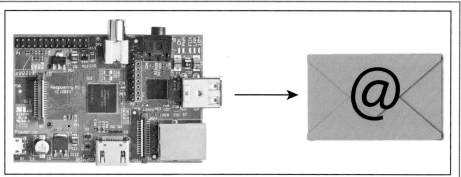

to send you messages, warnings, and notifications. For example, if you set up a home automation system, your Pi can send you an e-mail if the outdoor temperature drops below freezing.

Set a Static IP Address

You can simplify networking by giving your Pi a static IP address. IP, or Internet Protocol, addresses consist of four numbers separated by periods, for example 192.168.0.20.

For applications such as `ssh` you need to know your Pi's address. Your home router assigns network addresses automatically, but you can force it to assign an address of your choice to your Pi. You can then use this address when you want to access your Pi remotely.

Set a Static IP Address

1 At the command prompt or in LXTerminal, type `route` and press Enter.

Note: The route command shows important information about your network.

2 Make a note of the IP address under the Gateway heading.

Note: The first two numbers are usually 192.168 for home networks and 10.1 for business and college networks.

3 Make a note of the numbers at the bottom of the Genmask column, usually 255.255.255.0.

4 Type `ifconfig` and press Enter.

5 Find `eth0` if you have a wired network connection, or `wlan0` if you are using Wi-Fi.

Note: `eth0` is the Ethernet (cabled network) connection. `wlan` is a Wi-Fi connection.

6 Make a note of the address after `inet addr:`.

Note: On a home network, the third number is usually 0, 1, or 2. The last number is usually between 2 and 254.

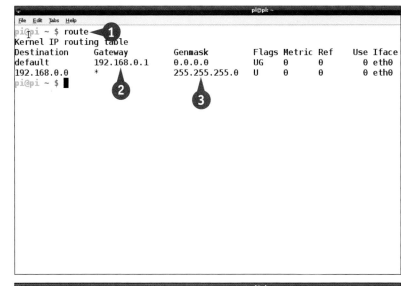

7 Type `sudo nano/etc/network/interfaces` and press **Enter**.

8 Find `dhcp` after `eth0 inet` or `wlan0 inet`. Delete it and replace it with `static`.

9 Add a new line with `gateway` followed by the number you noted in step **2**.

10 Add a new line with `netmask` followed by the number you noted in step **3**.

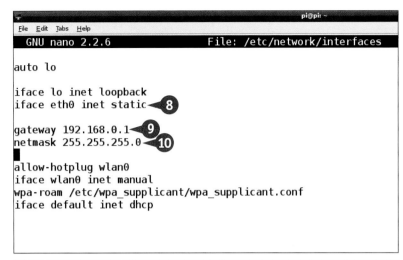

11 Add a new line with `address` and the address you noted in step **6**.

Note: This address is now your Pi's permanent static network address.

12 Press **Ctrl**+**O**, **Enter**, and **Ctrl**+**X** to save the changes and exit `nano`.

13 Type `sudo reboot` to restart your Pi.

The Pi reboots. Its IP address is set permanently to the address you typed in step **11**.

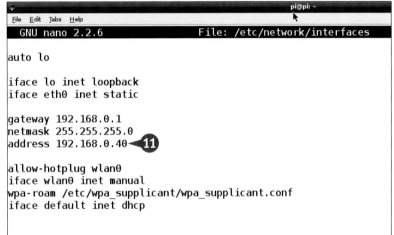

TIPS

Can I set a different permanent address?
If you understand how to find the range of addresses your network uses, you can pick any valid address from that range. If you do not, use the address you noted in step **11** because it is guaranteed to work; other addresses may not.

Do I need to set a broadcast address?
If you are familiar with DHCP, or Dynamic Host Configuration Protocol, you can add another line to the file with broadcast followed by your network's broadcast address. This is not usually necessary, but if your static address is not working, try adding this extra line. The broadcast address is shown in `ifconfig` after `Bcast:`.

Set Up ssh

Y ou can use a command called `ssh` (short for *secure shell*) to log in to your Pi from another computer and control it by typing commands. The Pi responds just as if you were typing commands from the Pi's own keyboard.

`ssh` is enabled by default. If you use your Pi as a public web server, you should disable it for security. Otherwise, your Pi could be hacked. If you use your Pi on your home network only and do not allow access from the Internet, you can skip this section.

Set Up ssh

1 Power up Raspberry Pi and wait for it to boot.

2 Type `sudo raspi-config` and press **Enter** at the command prompt.

Note: You can also launch the desktop and make the changes in LXTerminal, as shown here.

3 Press ⬆ and ⬇ to highlight Advanced Options, and press **Enter** to select.

4 Press ⬆ and ⬇ to highlight SSH, and press **Enter** to select.

5 Press ⬅ and ➡ to select **Enable** or **Disable**.

6 Press **Enter**.

Setup Options flashes a confirmation message.

7 Press **Enter** to select **OK** and return to the main Setup Options screen.

`ssh` is enabled or disabled, as you specified.

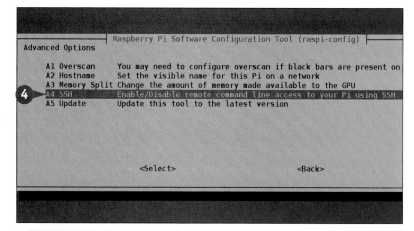

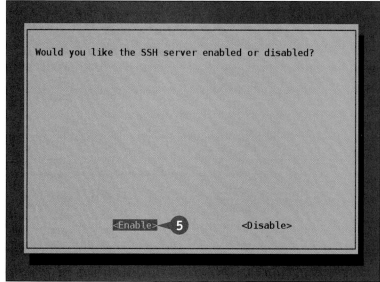

Using ssh for Remote Command Line Access

After you set up ssh on your Pi, you can log in to your Pi remotely from any computer on your network with an ssh client. On a Mac, you can use Terminal. On a PC, a popular choice is the free PuTTY application from www.chiark.greenend.org.uk/~sgtatham/putty.

ssh uses a random security key. By default, all copies of Raspbian have the same key. This makes your Pi very easy to hack. For maximum security, generate a unique key before using ssh.

Using ssh for Remote Command Line Access

1 At the command prompt, type sudo rm/etc/ssh/ ssh_host_* and press **Enter**.

Note: Step **1** deletes the existing security keys.

2 At the prompt, type sudo dpkg-reconfigure openssh-server and press **Enter**.

A The Pi generates new keys for ssh access and restarts the ssh server.

3 Using a terminal application on your remote computer, type ssh pi@*[your Pi's static IP address]* and press **Enter**.

Note: If your Pi's address is 192.168.0.40, type ssh pi@ 192.168.0.40 and press **Enter**. To set a static IP address, see the section "Set a Static IP Address."

Note: Type yes and press **Enter** if ssh asks you to confirm the connection.

4 Type the password for the Pi user.

B ssh logs you in. You can now use the Pi's command prompt remotely.

Note: If ssh notes that the key has changed, type ssh-keyscan *[your Pi's static IP address]* >> ~/.ssh/known_hosts and press **Enter** to validate the new key.

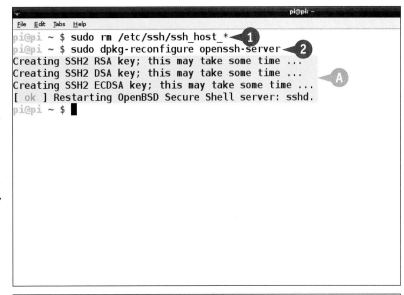

Set Up Remote Access with VNC

You can install a package called `tightvncserver` to allow remote desktop control of your Pi. You can then run `tightvncserver` manually to create a virtual desktop.

The virtual desktop does not appear on your Pi's monitor. You can only access it remotely from another computer over the network. If you have already launched the desktop with `startx`, `tightvncserver` creates another desktop. You cannot access the second desktop from your Pi.

Set Up Remote Access with VNC

Set Up Remote Access on the Pi

1 At the command prompt or in LXTerminal type `sudo apt-get install tightvncserver` and press **Enter**.

Note: Type `Y` and press **Enter** if asked to confirm.

Ⓐ Linux installs `tightvncserver`.

2 Type `tightvncserver -geometry 1024x768 -depth 24` and press **Enter**.

Note: You can set the desktop resolution by typing different numbers after `geometry`, up to 1920 × 1200.

Note: VNC is slow. Use the smallest acceptable resolution.

3 Type a password and type it again at the verify prompt.

4 Type and verify a view-only password.

Note: The two passwords can be the same. You will only be asked to type them the first time you launch `tightvncserver`.

Ⓑ `tightvncserver` creates an "invisible" desktop you can access from another computer.

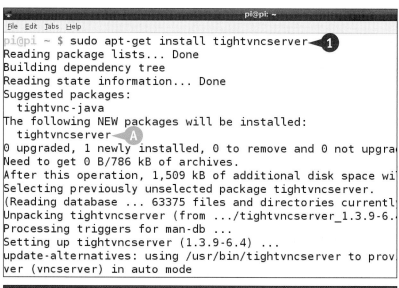

Access the Pi Desktop on a Mac

1 Launch Safari.

2 Type `vnc://[your Pi's static address]:5901` and press **Enter** into Safari's address bar.

C The Pi's desktop appears on your Mac. You can use the mouse and keyboard in the usual way.

Note: Screen updates are much slower than they are on the Pi.

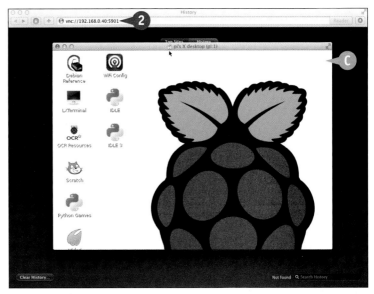

Access the Pi Desktop on a PC

1 Visit the Real VNC site at www.realvnc.com/download/viewer.

2 Download and install either the 32-bit or 64-bit viewer, depending on your version of Windows.

3 Launch the Viewer.

4 Type the Pi's IP address followed by `::5901` in the dialog box.

D The Viewer loads the Pi's desktop. You can control it with your PC's keyboard and mouse.

Note: To improve image quality at the expense of speed, or vice versa, select **Options** and click and drag the **Allow JPEG, set image quality** slider.

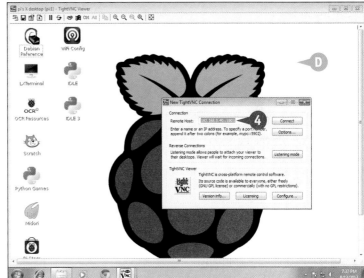

TIPS

Does VNC have limitations?
Yes. VNC lacks security. If you connect to your Pi over the Internet, your connection can be hacked. VNC is also slow. You can use VNC for basic text editing and web browsing, but it is too slow for animated games. VNC always creates its own desktop, so you cannot use it to control a desktop that is already running.

Are there better alternatives?
Yes. x11vnc is more powerful and more secure than VNC, but it is also more difficult to set up and does not work with Windows. You can install it by typing `sudo apt-get install x11vnc`. For configuration hints see www.raspberrypi.org/phpBB3/viewtopic.php?p=108862 - p108862.

Share Files with Samba

You can install an application called Samba to share the files on your Pi with other computers on your network. You can access files directly from Finder on a Mac or Windows Explorer on a PC. You do not need extra software.

Samba is easy to install, but the contents of the configuration file that controls Samba are critical. You must use the correct settings, or Samba does not work. This example sets up a configuration file that is known to work correctly.

Share Files with Samba

Note: You can find the code used in this section on this book's website, www.wiley.com/go/tyvraspberrypi.

1 At the command prompt or in LXTerminal, type sudo apt-get install samba and press Enter.

Note: Type y if asked to confirm.

Ⓐ Linux downloads and installs the main Samba package web server.

2 At the command prompt or in LXTerminal, type sudo apt-get install samba-common-bin and press Enter.

Ⓑ Linux downloads and installs supporting tools for Samba.

3 Type sudo rm /etc/samba/smb.conf and press Enter.

Note: This deletes the default configuration file, which does not work on the Pi.

4 Type sudo nano /etc/samba/smb.conf and press Enter.

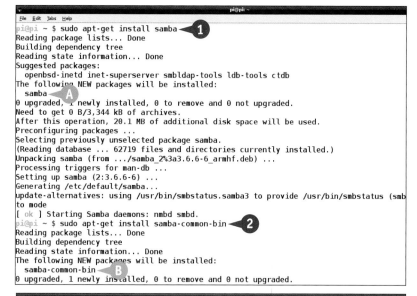

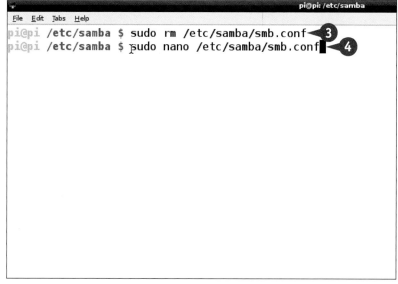

C nano creates an empty file.

5 On the first line, type
`sudoworkgroup =`
followed by the name of your
Windows workgroup, or
`WORKGROUP` if you do not
have one.

6 Type the rest of the text
exactly as shown in the
figure.

Note: This configuration sets up
a *share*, or access point, for the
Pi on your network.

7 Press `Ctrl`+`O`, `Enter`, and
then `Ctrl`+`X` to save the
file.

8 Type `sudo service
samba restart` and press
`Enter`.

D Samba restarts and loads the
new configuration.

After a few minutes, the Pi
appears on your network. You
can log in as a guest with no
password and access all files.

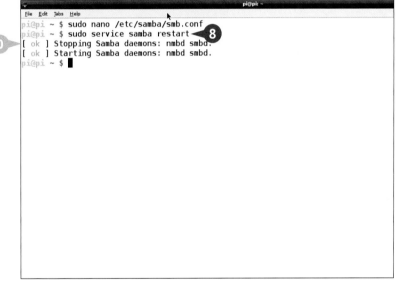

TIPS

Why does the Pi not appear in Finder on a Mac?
You may need to force Finder to recognize the Pi.
In Finder, click **Go** and then **Connect to Server**.
Type `smb://pi` or `smb://[your Pi's static IP address]` and press `Enter`.
Finder should then connect to the share. Double-click the **Share** icon to access the files on the Pi.

Why does the Pi not appear in Windows Explorer?
Windows has a complex relationship with Samba shares.
On XP, shares usually work. On Windows 7 and 8, support
is version dependent. Try selecting **Network** in Windows
Explorer and typing `//[your Pi's static IP address]` into the address bar. If your version of
Windows 7 or 8 supports Samba, the Pi should appear as
a share. Double-click it to access the files.

Set Up a Simple Web Server

You can use your Pi to set up a web server. When you type the Pi's IP address into a browser, it displays pages you have designed and uploaded to a special directory on the Pi. Pages can include static text and images. Your Pi can also generate smart pages that include live information, such as a temperature reading from a sensor or the contents of a Twitter feed.

You can install various web server packages. This example installs a simple web server called `lighttpd`, which is powerful enough to be useful, but is also easy to set up.

Set Up a Simple Web Server

1 At the command prompt or in LXTerminal, type `sudo apt-get install lighttpd` and press **Enter**.

2 Type `Y` when asked to confirm.

A Linux downloads and installs the `lighttpd` web server.

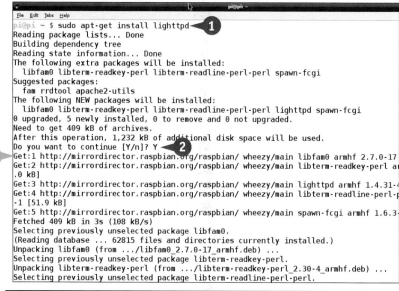

3 Type `sudo chown www-data:www-data /var/www` and press **Enter**.

4 Type `sudo chmod 775 /var/www` and press **Enter**.

5 Type `sudo usermod -a -G www-data pi` and press **Enter**.

Note: These "magic word" commands in steps **3** to **5** set up the web server's directory for web content, and give the Pi user access to it.

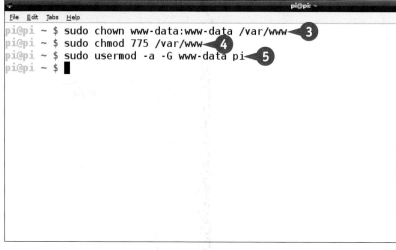

6 Type `sudo reboot` and press
Enter to reboot the Pi.

Note: You must reboot to force the
web server to notice your changes.

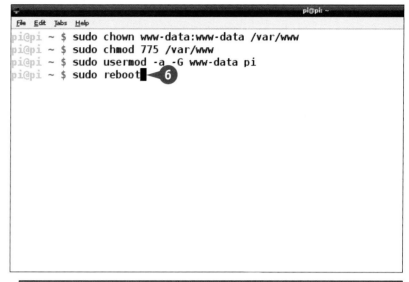

7 Type `startx` and press **Enter**
to launch the desktop.

8 Double-click the Midori icon to
launch the Midori web browser.

9 Type your Pi's static IP address
into the browser address box
and press **Enter**.

Ⓑ The browser loads a web page.
The page is hosted on your Pi.

Note: The placeholder content is in
/var/www/index.lighttpd.html.

Note: You can also access the server
on your Pi only by typing **localhost**
into a web browser address bar.

TIPS

What is Apache?

Apache is an industrial-strength web server
with many features. It is used by many
commercial web sites, but it can be difficult
to manage, so it is not used in this book.
You can install it with `sudo apt-get
install apache2`. For more details,
search online for "apache web server."

What are LAMP and MySQL, and do I need them?

MySQL is a database, or a tool for organizing and storing
complex information. MySQL, Apache, and a tool called PHP
are often installed together on Linux to create a widely used
professional tool called LAMP, from the initials of the
components. You do not need MySQL or Apache for the
projects in this book. PHP is introduced in the section
"Install PHP."

Create a Simple Web Page

You can create a simple web page on your Pi by writing a file called index.html to the /var/www directory. The file can contain any valid fixed HTML. The web server looks for a file starting with "index" when it receives a request to display a page.

This example creates a page that displays a line of text. If you have web programming experience, you can create a more complex web page by adding more content to index.html.

Create a Simple Web Page

1 At the command prompt or in LXTerminal type `sudo nano/var/www/index.html` and press **Enter**.

Linux launches `nano`.

2 Type `<p>Hello, World!</p>`.

3 Press **Ctrl**+**O**, **Enter**, and **Ctrl**+**X** to save and close the file.

Note: This very simple demo content does not include all the code used on commercial web pages, but all browsers display it without errors.

4 Type `startx` and press **Enter** to launch the desktop if it is not already running.

5 Double-click the Midori icon to launch the Midori web browser.

6 Type your Pi's static IP address into the address bar and press **Enter**.

Ⓐ The browser loads the page you created.

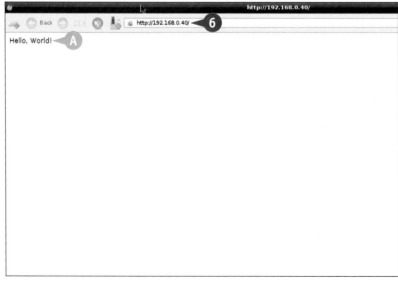

Note: If you are not familiar with HTML you can find many tutorials and examples online, such as the course at www.w3schools.com.

Install PHP

You can install PHP (short for PHP: Hypertext Processor) to enhance your web server so it can generate smart web pages. If you do not install PHP, you can only create static web pages with fixed text and images.

With PHP, your web server can generate *smart* web pages that can read information, process it, and display the results. PHP is complex and has many features. You can generate graphics, format text in creative ways, save and load information, and create complex custom web applications.

Install PHP

1 At the main command prompt or in LXTerminal, type sudo apt-get install php5-common php5-cgi php5 and press Enter.

2 Type Y and press Enter when asked to confirm.

Ⓐ Linux downloads and installs the elements that make up PHP.

3 Type sudo lighty-enable-mod fastcgi-php and press Enter.

Note: This tells lighttpd that PHP is available.

4 Type sudo service lighttpd force-reload and press Enter.

Ⓑ Linux restarts the web server. You can now create web pages that include PHP scripts.

Note: To find out more about PHP, view the free introductory course at www.w3schools.com.

```
                                              pi@pi: ~
File  Edit  Tabs  Help
pi@pi ~ $ sudo apt-get install php5-common php5-cgi php5      ◀─1
Reading package lists... Done
Building dependency tree
Reading state information... Done
The following extra packages will be installed:
  libonig2 libqdbm14
Suggested packages:
  php-pear
The following NEW packages will be installed:
  libonig2 libqdbm14 php5 php5-cgi php5-common
0 upgraded, 5 newly installed, 0 to remove and 0 not upgraded.
Need to get 5,680 kB of archives.
After this operation, 15.9 MB of additional disk space will be used.
Do you want to continue [Y/n]? Y   ◀─2
Get:1 http://mirrordirector.raspbian.org/raspbian/ wheezy/main php5-common
4 kB]
Get:2 http://mirrordirector.raspbian.org/raspbian/ wheezy/main php5 all 5.
Get:3 http://mirrordirector.raspbian.org/raspbian/ wheezy/main libonig2 an
Get:4 http://mirrordirector.raspbian.org/raspbian/ wheezy/main libqdbm14 a
Get:5 http://mirrordirector.raspbian.org/raspbian/ wheezy/main php5-cgi an
 kB]
24% [5 php5-cgi 532 kB/4,847 kB 11%]
```

```
Selecting previously unselected package php5.
Unpacking php5 (from .../php5_5.4.4-14+deb7u3_all.deb) ...
Processing triggers for man-db ...
Setting up php5-common (5.4.4-14+deb7u3) ...

Creating config file /etc/php5/mods-available/pdo.ini with new version
Setting up libqdbm14 (1.8.78-2) ...
Setting up libonig2 (5.9.1-1) ...
Setting up php5-cgi (5.4.4-14+deb7u3) ...

Creating config file /etc/php5/cgi/php.ini with new version
update-alternatives: using /usr/bin/php5-cgi to provide /usr/bin/php-cgi (p
update-alternatives: using /usr/lib/cgi-bin/php5 to provide /usr/lib/cgi-bi
to mode
Setting up php5 (5.4.4-14+deb7u3) ...
pi@pi ~ $ sudo lighty-enable-mod fastcgi-php   ◀─3
Enabling fastcgi-php: ok
Run /etc/init.d/lighttpd force-reload to enable changes
pi@pi ~ $ sudo service lighttpd force-reload   ◀─4
[ ok ] Reloading web server configuration: lighttpd.
pi@pi ~ $ ▮
```

Create a Smart Web Page

After you install PHP, you can create a smart web page that uses PHP to run a Linux command or script, and display the results. Save your PHP code in index.php file in /var/www. (If index.php exists, the server ignores index.html.)

This example runs a Linux command that checks the Pi's internal temperature and displays it. Although this example is very simple, it demonstrates how you can run a script and show the results in a web page.

Create a Smart Web Page

1 At the command prompt or in LXTerminal type `sudo usermod -a -G video www-data` and press **Enter**.

Note: This is a "magic word" command that allows the web server to read the Pi's temperature.

Note: Somewhat unexpectedly, the Pi's temperature sensor is part of its video system.

2 Type `sudo reboot`, press **Enter**, and wait for the Pi to reboot.

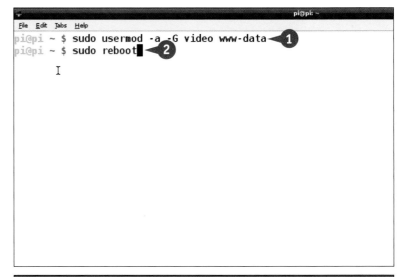

3 At the command prompt or in LXTerminal type `sudo nano /var/www/index.php` and press **Enter**.

4 Type `<?php` and press **Enter**.

Note: This line tells the web server to interpret what follows as a PHP script.

5 Type `$result = shell_exec('/opt/vc/bin/vcgencmd measure_temp');` and press **Enter**.

Note: In PHP, `shell_exec` runs a Linux command. The "magic word" command that follows displays the Pi's temperature.

6 Type echo ("The Pi's
".$result); and press Enter.

Note: This line uses PHP's echo command to display a result.

7 Type ?>.

Note: This line tells the web server the PHP script is complete.

8 Press Ctrl+O, Enter, and Ctrl+X to save and close the file.

Note: nano automatically colorizes PHP scripts. Text strings are colored yellow. The text remains black while you type.

9 Type startx and press Enter to launch the desktop.

10 Double-click the Midori icon to launch the Midori web browser.

11 Type your Pi's static IP address into the address bar and press Enter.

A The browser loads a web page that runs a script to display the Pi's current temperature. To update the reading, reload the page.

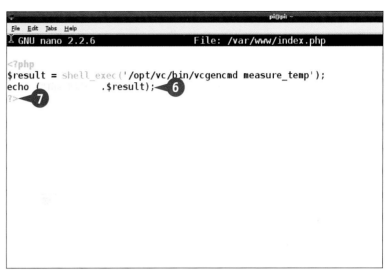

TIPS

What is the difference between Python, PHP, and Linux scripts?

PHP is specifically designed for web applications. It is a complex tool with many features, but you can use small parts of it without having to learn it all. Linux scripts are limited to combinations of Linux commands. Python is designed for general programming. Some Pi projects use only one tool. Others use all of them.

Do I need expert knowledge of web design, PHP, Python, and Linux?

The more you know, the more you can do with your Pi. But even if you have no previous experience you can still do a lot with very simple web pages, programs, and scripts. As you gain more experience, you can work on more complex projects.

Send E-Mails

Y ou can install an e-mail package to send e-mails using Linux commands. The Pi is not powerful enough to be a full desktop replacement, so this option works well for automated e-mails generated by scripts or custom software you create with PHP or Python. For example, you can send e-mails with temperature warnings, weather alerts, or timed reminders. You can also grab frames from a webcam and send them in attachments.

This example uses a simple e-mail package called `ssmtp` to forward e-mail via a Gmail account. You can send e-mail to any address, but it appears to come from the Gmail account.

Send E-Mails

1 At the command prompt or in LXTerminal, type `sudo apt-get install ssmtp` and press Enter.

A Linux downloads and installs the `ssmtp` mail sender.

2 Type `sudo apt-get install mailutils` and press Enter.

B Linux downloads and installs extra e-mail tools used by `ssmtp`.

Note: Visit http://mail.google.com to set up a Gmail account.

3 Type `sudo nano/etc/ssmtp/ssmtp.conf` and press Enter.

4 Repeat Ctrl+K to delete every line.

5 Add the following lines:

`AuthUser=` *[yourname@ gmail.com]*

`AuthPass= [yourpassword]`

6 Continue adding lines:

mailhub=smtp.gmail.
com:587

UseSTARTTLS=YES

FromLineOverride=YES

7 Press Ctrl+O, Enter, and Ctrl+X to save the file.

8 At the command prompt, type echo "message text" | mail -s "subject text" email@address.com and press Enter.

C The command prompt disappears for a few seconds while Linux sends the e-mail.

Linux sends the e-mail to the address you specify with the subject and message in the command.

Note: When the e-mail arrives, it appears to come from your Gmail account.

TIPS

Do I have to send e-mail via Gmail?
No. You can use other services such as Yahoo!, AOL, or your own private e-mail server. But Gmail is simple, reliable, and easy to set up. Finding the "magic words" for other services, and including the correct port number and encryption settings, can take a lot of trial and error.

How can I receive e-mails or add attachments?
To receive mail, investigate a package called fetchmail. fetchmail is challenging to set up. You can find instructions online. To send attachments, investigate a package called mpack. After installing mpack with apt-get you can e-mail an attachment with mpack -s "subject text"/path/file name@address.

Get Started with curl and wget

You can the `curl` and `wget` commands to access information on web sites directly from the command line or a script, without having to use a browser.

Most popular sites, including Twitter, Facebook, and public utility sites such as transport authorities offer an API, or Application Programming Interface, to their web services. You can use `curl` and `wget` commands to exchange information with these sites. This example introduces `curl` and `wget` but does not attempt to work with any specific API.

Get Started with curl and wget

curl

1 At the command prompt or in LXTerminal, type `curl http://www.bbc.co.uk/news/` and press `Enter`.

Note: Remember to add the final / character. You will see an error message if you do not include it.

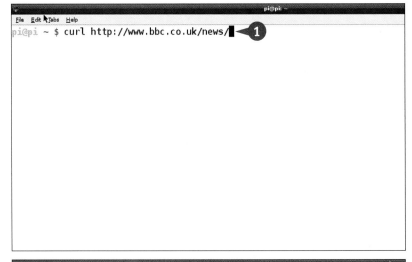

A `curl` downloads and displays the raw HTML used by the BBC news site.

Note: The raw HTML is many pages. You can stop scrolling at any time by pressing `Ctrl`+`C`.

wget

1 At the command prompt or in LXTerminal, type wget http://www.bbc.co.uk/news/ and press Enter.

B Linux downloads the raw HTML into a file called index.html.

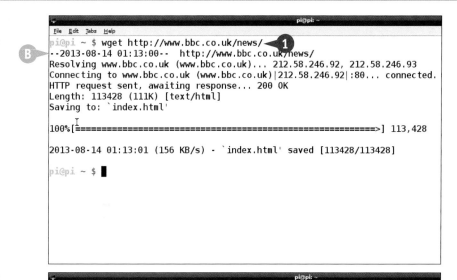

2 Type less index.html and press Enter to view the file.

C Linux displays the contents of index.html, split into screens.

Note: wget and curl download exactly the same content.

Note: If you repeat wget, it generates files called index. html.1, index.html.2, and so on.

TIPS

What can I do with the raw HTML of a site?
You can use grep, sed, or Python to trawl through the raw data to extra useful information from sites that do not provide an API. This is an intermediate topic and requires some programming skill.

Why do I get errors if I try to use curl and wget?
Many sites, including Twitter and Facebook, require *authentication*: Before you can access the API you must log in and present a digital key previously supplied by the site. For details, search the web for "API" and the site's name. Some sites also require a user agent switch to fool the site into believing the request comes from a web browser. For details, search the web for "user agent" and "curl" or "wget."

Put Your Pi on the Internet

You can put your Pi on the Internet and make your web server accessible from any location. If your Internet provider gives you a *static IP address,* or an online address that never changes, you can put your Pi online by making some simple changes to the settings in your router to set up port forwarding. *Port forwarding* tells your router to send web requests to your Pi.

Note that all routers are different. You will probably not see the pages shown here. But you can usually find similar settings. Most router manufacturers and ISPs provide detailed instructions.

Put Your Pi on the Internet

① If you do not know your router's address, type `route` at the command line or in LXTerminal.

② Note the Gateway address.

Note: See the section "Set a Static IP Address" earlier in this chapter for an example.

③ Open a web browser on the Pi or any other computer.

④ Type the Gateway address to view your router's login screen.

⑤ Type a username and password to log in to your router.

⑥ If your router has an Advanced Settings option, click it to select it.

Note: As in this example, you may be asked to click a button to confirm that you want to access the advanced settings.

7 Select **Port Forwarding**.

Note: Port Forwarding may be part of another option labeled NAT.

Your router displays a table of forwarding options.

Note: The table may have different graphics, but is likely to show similar information.

8 Type the static IP address you set in the section "Set a Static IP Address" under LAN IP Address.

9 Select **TCP&UDP** if there is a Protocol Type option.

10 Type **80** for the LAN Port setting.

Note: This option sends web traffic to your Pi.

11 Type **8080** (or some other number) for the Public Port or WAN Port setting.

Note: You can set this to 80, but it may not work and is less secure than using another port number.

12 Click **Enable** (☐ changes to ☑).

The Pi's web server should now be visible on the Internet.

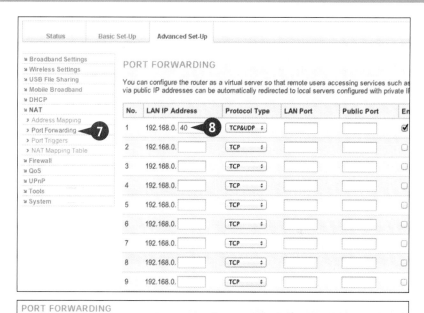

TIP

How can I check if my Pi is online?

You can only check if your Pi is online from a remote location or from another network, such as a neighbor's Wi-Fi, or a mobile network. Open a browser, and type the static IP address provided by your ISP into the address bar. (Type `curl ident.me` at the Pi's command line if you do not know it.) If are not using port 80, type a colon followed by your custom port number. Your Pi's web server should display your custom web content. Note that if your ISP does not provide a fixed address for your connection, you will need to sign up with a service such as www.no-ip.com to redirect traffic automatically.

## CHAPTER 8

Getting Started with Sound and Video

Your Pi can produce sound and video, but you need to set it up correctly first.

Understanding Media on the Pi

You can play audio and video on the Pi, which has unexpectedly powerful hardware given the low price. But configuring and managing media support in Raspbian can take some time and effort.

Understanding Monitor Resolution

When you first boot your Pi it defaults to the maximum resolution available on your monitor, or 1920 × 1200 @ 60Hz, whichever is smaller. At high resolutions, text is tiny and difficult to read. You can lower the resolution and increase the size of the text by hand-editing settings in the /boot/config.txt file.

Understanding Overscan

Some monitors display black boxes around the sides of the screen. Others spill text off the edges of the screen. You can fix both problems by manually adjusting the overscan settings in /boot/config.txt.

Understanding Audio

The Pi uses ALSA, or Advanced Linux Sound Architecture. The Pi board includes an audio jack for headphones or an external amplifier, driven by a converter chip. You can also play audio through an HDMI connection to TVs and monitors with built-in speakers. For hi-fi applications, you can connect an external USB DAC (digital-to-analog converter). The command line `aplay` application plays a limited selection of audio file types. On the desktop, you can install a package called LXMusic to play an extended range of audio file types, including MP3 and FLAC.

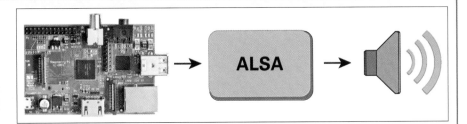

Understanding Video Support

The Pi is fast enough to play video files, and if you use the HDMI monitor connector you can view the video on a compatible TV. However, Raspbian includes very limited software support for video playback. You can use the `omxplayer` command to play video from the command line. There is no video equivalent to LXMusic. If you want to use your Pi as a video player, consider using an alternative media center operating system.

Understanding Media Center Options

You can install an alternative operating system called XBMC on your Pi to turn it into a full media center with support for playlists, online streaming, and many kinds of audio and video files. XBMC is free and highly customizable. Two versions are included with the NOOBS software introduced in Chapter 2. You can install either version by copying it to a spare SD card and booting your Pi from the new card. For more information, see Chapter 2.

Understanding Video Codecs

Video files come in many formats. Out of the box, the Pi can play video files in the MP4 format, which are created by mobile phones. You can buy optional *codecs* — software plugins — to expand this range. Codecs are available for VC-1 files, which are used in some BluRay discs, and MPEG-2 files, which are used in DVDs. If you want to view these files in XBMC or Raspbian, you must purchase the codecs. Both codecs are available at a low price.

Set Monitor Resolution and Overscan

You can change the size of the text on your monitor or TV by changing the Pi's screen resolution. If black bars appear around the screen you can adjust overscan settings to remove them, and center the image.

To access these settings, use nano to open the /boot/config.txt file. To select the resolution, set an hdmi_group and hdmi_mode number using the table at http://elinux.org/RPi_config.txt. Use hdmi_group=1 to set a standard video resolution, for example, 720p, or hdmi_group=2 to set the resolution in pixels, for example, 1024 × 768. To modify overscan, set pixel offsets for the top, bottom, left, and right of the screen.

Set Monitor Resolution and Overscan

1 In LXTerminal or at the command prompt, type `sudo nano /boot/config.txt` and press **Enter**.

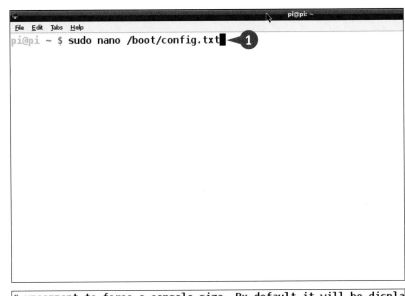

The Pi loads the config.txt file for editing.

2 Use ⬇ to scroll down to the line starting #hdmi_group=1.

3 Delete # from the beginning of the line.

4 If you are using a computer monitor instead of an HDMI TV, change the 1 to a 2.

Note: Lines beginning with # are comments and are inactive. Removing a # makes the setting on a line "live."

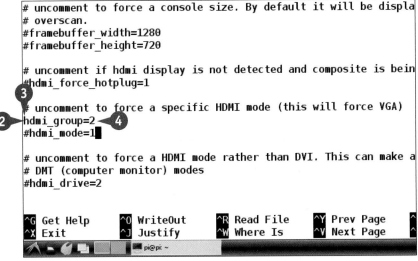

5 Open a web browser and visit http://elinux.org/RPi_config.txt.

Note: You can use Midori on the Pi, or another browser on another computer.

6 Pick a resolution from the group 1 or group 2 (not shown) tables and note its code.

Note: Refer to your monitor or TV specifications to find the maximum compatible resolution. You may want to use a lower resolution to make text on the screen larger and easier to read.

7 Return to config.txt in nano.

8 Remove the # at the start of the mode line, and change the number to match the code you noted in step **6**.

9 If you see black bars around your screen or the text is cut off at one edge, remove the # characters and change the numbers to fix the overscan.

10 Press Ctrl+X, Enter, and Ctrl+O to save the file.

You can now reboot with sudo reboot. After reboot, the Pi switches to the resolution you selected.

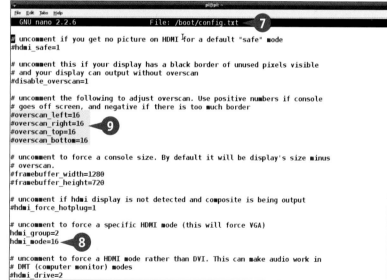

TIPS

What do the Hz numbers mean?

The Hz, or Hertz, number is the *refresh rate*, which is how often the image on the screen is redrawn. Use 60Hz for all monitors and U.S. TVs, and 50Hz or 60Hz for U.K. HDMI TVs. If you set a lower rate, the screen flickers. If you set a higher rate, your monitor or TV may not be compatible.

What is the highest possible resolution?

hdmi_mode=68 is the maximum possible for the Pi. If your monitor does not support this resolution, the Pi falls back to a minimum resolution of 640 × 480 and displays giant text. Good working resolutions are 1024 × 768 (hdmi_group=2, hdmi_mode=16) and 720p (hdmi_group=1, hdmi_mode=4).

Set Up Audio

You can play audio files on your Pi through the built-in earphone socket, through the HDMI connector, or through an external USB audio DAC (digital-to-analog converter). The earphone socket produces very poor-quality audio. For better results, use one of the alternatives.

Audio support for WAV files is enabled and installed automatically. However, audio is routed through a *mixer* that steers the audio through the various possible outputs. You may need to change the mixer settings before you hear any sound.

Set Up Audio

① At the command prompt or in LXTerminal, type cd /usr/share/sounds/ alsa and press Enter.

② Type ls and press Enter.

Ⓐ Linux lists a selection of the WAV preinstalled on the Pi. You can use these files to test audio.

③ Depending on your audio hardware, either insert earphones into the Pi's audio jack, use a cable to connect the jack to an amplifier and speakers, or turn up the volume on your HDMI monitor or TV, if it has speakers.

④ Type aplay Front_ Center.wav and press Enter.

Ⓑ Linux displays information about the sound file as it plays it.

If you hear audio, your Pi is set up correctly.

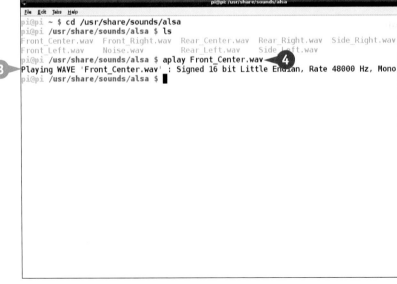

⑤ If you do not hear audio, type
`amixer cset numid=3`
`1` and press `Enter`.

Note: This command forces the Pi to play audio through the earphone socket. To play audio through the HDMI output, replace the final 1 with a 2.

Note: For technical reasons HDMI audio does not always work correctly. If you cannot make it work, use the earphone socket and external speakers or earphones.

⑥ To set the volume, type
`alsamixer` and press
`Enter`.

Ⓒ The command displays a volume control with a bar graph.

⑦ Use ⬆ and ⬇ to set the volume.

Note: You can also type `amixer cset numid=1 -- 100%` and press `Enter` where the last number sets the volume.

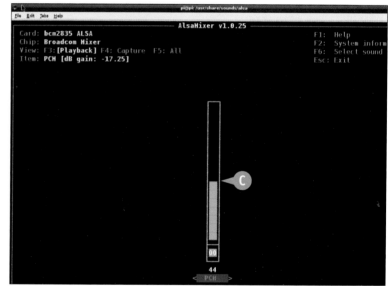

TIPS

Why does my USB DAC not work?

The Pi's audio system uses default Linux drivers that work with class compliant audio hardware. Most USB DACs are class compliant and should work. DACs that need custom drivers are not compatible. Check your DAC's documentation for details.

How can I play MP3 or FLAC files?

A package called mpg321 can play mp3 files from the command line. You can also install a full desktop music player and a set of plugins for most audio types. Use `sudo apt-get` to install `xmms2-plugin-all` and `lxmusic`. Launch the desktop with `startx`. A new folder called Sound & Video appears in the Start menu. It contains a new application called Music Player that can load and play almost any audio file.

Play Video with omxplayer

You can play video with the `omxplayer` command. `omxplayer` works from the command line and displays video on your monitor or TV. Audio is sent to an HDMI monitor or TV or your Pi's earphone jack automatically.

`omxplayer` can play files recorded using a technology known as H.264. Many camera phones produce compatible video. Many downloaded files with an MP4 extension are also likely to be compatible. To play files with an MP2 extension, see the next section, "License Extra Video Formats."

Play Video with omxplayer

1 Click the **Midori** icon on the desktop to open the Midori web browser.

2 Search the web for sample MP4 files.

Note: There are many MP4 sites. One possible example is www.longtailvideo.com/support/open-video-ads/13051/sample-ads.

3 Right-click a downloadable file.

4 Click **Save As**.

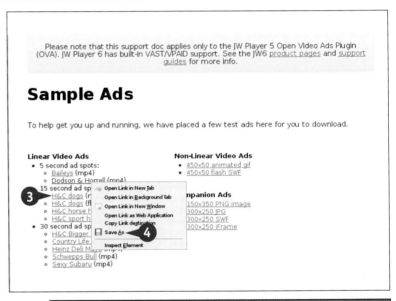

5 Type **test.mp4** into the Name field.

6 Click **Save**.

⑦ At the command line or in LXTerminal, type `omxplayer test.mp4` and press Enter.

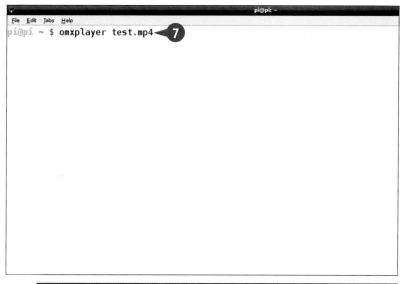

`omxplayer` plays the video.

Note: The video appears on top of other screen content. It does not appear in a window. The video frame does not disappear when `omxplayer` finishes the video.

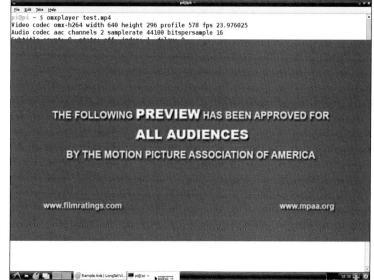

TIPS

How can I play video on a clear screen?

`omxplayer` does not include an option to clear the screen, so you must clear it manually. Many users create a custom script to clear the screen to black and hide the flashing cursor. For one possible script, see http://raspberrypi.stackexchange.com/questions/3268/how-to-disable-local-terminal-showing-through-when-playing-video.

Why is there no sound?

For technical reasons, some HDMI monitors with speakers do not play audio correctly. You can use the `amixer` command introduced in the section "Set Up Audio" to route audio to try to force audio to play through your HDMI display, or to route it to the earphone socket if you cannot make it work.

License Extra Video Formats

You can license extra video *codecs*, or plugins, to make your Pi compatible with a wider selection of video files. If you are not interested in video, you can ignore this option. But the codec licenses are very affordable, and you must buy them to use your Pi as a media center.

The codecs are already built in to the Pi. When you buy a license, you receive an access code by e-mail to unlock them. To install the license, you must edit a configuration file with `nano` and reboot.

License Extra Video Formats

1 On the desktop, double click **LXTerminal** to launch it.

2 Type `cat /proc/cpuinfo` and press **Enter**.

3 Drag your mouse over the numbers at the end of the line beginning with Serial to highlight them.

4 Right-click and select **Copy** from the context menu.

Note: These steps reveal your Pi's unique serial number and copy it to the system clipboard.

5 Launch the Midori browser and visit www.raspberrypi.com/license-keys.

6 Click **Option 1** or **Option 2** (not shown) to select either an MPEG-2 or a VC-1 license key.

Note: As of summer 2013 there are two choices. The Other Items boxes on the page simply repeat them.

7 Right-click the Serial Number field.

8 Click **Paste** from the context menu.

9 Click **Add To Cart**.

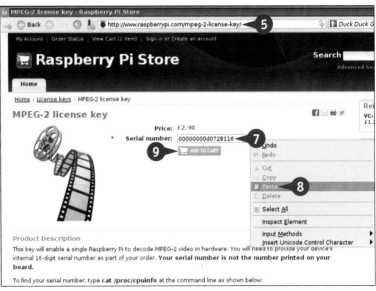

10 Either click through to the checkout or repeat the steps to add the other codec to your cart, and then click through.

11 Click **Register an account** to register as a customer, or **Checkout as a guest** to pay without registering (⊙ changes to ⦿).

12 Step through the standard billing and order confirmation options.

The site sends an initial confirmation e-mail. Within 72 hours it sends a further e-mail with your license key or keys.

13 At the command line or in LXTerminal, type sudo nano /boot/config.txt.

14 Copy the key or keys included in your license e-mail into the file, as shown.

Note: Prefix the MPEG2 code with decode_MPG2=. Prefix the VC-1 code with decode_WVC1=.

15 Press Ctrl+O, Enter, and Ctrl+X to save the file.

After you reboot, your Pi can play MPEG2 and/or VC-1 files.

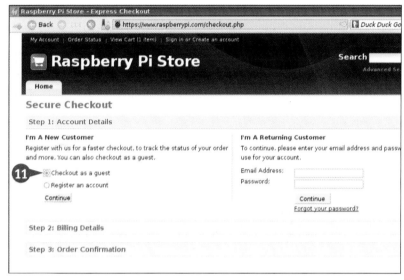

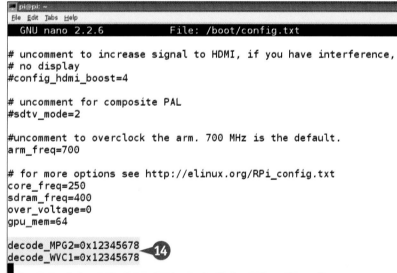

TIPS

Can I play videos from a DVD or BluRay drive?

Not easily. Commercial discs include copy protection. Commercial players include circuitry and software to remove the copy protection. Your Pi does not. You can try to install it, but this is a complex process. For notes about one attempt see http://raspi.tv/2012/watch-encrypted-dvd-on-raspberry-pi-by-streaming-to-omxplayer.

Video playback is jerky. Can I improve it?

The Pi struggles with videos in the 1080p HD format. You can improve performance by overclocking, although this can shorten the life of your Pi. For details, see Chapter 3.

Connect a USB Media Drive

If you have a drive with a collection of media files, you can connect it to your Pi. On the Linux desktop, connecting a drive works as long as it holds information in a format Linux recognizes. On the command line, you must create a *mount point*, or a dummy directory for the information on the drive. Then you tell Linux to mount the drive. The information on the drive appears in the dummy directory. When you mount a drive, you must tell Linux whether the drive is compatible with Linux, Windows, or OS X.

Connect a USB Media Drive

1 Plug your drive into a USB hub.

2 At the command line or in LXTerminal, type `dmesg|tail` and press Enter.

3 Make a note of the line starting with `sd` and ending in a number, `sda1` in this example.

Note: If your drive has more than one *partition*, that is, more than one subdisk, you see more than one numbered entry here. If you have more than one disk, you may see `sdb`, `sdc`, and so on.

```
pi@pi: ~
File   Edit   Tabs   Help
pi@pi ~ $ dmesg | tail          2
[ 9862.692198] scsi0 : usb-storage 1-1.3.2:1.0
[ 9863.693413] scsi 0:0:0:0: Direct-Access     WDC WD32 00SD-01KNB
[ 9863.697309] sd 0:0:0:0: [sda] 625142448 512-byte logical blocks
[ 9863.698318] sd 0:0:0:0: [sda] Write Protect is off
[ 9863.698353] sd 0:0:0:0: [sda] Mode Sense: 34 00 00 00
[ 9863.699457] sd 0:0:0:0: [sda] Write cache: disabled, read cache
FUA
[ 9863.712568]   sda: sda1      3
[ 9863.717807] sd 0:0:0:0: [sda] Attached SCSI disk
[ 9864.599262] NTFS driver 2.1.30 [Flags: R/W MODULE].
[ 9864.747456] NTFS volume version 3.1.
pi@pi ~ $ █
```

4 To create an access point for the disk, type `sudo mkdir /media/[auniquename]` and press Enter.

Note: A unique name can be any combination of letters without spaces. You only need to perform step 4 once.

5 Type `sudo apt-get install ntfs-3g` and wait while Linux installs drivers for Windows NTFS disks.

Ⓐ Linux downloads and installs drivers for disks created on a Windows PC.

```
FUA
[ 9863.712568]   sda: sda1
[ 9863.717807] sd 0:0:0:0: [sda] Attached SCSI disk
[ 9864.599262] NTFS driver 2.1.30 [Flags: R/W MODULE].
[ 9864.747456] NTFS volume version 3.1.
pi@pi ~ $ sudo mkdir /media/bigdisk     4
pi@pi ~ $ sudo apt-get install ntfs-3g     5
Reading package lists... Done
Building dependency tree
Reading state information... Done
The following NEW packages will be installed:
  ntfs-3g     A
0 upgraded, 1 newly installed, 0 to remove and 0 not upgraded.
Need to get 694 kB of archives.
After this operation, 1,513 kB of additional disk space will be use
Get:1 http://mirrordirector.raspbian.org/raspbian/ wheezy/main ntf
4 kB]
Fetched 694 kB in 4s (148 kB/s)
Preconfiguring packages ...
Selecting previously unselected package ntfs-3g.
```

Note: You only need to perform step **5** once.

6 Type the "magic word" command `sudo mount -o uid=pi, gid=pi /dev/ [sd+number]/[access point]` and press Enter.

Note: See step **3** for `[sd+number]`. See step **4** for `[access point]`.

Linux mounts the disk and makes it available.

7 To check that the disk is available, use `cd` to navigate to the mount point, and `ls` to list files.

B If the disk is mounted, `ls` lists the contents.

TIPS

Can I unmount a drive?

In theory you can use the `umount` command to unmount a drive so you can remove it safely. In practice, as soon as you mount a drive, many parts of Linux start using it. So you cannot unmount most drives without stopping Linux or rebooting. Never simply unplug a drive: You may corrupt the files on it.

Can I mount a disk automatically when the Pi boots?

Yes, with caution. Type `sudo nano/etc/fstab`. Add a new entry. You must include five items: the `/dev/` reference used to mount the drive (for example, `/dev/sda1`), the access directory, the format, the word `defaults`, and two zeroes. For detailed examples, see http://elinux.org/RPi_Adding_USB_Drives. If you are using multiple external drives, use UUIDs — explained in the article — instead of `/dev/. . .` references.

## CHAPTER 9

Programming with Scratch

Scratch is an easy-to-learn toy programming language for kids. Scratch is preinstalled on the Pi desktop, so you can start learning how to make simple games and animations right away.

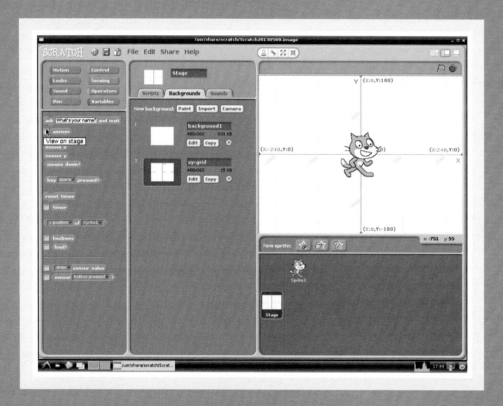

Understanding Scratch

You can use an application called Scratch to learn programming on your Pi. Scratch is a toy language created at MIT for use in schools. It introduces many basic features of programming and software, and is also fun to play with.

Understanding the Stage

In Scratch, everything happens on the stage. Initially the stage is a plain white rectangle, but you can set a background. A typical Scratch project makes images and animations appear on the stage. Then simple programming code moves them around, makes them respond to collisions and key presses, and so on. To help you position items, the stage is divided into horizontal (x) and vertical (y) steps. Step 0,0 is the center of the stage. Negative x steps are in the left half of the stage, positive x steps in the right half, negative y steps in the bottom half, and positive y steps in the top half.

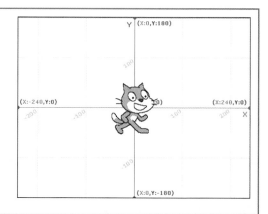

Understanding Sprites

The items on the stage are called *sprites*. Each sprite has a selection of *costumes*, or images. You can keep a single costume for a sprite, or switch between different costumes to animate the sprite or make it respond to events. Each sprite has an x,y position on the stage, and you tell Scratch to move it.

Understanding Blocks

You can control sprites by connecting Scratch blocks together. There are many blocks, and each does something different. For example, you can use a block to move a sprite by a certain number of steps or to glide a sprite to a position on the stage. Blocks can play sounds, show or hide sprites, and make think and speech bubbles appear next to a sprite.

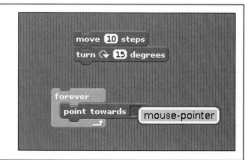

Understanding Block Types

Scratch on the Pi includes eight kinds of blocks. *Motion* blocks can rotate a sprite and set its position. *Looks* blocks change the size and color of a sprite, select costumes, and add speech and think bubbles. *Sound* blocks play notes and sounds. *Pen* blocks can draw lines on the stage. *Control* blocks repeat other blocks and perform tests. *Sensing* blocks create timers, check colors and sprite positions, and report the mouse position. *Operators* perform arithmetic and combine test results. *Variables* hold settings.

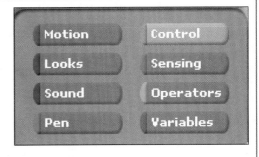

Understanding Scripts

You can drag blocks from the block palette and connect them like puzzle pieces. A sequence of blocks is called a *script*. With scripts, you can combine all the different blocks to make sprites respond in complex ways. Sprites can hold more than one script, but only one script can be active at a time.

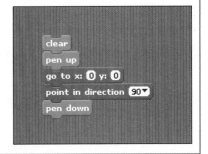

Understanding Sharing

Scratch is associated with the website http://scratch.mit.edu. You can upload your Scratch projects to the site and download projects created by other people. You can find out more about Scratch from the shared Scratch WIKI at http://wiki.scratch. mit.edu. Note that the version of Scratch on the Pi is not the most recent version, and some features mentioned in the Wiki are not available on the Pi.

Import a Costume

You can import one or more costumes to clothe a sprite. A sprite is really just a blank object with a position on the stage. To make the sprite visible, you import a costume and switch it to select it.

When you launch Scratch, it loads a default sprite named Sprite1. The default costume is a cartoon cat. Scratch includes a costume library with many predrawn costumes. You can import one or more costumes from this library. To clothe a sprite with a costume, click a costume image in the costume area.

Import a Costume

1 If the desktop is not running, launch it with `startx`.

2 Double click **Scratch**.

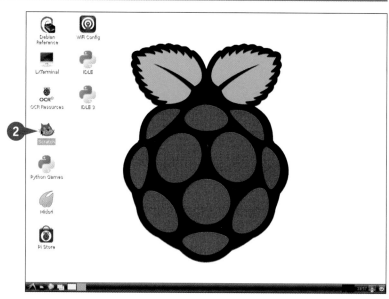

Scratch loads and displays the default project with a single sprite on a blank stage.

3 Click the **Costumes** tab.

4 Click **Import**.

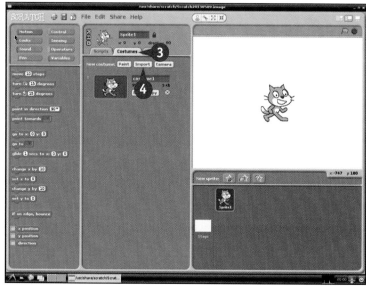

Scratch opens the Import Costume dialog box.

6 Double-click the **Animals** folder.

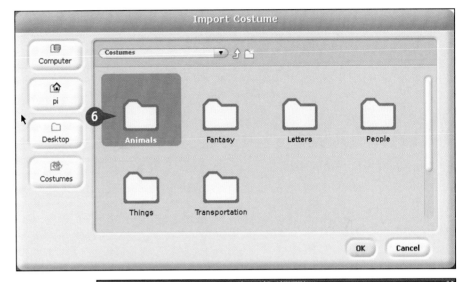

7 Click a costume, **bat1-a** for example.

8 Click **OK**.

A Scratch imports the bat1-a costume and adds it to the list of costumes available for Sprite1.

TIP

Why do some costumes have a and b versions?
The a and b versions are for simple animations. For example, you can load a and b versions of the bat costume and then create a script to switch the costumes. When the script runs, the bat appears to flap its wings. Some of the costumes in the People folder have multiple versions. You can create longer scripts to make the sprite look like it is walking or dancing.

Switch a Costume with Blocks

You can switch a costume by clicking it in the Costumes tab. But you can also use blocks to switch costumes. Blocks make switching automatic, so you can create simple animations with two or more costumes, or you can create more complex effects where the costume changes when a sprite bounces off an object or collides with another.

Switch a Costume with Blocks

1 Import the bat1-a and bat1-b costumes.

Note: See the previous section, "Import a Costume," for details about importing costumes.

2 Click the **Scripts** tab.

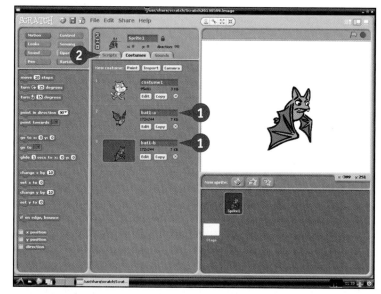

A Scratch shows the empty scripts area for Sprite1.

3 Click **Looks**.

B Scratch displays a collection of Looks blocks.

4 Click the **switch to costume** block, drag it to the Scripts area, and release it.

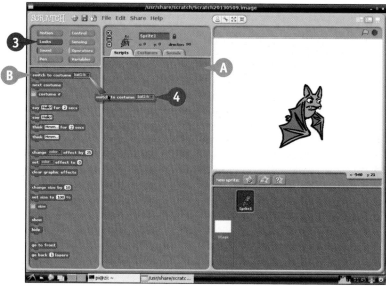

5 Click and drag another copy of the **switch to costume** block to the Scripts area.

6 In either block, click the area showing a costume name.

7 Select the **bat1-a** costume.

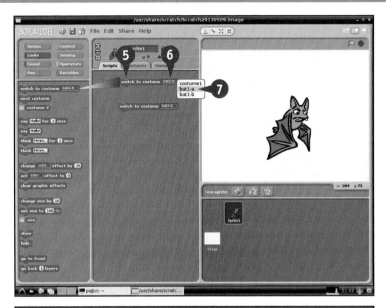

8 Click the blocks in turn.

C Clicking a block selects a different costume.

The bat appears to flap its wings.

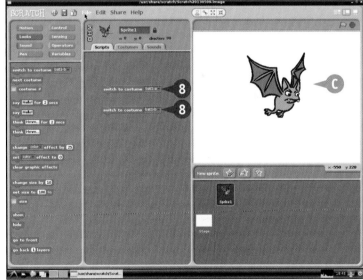

TIPS

Can I switch costumes automatically?
Yes. You can add other blocks to the script to switch the costumes automatically. For details, see the next section, "Create a Loop."

Is there a limit to the number of costumes?
No. However, most projects use just a few costumes for each sprite. In theory, you could use every possible costume with a single sprite. Users recognize costumes, not sprites. So switching among too many costumes can confuse users.

Create a Loop

You can use *control blocks* to repeat other blocks in a script. You can also use them to make decisions — for example, to change a sprite's costume or modify its behavior when it is in a certain part of the screen.

To loop part of a script, use the `forever` block. To repeat part of a script a set number of times, use the `repeat` block, which includes a repeat count. You can use the `delay` block to make the script pause during the loop.

Create a Loop

1 Starting with a blank Scripts area, import two costumes and add two costume switching blocks.

Note: For instructions, see the sections "Import a Costume" and "Switch a Costume with Blocks."

2 Click **Control**.

3 Drag a `wait` block from the Blocks area onto the lower edge of a costume switching block.

A Scratch draws a white border.

Note: The border indicates that if you drop the floating block, it joins the other block.

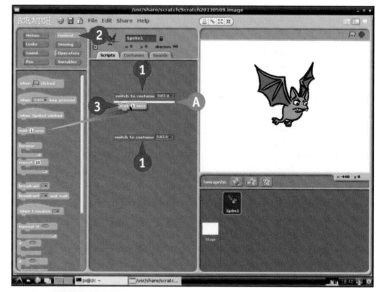

4 Release the block to connect it.

B Scratch joins the blocks to show they work in sequence.

Note: You can drop blocks above or below other blocks.

Note: You can only connect blocks if they have a matching tab and notch. Some blocks have a rounded top edge. You cannot drop blocks on top of them.

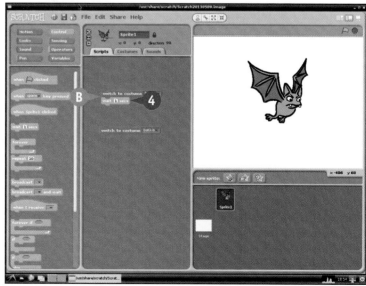

5 Drop another `wait` block under the other costume switch block.

6 Drag the bottom pair of blocks and drop them on the bottom edge of the top pair of blocks.

Scratch joins all four blocks together to make a single script.

7 Click any block in the script to run it.

C The bat flaps its wings once.

Note: You can join any number of blocks together in any combination.

Note: Clicking any block runs the whole script.

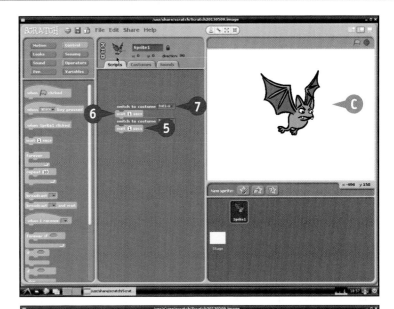

8 Drag a `forever` block from the blocks area.

9 Drag the block to the top of the group.

Note: The bracket automatically expands around the group.

Note: You can also drop the block lower; the bracket expands around just some of the group.

10 Click any block.

D The bat flaps its wings forever.

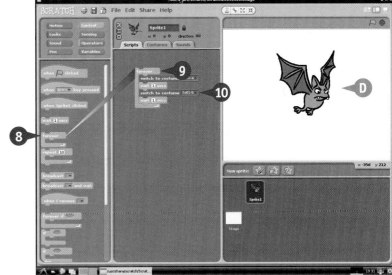

TIPS

Why do some blocks have a curved top?
Hat blocks mark the start of script. Usually, you run a script by clicking it in the Scripts area. If you start a script with a hat block, you can run it in other ways — for example, by clicking a sprite, by pressing a key, or by clicking the green flag icon at the top right above the stage.

How do I stop a script?
To stop a script, click a block or group that is running. Running scripts are outlined in white. The first time you click a block, it runs. The next time you click it, it stops. Clicking it runs it again, and so on.

Move a Sprite

You can use *motion blocks* to change the position of a sprite on the stage. To move a sprite, change its x position to move it left and right, and its y position to move it up and down. You can use a `go to` block to make a sprite jump from one location to another. Use a `glide` block to make the sprite move smoothly. You can set a relative position with a `move...steps` block. Step moves depend on the sprite's *direction* — its angle on the stage sets where it points. You can use *sensing* blocks to make the sprite follow the mouse cursor, or the position of another sprite.

Move a Sprite

1 Launch the desktop and Scratch, if they are not already running.

2 Click **Motion** if it is not already selected.

3 Drag a `move 10 steps` block to the Scripts area.

4 Join a `turn 15 degrees clockwise` block under it.

5 Click either block.

A The sprite moves 10 steps to the right and turns 15 degrees clockwise.

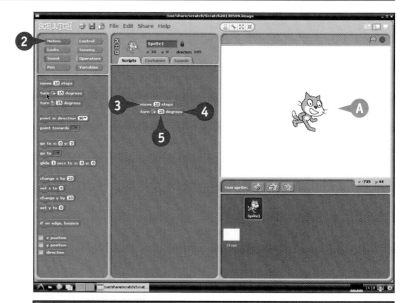

6 Drag a `point towards` block to the Scripts area.

7 Drag a `forever` block to the Scripts area around the `point towards` block.

8 Click the box in the `point towards` block and select **mouse-pointer**.

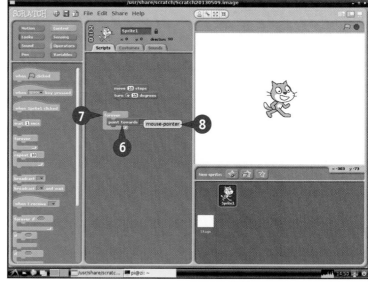

9 Click the **forever** block to run the script.

B The sprite rotates to follow the mouse pointer.

10 Drag a glide block from the Blocks area and drop it above the point toward block.

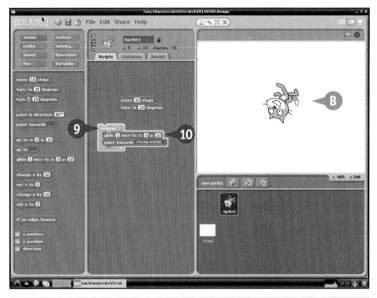

11 Click **Sensing**.

12 Drag a mouse x block onto the x: slot in the glide block.

13 Drag a mouse y block onto the y: slot in the glide block.

Note: The mouse x and mouse y blocks read the current mouse position.

C The sprite chases the mouse pointer around the stage.

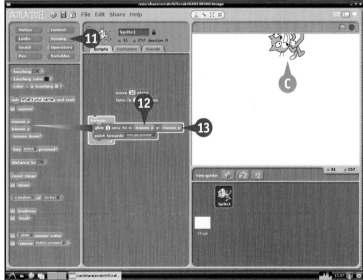

TIPS

What does the number after glide do?
The number sets how quickly the sprite glides toward its next position. Click the number to change it. If you make it 10, the sprite takes 10 seconds to glide. Make it 0, and the sprite moves almost instantly.

What do the sensor blocks do?
You can buy an optional hardware kit to work with Scratch, with buttons and sliders. Unfortunately, this kit does not work with the Pi, so you cannot use these blocks.

Add a Bounce

You can use an `if on edge, bounce` block to make sprites bounce off the edges of the screen. Bouncing a sprite changes its direction. By default, sprites can rotate in any direction, so when the sprite bounces, Scratch draws it upside down.

If this is not what you want, you can fix it by using three small buttons in the area next to the sprite preview at the top of the screen. The top button (⟳) allows full rotation. The middle button (↔) allows the sprite to point left or right. The bottom button (■) turns off all rotation.

Add a Bounce

1. Launch the desktop and Scratch, if they are not already running.

2. Click **Motion** if it is not already selected.

3. Drag a `move 10 steps` block onto the Scripts area.

4. Drag an `if on edge, bounce` block under it.

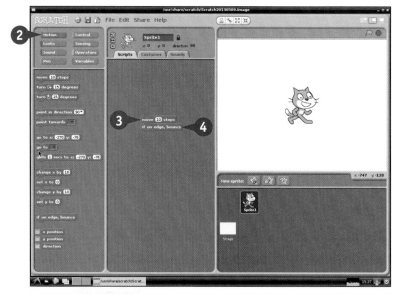

5. Click **Control**.

6. Drag a forever block around the motion blocks.

7. Click any block.

Ⓐ The sprite bounces off the edges of the screen and turns upside down on each bounce.

Note: If you did not reset the sprite direction in step 4, the sprite may bounce around the stage diagonally.

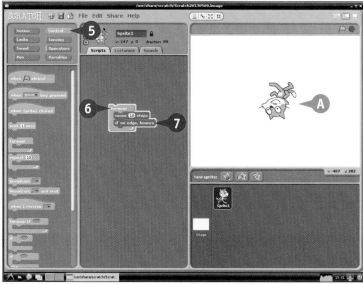

8 Click the **only face left and right** button (↔).

B When the sprite bounces, it faces left or right only.

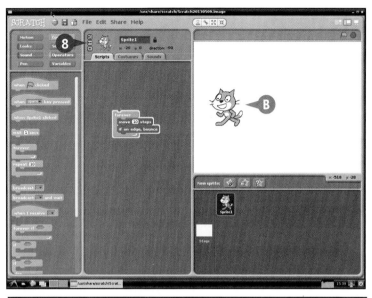

9 Click the **do not rotate** button (■).

C The sprite always faces the right.

TIPS

How can I set the starting direction and position?
Add a go to and point in direction block before the forever loop. Set the go to position to x:0 and y:0. Set the point in direction to 90. This moves the sprite to the middle of the stage and makes it face the right.

Why does the sprite bounce diagonally?
Fixing the rotation does not change the direction. If the sprite's starting direction is not exactly 90 or –90, the sprite bounces diagonally.

Check for Collisions

You can use the `touching` block in the Sensing group to check if a sprite is touching another sprite, or the edge of the stage. To use the touching block, embed it in a control block that makes a decision. The `repeat until` block is a good way to keep moving or changing a sprite until it collides with another one.

You can make your sprites behave in complex ways by chaining control blocks together. For example, you can make a sprite move from the right of the screen, stop when it reaches another a sprite, display a message, wait a while, and then move back again.

Check for Collisions

1 Launch the desktop and Scratch, if they are not already running.

2 Drag the default sprite to the right edge of the screen.

3 Right-click **Sprite1** in the Sprite area.

4 Click **duplicate** to make a copy.

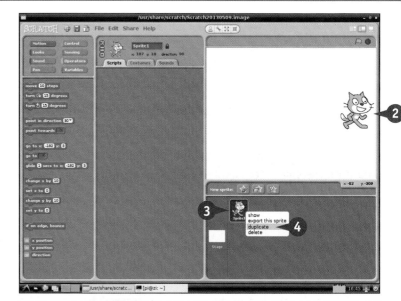

5 Click **Sprite2**.

6 Click **Motion** if it is not already selected.

7 Drag a `go to` block to the Scripts area and set x to **–330** and y to **0**.

Note: You can set a field by clicking it, typing a number, and then pressing Enter.

8 Drag a `point in direction` block to the bottom of the `go to` block.

Note: The direction should be 90. If it is not, click it and select **90**.

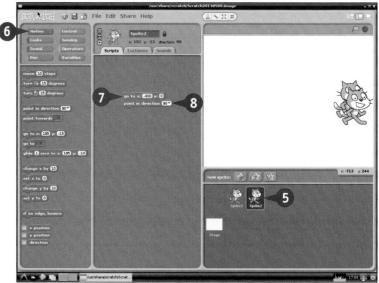

9 Click **Control**.

10 Drag a `repeat until` block and join it to the bottom of the `point in direction` block.

11 Click **Motion**.

12 Drag a `move 10 steps` block into the `repeat until` bracket.

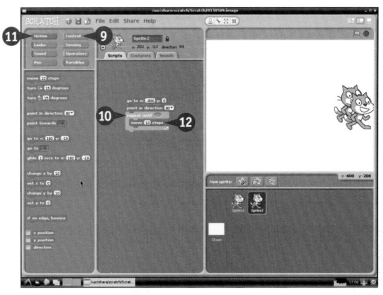

13 Click **Sensing**.

14 Drag a `touching` block and drop it on the empty test field in the `repeat until` bracket.

15 Click the box and select **Sprite1** from the pop-up menu.

16 Click any block to run the script.

A Sprite2 jumps to the left of the screen, glides to Sprite1, and stops when the sprites touch.

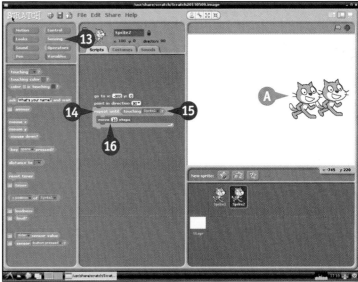

TIPS

How can I control how fast the sprite moves?
You can change the number in the `move...` `steps` block. The bigger the number, the more quickly the sprite moves, but big numbers create jerky movement. You can also add a `wait` block. To slow down the sprite, set the time to half a second. To make it much slower, set it to more than a second.

Why not use a glide-to block?
You could use a `glide-to` block to animate movement and collisions. For an example, see the section "Move a Sprite." If you use sensing to control movement and check for collisions you have more control over how sprites respond to each other. For example, you might use the `say` block in Looks to make one sprite say something when the sprites touch.

Respond to the Mouse and Keyboard

You can use sensing and control blocks to make your sprites respond to mouse clicks and keyboard taps. Sensing blocks do nothing until you embed them in the hexagonal spaces of a control block.

The most useful sensing blocks are `mouse down` and `when...key pressed`. The `mouse down` block checks if a mouse button is pressed. The `when...key pressed` block checks one key on the keyboard. You can pick a key to test by clicking the small box on the block and selecting the key from a pop-up menu.

Respond to the Mouse and Keyboard

1 Launch the desktop and Scratch, if they are not already running.

2 Click **Control** if it is not already selected.

3 Drag a `when...key pressed` block to the Scripts area.

4 Drag a `repeat until...` block under the `when... key pressed` block.

Note: You can change the key the `when...key pressed` block responds to by clicking the space box and selecting a different key.

5 Click **Sensing**.

6 Drag a `mouse down` block and drop it on the hexagonal area of the `repeat until...` block.

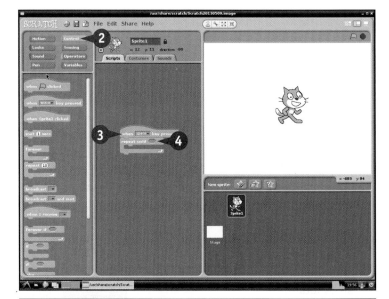

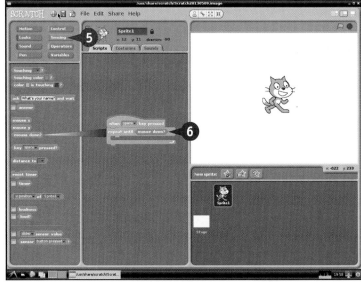

7 Click **Motion**.

8 Drag a `point towards...` block inside the `repeat until...` bracket.

9 Click the box and select **mouse-pointer**.

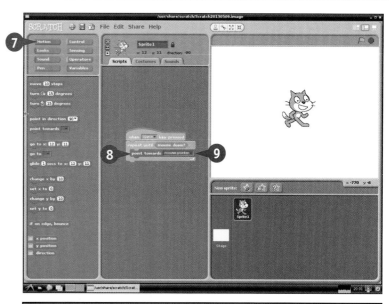

10 Press `Spacebar` on your keyboard.

A The sprite rotates to follow the mouse position.

Note: If nothing happens click the **can rotate** button (⟳) to allow sprite rotation.

11 Click the mouse button.

The script ends and the sprite stops rotating.

Note: You can press `Spacebar` again to make the sprite rotate, and click the mouse again to stop it.

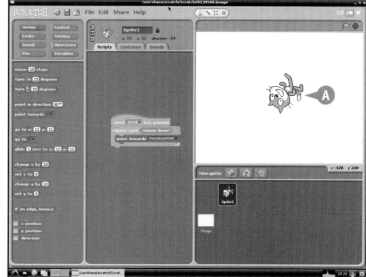

TIPS

How can I make a sprite respond to different keys?

Create a different script for each key. Start each script with a `when...key pressed` block and select a different key in each one. For a simple game you might make one key glide a sprite to the far left of the stage and another key glide a block to the far right.

How can I combine checks?

Click **Operators** and select the `...and...` block or the `...or...` block. Drop different sensing blocks into the hexagonal spaces on the operator. Then drop the completed operator block into a hexagonal space in a control block. Use the `...and...` operator when you want both checks to be true and the `...or...` operator when you want either to be true.

Edit a Costume

Scratch includes a simple editor for costumes. You can use it to draw a costume from scratch or to change an existing costume.

Drawing a recognizable costume requires some artistic skill. Even if your skills are very basic, you can still use the editor to experiment with custom shapes and images. If you have no drawing skills you can experiment by changing the existing costumes.

Edit a Costume

1 Launch the desktop and Scratch, if they are not already running.

2 Click the **Costumes** tab.

3 Pick a sprite and click the **Edit** button next to it.

Note: This example edits the default costume.

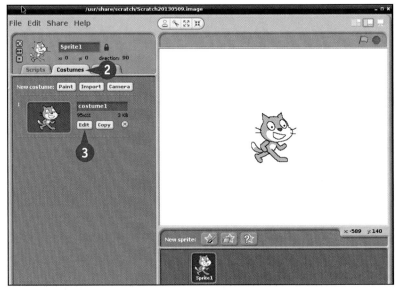

Scratch loads the Paint Editor.

4 Click the black color in the color palette.

A Scratch sets black as the foreground color.

5 Click the **Fill** tool (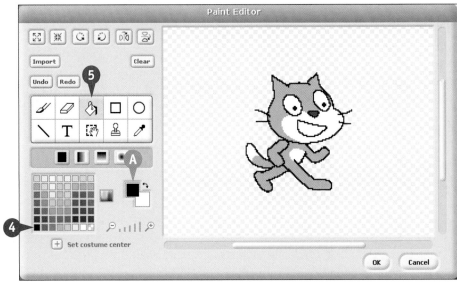).

Note: The Fill tool paints entire areas with a single color.

6 Click one of the orange areas on the cat to paint it black.

Note: The Fill tool fills areas of color that match where you click.

7 Click the remaining orange areas to paint the whole cat black.

8 Click the **Zoom** icon (⟨⊕⟩) to make the image bigger.

Note: You can move the image by dragging the scroll bars under and to the right of the edit area.

9 Click the remaining orange pixels to make them black.

10 Click **OK**.

Note: Scratch saves the modified sprite when you click **File** and then **Save As** and save the project.

Note: Editing a costume does not change it permanently.

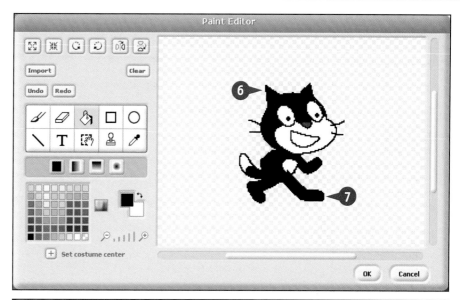

TIPS

Can I use a different editor?
Scratch's costume files are in /usr/share/scratch/media/ costumes. You use any editor on any computer to create a file and save it to this directory. Files should be smaller than 150 pixels or so and saved as a GIF or PNG file. Delete white space around the image before saving.

Are GIF files animated?
No. Scratch does not support animated GIF images. To create animations, save each animation frame as a separate costume. Use costume swapping to cycle through the frames. See the section "Import a Costume" for details.

Change the Stage Background

You can replace the default white stage with a photo or some other background. Changing the stage does not change how scripts work or how sprites look. It simply provides a different backdrop.

Scratch includes a selection of photos and images you can import to change the look of a stage. Most are decorative, but one is very useful — an xy backdrop that you can use as a guide when placing and moving sprites.

Change the Stage Background

1 Launch the desktop and Scratch, if they are not already running.

2 Click **Stage**.

3 Click **Import**.

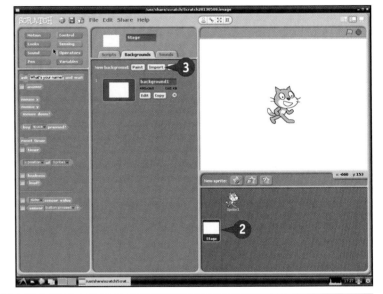

The Import Background dialog box opens.

4 Click **xy-grid**.

5 Click **OK**.

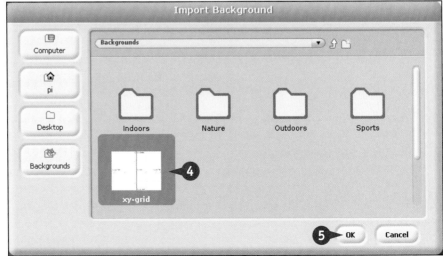

A Scratch changes the background to an x y guide.

Note: The numbers and points are x y values. You can use them as a guide for the numbers to use when you place sprites on the stage with motion blocks.

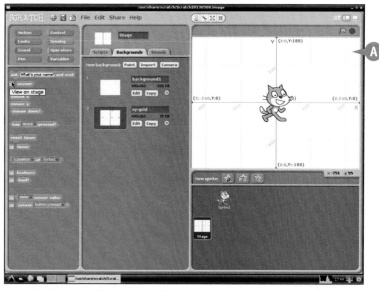

6 Click **Import**.

The Import Background dialog box opens.

7 Double-click any folder (not shown).

Note: This example shows the contents of the Nature folder.

8 Click any photo or image.

9 Click **OK**.

B Scratch loads the photo as a background.

TIPS

Can I edit a background?
Yes. You can use the built-in editor to change any photo or image. For details, see the previous section, "Edit a Costume." Note that editing photos is difficult. You may get better results by starting with a blank white stage and drawing your own background.

Can I use my own photos?
Yes. The background files are in /usr/share/scratch/media/backgrounds. You can create your own backgrounds using any camera or photo-editing tool on any computer. If you save them to this folder, you can load them into Scratch. The standard size is 480 × 360 pixels.

Play Sounds

Y ou can play sound and music in Scratch with sound blocks. On the Pi, you can play samples, melodies, and simple drum sounds. In theory, you can select different instruments. In practice, all instruments sound the same.

Versions of Scratch on other computers support a full palette of sounds known as the *General MIDI Specification*, which includes simple emulations of popular instruments and many drum sounds. Unfortunately you cannot use these instruments on the Pi, because it does not have a General MIDI synthesizer.

Play Sounds

1 Launch the desktop and Scratch, if they are not already running.

2 Click **Sound**.

3 Drag a `play sound...` block to the Scripts area.

4 Click the block to play the sound.

Note: If you do not hear sound, see Chapter 8 for more information about setting up audio.

5 Click **Import**.

The Import Sound dialog box opens.

6 Double-click any folder to open it (not shown).

Note: This example shows the contents of the Animal folder.

7 Click a sound to hear it.

8 Click **OK** to import it.

You can now select the sound in a `play sound...` block.

Note: If you cannot hear a sound or you see an error when you try to import it, install the extra audio player options described in Chapter 8.

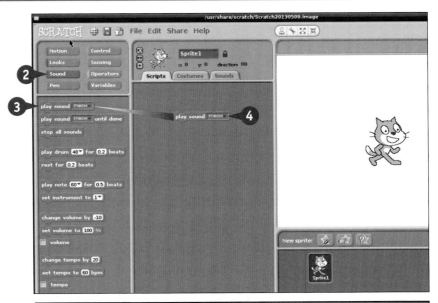

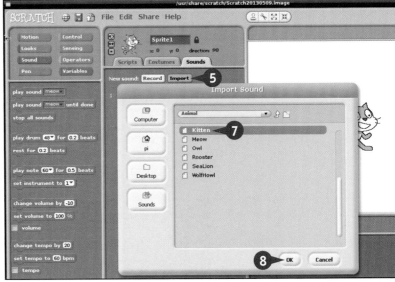

9 Drag a `play drum...` block to the Scripts area.

10 Click the block to play the sound.

11 Click the number box to see a list of drum sounds.

12 Click any menu item.

Scratch plays a slightly different version of the original sound.

Note: Scratch does not play a different drum sound, because no synthesizer application is installed.

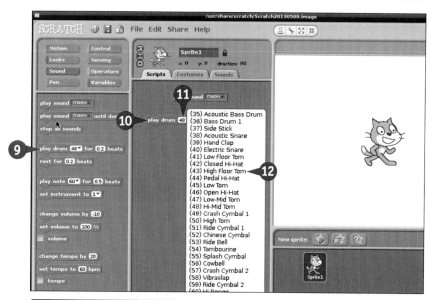

13 Drag a `play note...` `for... beats` block to the Scripts area.

14 Click the block to play a note.

Scratch plays a clean, flute-like note.

15 Click the number to change the note.

16 Click a note on the keyboard to change the note.

Note: You can also click the number once and type in a different number.

Note: Note 60 is middle C.

Note: To play a simple tune connect seven blocks and set their numbers to **60**, **60**, **67**, **67**, **69**, **69**, and **67**.

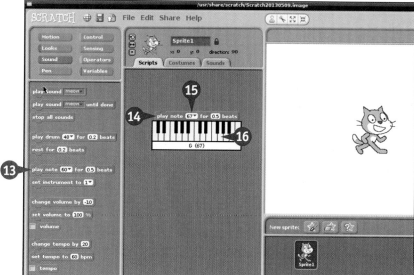

TIPS

Can I record sounds?
The record feature only works on the Pi if you have an external USB converter that allows recording. By default, the Pi cannot record sounds.

Can I play more than one sound at a time?
No. Scratch on the Pi does not mix sounds. You can play more than one note at a time using `play note...` blocks. Use a set volume block to lower the volume; otherwise, the sound distorts. If you play three notes at a time, set the volume to 33%.

Work with Variables

You can use variables to make scripts more powerful. *Variables* store a value that you can change at any time. Instead of using a fixed number in a block, you can use a variable, and do math on the variable when you need to change it.

By default, variables appear on the stage in a box. You can choose the appearance of the box: a small number with the variable name; a large number; or a small number, the name, and a slider. If you choose the slider option you can change the variable by dragging the slider.

Work with Variables

1 Launch the desktop and Scratch, if they are not already running.

2 Click **Variables**.

3 Click **Make a variable**.

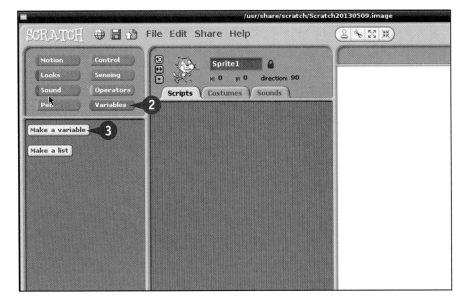

4 Type a name for the variable.

Note: In this example the variable is named distance.

5 Click **OK**.

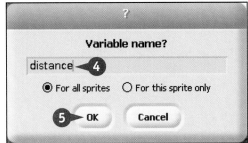

A Scratch adds the variable to the Variables blocks.

B Scratch also adds the variable to the stage.

C You can optionally right-click the box and select one of the display options.

6 Drag the `variable` block to the Scripts area.

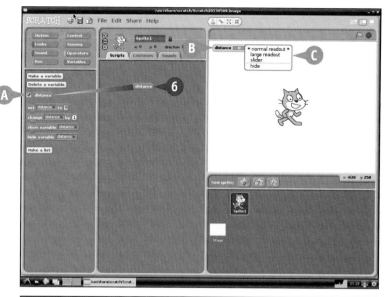

7 Click **Motion**.

8 Drag a `move...steps` block to the stage.

9 Drag the `distance` block and drop it on the 10 in the `move...steps` block.

Note: This step replaces the old fixed number with the value of the variable.

10 Click the `move...steps` block.

The sprite does not move. The variable value of 0 has replaced the default 10.

Note: To make the sprite move, change the variable value and click the `move...steps` block again.

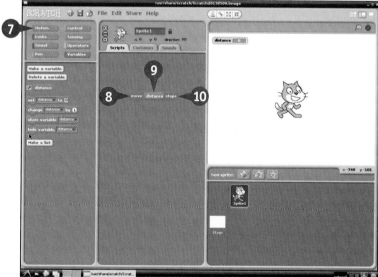

TIPS

How do I set a variable?
You can use the `set...` and `change...` blocks in Variables. Use the `set...` block to set the variable. Use the `change...` block to add or subtract a number from variable. You can replace the numbers in both blocks with other variables. When a slider display is visible on the stage, you can set a variable by moving its slider.

Do variables have to hold numbers?
No. Variables can also hold words and sentences — known as *strings*. But Scratch has very basic tools for working with words and sentences, so variables usually do hold a number.

Using the Pen

You can use the pen in Scratch to draw lines and shapes. After a `pen down` block, a sprite leaves a line as it moves. Use a `pen up` block to stop drawing, and a `clear` block to remove all lines. You can also set the pen color, change the pen color by a step to cycle through colors, and change the width of the line the pen draws.

The pen is a good way to learn how to draw shapes. This example draws a complicated shape with simple rules. Turning by 89 degrees after each line draws a square shape that rotates and never closes.

Using the Pen

1 Either continue from the previous section, "Work with Variables," or repeat the steps to create a variable called `distance` in a `move...steps` block.

2 Click **Pen**.

3 Drag a `clear` block to the scripts area and drag and join a `pen up` block under it.

4 Drag a `pen down` block to the scripts area but do not join it.

5 Click **Motion**.

6 Drag/join a `go to...` block under the `pen up` block.

7 Drag/join a `point in direction...` block under the `go to...` block.

Note: By default, x and y should be 0, and the direction should be 90. If you have changed the defaults, change them back in the `script` blocks.

8 Join the `pen down` block under the `point in direction...` block.

9 Drag/join a `turn clockwise` block under the `move...steps` block, click the value, and type **89**.

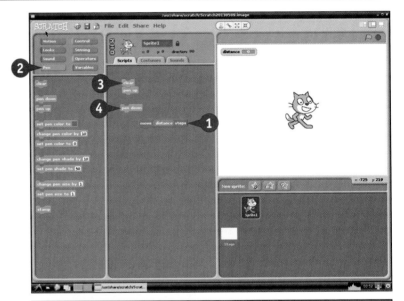

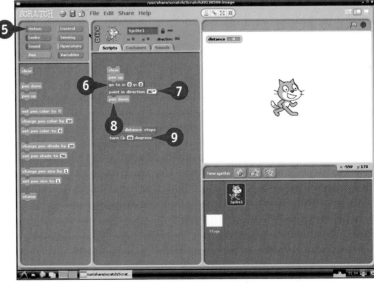

10 Click **Variables**.

11 Drag/join a `set distance...` block under the `pen down` block.

12 Drag a `change distance...` block under the `turn clockwise...` block.

Note: If you created other variables, click the selection box to select distance.

Note: The set value should be 0, and the change value should be 1. If they are not, click them and type the correct value.

13 Click **Control**.

14 Drag a `repeat...` block around the `move/turn/change` blocks.

15 Click the number and type **250**.

16 Drag the `repeat...` block up to join it to the bottom of the `set distance...` block.

17 Click any block in the script to run it.

A The sprite moves around the stage and draws a pattern.

Note: The distance variable also shows the number of lines drawn so far.

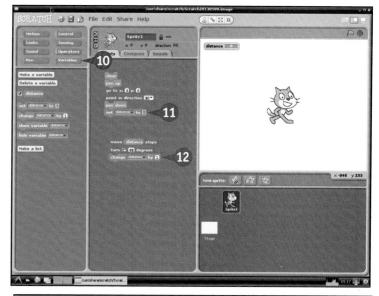

TIPS

How can I add more color?
Try inserting a `change pen color by...` block into the `repeat` bracket. Set the value to 1 to make the color of each line change slowly.

How can I share my projects?
Go to the website at http://scratch.mit.edu and follow the simple instructions to create an account. Make a note of your login name and password and keep them safe. In Scratch, click **Share** and **Share This Project Online** and then fill in the details. Your project appears on the site and other Scratch users can download it.

## CHAPTER 10

Getting Started with Python

Python is a simple but powerful programming language — a tool for creating software applications. Your Pi desktop includes IDLE, which is a Python development tool. Python is a good tool for general programming, including basic game development.

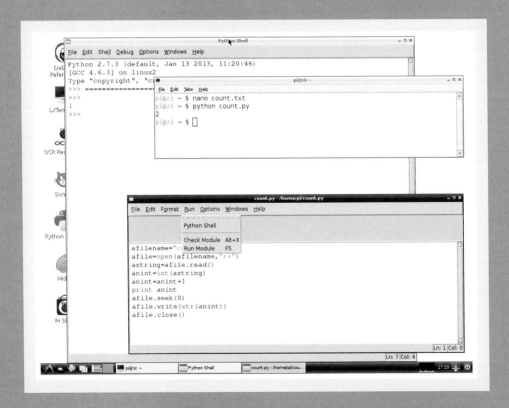

Introducing Python

You can use a programming language called Python to create software for your Pi. Python is free and included in Raspbian. It is relatively easy to learn, but powerful enough to be useful.

Understanding Software Applications

Computers are useless without software. The Pi's desktop, the LXTerminal application, the command line bash shell, and the Midori web browser are all examples of software applications. You can use Python to create your own applications. With an extension called Pygame, introduced in Chapter 12, you can create simple games. If you connect switches, buttons, sensors, and lights to your Pi, you can use Python to make them work together.

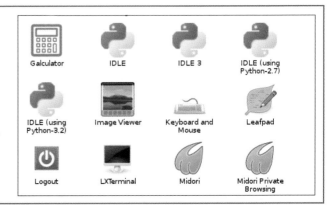

Understanding Programming Languages

To create an application, you write a list of instructions — often called *code* — in a programming language. In most languages, you define instructions with a limited selection of English words, basic math symbols, and punctuation. Compared to other languages, the instruction definitions in Python are simple and unfussy. This makes Python easy to learn. But Python still includes powerful features, so you can do a lot with it.

Understanding the python Command

You can create Python instructions with any text editor, including `nano`, and run them like the scripts described in Chapter 6. Python instructions are different from Linux instructions. But you can run a Python application from the command line with the `python` command, like this: `python ascript.py`. If your application generates text, the text appears after the command.

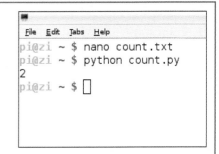

Understanding IDLE

Raspbian includes an application called IDLE, which includes a text editor for writing Python applications, and a shell you can use to test them. If you type Python instructions into the shell, it runs them immediately. For example, if you type 1+1 and press **Enter** the shell responds with 2. You can also run complete applications. If they generate text, it appears in the Python Shell window.

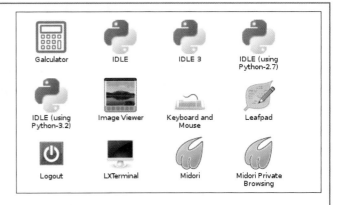

```
                                              Python Shell
File  Edit  Shell  Debug  Options  Windows  Help
Python 2.7.3 (default, Jan 13 2013, 11:20:46)
[GCC 4.6.3] on linux2
Type "copyright", "credits" or "license()" for
>>> 1+1
2
>>> 12345*5678
70094910
>>> 15/3
5
>>> 16/3
5
>>> |
```

Understanding IDLE and IDLE3

Raspbian includes two versions of Python. IDLE runs Python version 2.7.3. IDLE3 runs Python version 3.2.3. The newer version of Python has some technical improvements, but is still slightly experimental. Most Python examples on the Internet are compatible with version 2, so this book uses IDLE instead of IDLE3. For personal experimentation, you can use either, but be aware that applications you create with IDLE are unlikely to work in IDLE3, and vice versa.

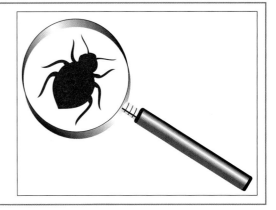

Understanding Debugging

In computer programming, mistakes are called *bugs*. IDLE includes a tool called a *debugger* to help you find and eliminate bugs. The debugger is not very smart. It cannot find bugs for you. But you can use it to step through your code line by line, so you can check that each line does what it should.

Launch IDLE

You can use the IDLE application to create, run, and test Python applications. IDLE is included in Raspbian as an icon on the default desktop. To launch it, start the desktop, and double-click the IDLE icon. You can use IDLE to create complete applications or to experiment with Python instructions. (Technically, IDLE is an *interpreter* — it runs instructions one at a time, instead of converting them into a finished application.) Most applications store information in various ways. In IDLE, you can view the information whenever you need to, so you can always see what your application is doing.

Launch IDLE

1 If the desktop is not running, launch it with `startx`.

```
Mon Jun 17 11:58:05 2013: Starting dphys-swapfile swapfile setup ...
Mon Jun 17 11:58:05 2013: want /var/swap=100MByte, checking existing: ke
Mon Jun 17 11:58:05 2013: done.
Mon Jun 17 11:58:05 2013: [ ok ] Starting bluetooth: bluetoothd rfcomm.
Mon Jun 17 11:58:06 2013: [ ok ] Starting network connection manager: Ne
Mon Jun 17 11:58:08 2013: [ ok ] Starting NTP server: ntpd.
Mon Jun 17 11:58:08 2013: [ ok ] Starting web server: lighttpd.
Mon Jun 17 11:58:09 2013: [ ok ] Starting OpenBSD Secure Shell server: s

Debian GNU/Linux 7.0 pi tty1

pi login: pi
Password:

Last login: Mon Jun 17 11:52:33 BST 2013 on tty1
LINUX PI 3.6.11+ #456 PREEMPT Mon May 20 17:42:15 BST 2013 armv6l

The programs include with the Debian GNU/Linux system are free software:
the exact distribution terms for each program are described in the
individual files in /usr/share/doc//*/copyright

Debian GNU/Linux comes with ABSOLUTELY NO WARRANTY, to the extent
permitted by applicable law.
Mon Jun 17 12:24:04 BST 2013
pi@pi ~ $ startx     1
```

2 Double-click the **IDLE** icon.

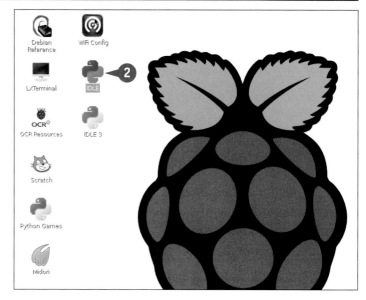

The Python Shell window appears.

(A) The current version of Python is listed at the top of the window.

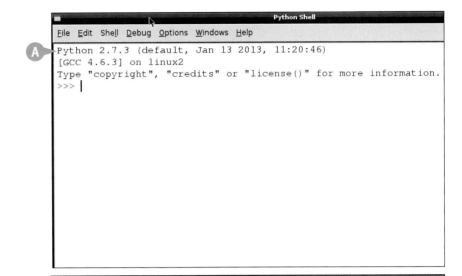

3 Type print 'Hello, world' and press (Enter).

Note: Include the single quotes.

(B) Python prints your text.

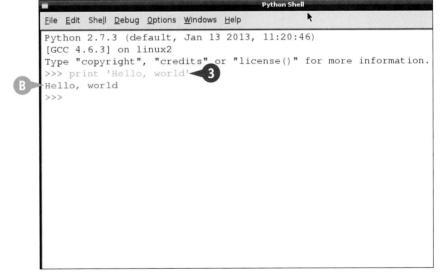

TIPS

What does 'Hello, world' mean?
Traditionally, a *hello world application* is a very simple software project that prints a message saying 'Hello, world.' The contents of the message do not matter at all — you can repeat step **3** with any text between the quotes, and Python repeats whatever you type.

What do the colors mean?
For clarity, Python automatically colorizes text as you type. Python instructions appear in red, Python output is blue, text messages (also known as strings) are green, and other information is black.

Work with Numbers

Y ou can use Python to do arithmetic. Like most programming languages, Python treats *integers*, or whole numbers, and *floating point numbers*, or numbers with decimals after a decimal point, differently.

Arithmetic with integers always produces another integer. This gives the correct answer for addition, subtraction, and multiplication. You should not divide integers unless you want an answer rounded down to the nearest whole number. You can force Python to use floating-point numbers for division by adding .0 to at least one number in the calculation.

Work with Numbers

1 Launch the desktop and IDLE, if they are not already open.

2 Type 1+1 and press Enter.

A Python calculates and displays the answer.

3 Type 12345*5678 and press Enter.

B Python calculates and displays the answer.

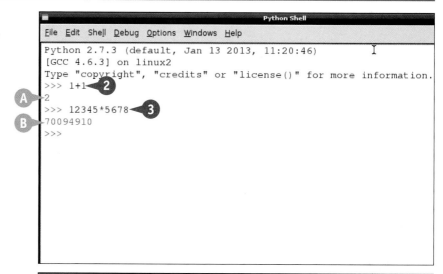

4 Type 15/3 and press Enter.

C The answer is a whole number, and is correct.

5 Type 16/3 and press Enter.

D The answer is rounded down to the nearest whole number, and is not correct.

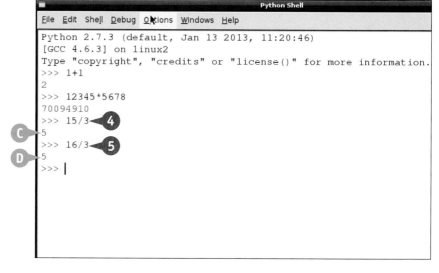

6 Type `16.0/3` and press **Enter**.

7 Type `float(16)/3` and press **Enter**.

E Python does both calculations with decimals instead of whole numbers, and gives the right answer.

Note: You can force Python to do calculations with decimals either by adding `.0` to a number, or by typing `float` and the number in brackets after it.

8 Type `21% 5` and press **Enter**.

F Python does *modulo*, or remainder, division.

Note: The % sign in this context means "divide two numbers and show only the remainder." The % sign does not calculate percentages.

9 Type `2 ** 0.5` and press **Enter**.

G Python raises 2 to the power of 0.5, which is the same as taking the square root of 2.

```
                              Python Shell
File  Edit  Shell  Debug  Options  Windows  Help
Python 2.7.3 (default, Jan 13 2013, 11:20:46)
[GCC 4.6.3] on linux2
Type "copyright", "credits" or "license()" for more information.
>>> 1+1
2
>>> 12345*5678
70094910
>>> 15/3
5
>>> 16/3
5
>>> 16.0/3      6
5.333333333333333
>>> float(16)/3      7
5.333333333333333
>>> |
```

```
                              Python Shell
File  Edit  Shell  Debug  Options  Windows  Help
Python 2.7.3 (default, Jan 13 2013, 11:20:46)
[GCC 4.6.3] on linux2
Type "copyright", "credits" or "license()" for more information.
>>> 1+1
2
>>> 12345*5678
70094910
>>> 15/3
5
>>> 16/3
5
>>> 16.0/3
5.333333333333333
>>> float(16)/3
5.333333333333333
>>> 21 % 5      8
1
>>> 2 ** 0.5      9
1.4142135623730951
>>> |
```

TIPS

Why are some decimal divisions wrong?
10.0/3 gives a long string of 3s with a 5 on the end. The 5 is wrong; it should be a 3. Computers calculate in binary, and binary cannot handle some decimal arithmetic accurately. For most calculations, the errors are so small you can ignore them.

Does the order of calculations matter?
Yes. Like most programming languages, Python uses operator precedence. It does power calculations, multiplication and division next, and then addition and subtraction. So `1+4*3**2` is 37. You can change the order by adding brackets. For example, `((1+4)*3)**2` is 225.

Create Variables

You can use *variables* to store numbers, text, and other information. A variable is a convenient way to store a value or setting. To create a variable, give it a name starting with at least one letter. (You cannot start a variable name with a number.) You can then use the = character to store information in it.

Although you can use very short names for variables like a, b, and c, you can make your code easier to read by using more descriptive names like age, speed, and x_position. Good code uses clear, obvious names for variables.

Create Variables

1 Launch the desktop and IDLE, if they are not already open.

2 Type a=3 and press **Enter**.

Python creates a variable called a and puts integer 3 in it.

3 Type a and press **Enter**.

A Python displays the value stored in a.

Note: Typing a variable name and pressing **Enter** tells Python to display its value.

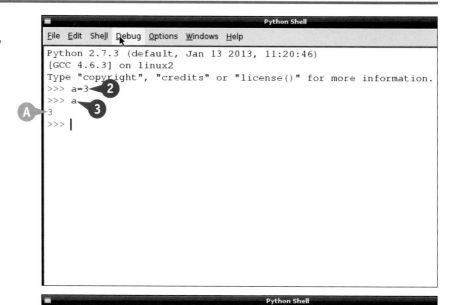

4 Type b=7 and press **Enter**.

Python creates a variable called b and puts integer 7 in it.

5 Type a*b and press **Enter**.

B Python calculates the value of a x b and displays it.

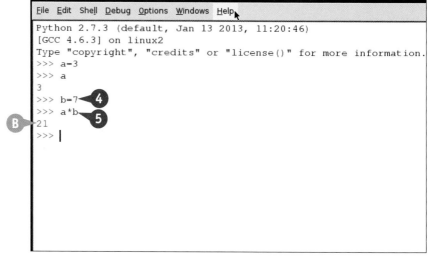

6 Type b=10 and press **Enter**.

Python changes the value of b to 10.

7 Type a*b and press **Enter**.

C Python calculates a x b. Because you changed b, the result is different.

Note: Changing a variable is sometimes called *assigning a new value* to a variable.

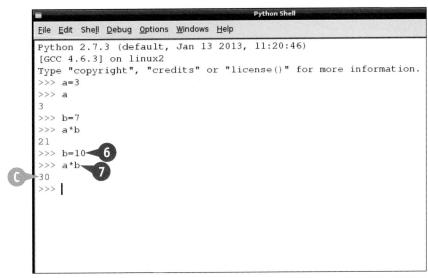

8 Type b/a and press **Enter**.

D Python performs an integer division of b/a and displays the result.

9 Type float(b)/a and press **Enter**.

E Python "promotes" b to a floating point number, and displays a result with decimal digits.

Note: Changing one kind of variable into another is sometimes called a *cast*.

TIPS

Why would I promote an integer to a float?

Software often has to convert whole numbers to numbers with decimals, and vice versa. In an application that converts dollars to another currency, users will probably type a whole number, but to get the right answer you must promote the whole number to a float.

What are variable types?

In some languages, variables have a *type* — you *declare* a variable before you use it by telling the computer if it is an integer or a float or holds some other kind of information. When your code works with the variable, the computer checks that you are not trying to do something impossible, such as adding a number to a word. Python includes basic type checking of this kind, but is not as fussy about variable types as other languages.

Get Started with Strings

You can use *string variables* to store and manipulate text. Strings — the name means "string of text characters" and has nothing to do with string — are often used to read information from the Internet or from a file, and to create useful messages for your users. Strings are written with single quotes: `'string'`.

Python includes many features for working with strings. You can split strings, join strings, search for text in a string, remove text from a string, and convert numbers to and from strings.

Get Started with Strings

1 Launch the desktop and IDLE, if they are not already open.

2 Type `a='a string'` and press **Enter**.

Python creates a variable called `a` and puts the text `'a string'` in it.

3 Type `a` and press **Enter**.

Ⓐ Python displays the value stored in `a` with quote marks to show it is a string.

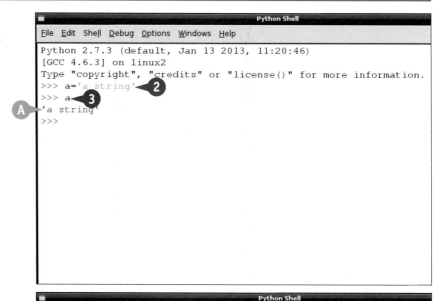

```
                                    Python Shell
File  Edit  Shell  Debug  Options  Windows  Help
Python 2.7.3 (default, Jan 13 2013, 11:20:46)
[GCC 4.6.3] on linux2
Type "copyright", "credits" or "license()" for more information.
>>> a='a string'
>>> a
'a string'
>>>
```

4 Type `print a` and press **Enter**.

Ⓑ Python displays the string without quotes.

Note: Printing a variable displays its value in the Python window. The value of a string is just the text, without quotes.

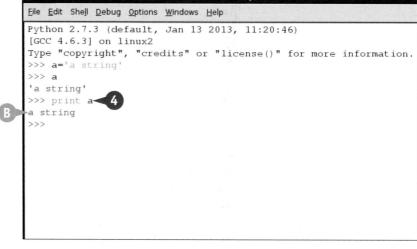

```
                                    Python Shell
File  Edit  Shell  Debug  Options  Windows  Help
Python 2.7.3 (default, Jan 13 2013, 11:20:46)
[GCC 4.6.3] on linux2
Type "copyright", "credits" or "license()" for more information.
>>> a='a string'
>>> a
'a string'
>>> print a
a string
>>>
```

⑤ Type b='another string' and press `Enter`.

⑥ Type print a+b and press `Enter`.

Note: You can use + to join strings together.

Ⓒ Python prints a and b in order.

Note: Python does not include a space between a and b because you did not tell it to. To include spaces, you must tell Python you want them.

⑦ Type print a+' '+b and press `Enter`.

Ⓓ Python prints a, a space, and b.

⑧ Type c=a+' '+b and press `Enter`.

⑨ Type print c and press `Enter`.

Ⓔ Python prints c, which holds the joined strings.

Note: You can combine strings into another string, and print it.

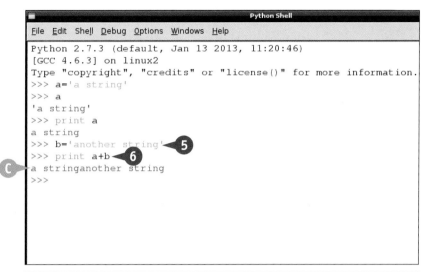

```
Python 2.7.3 (default, Jan 13 2013, 11:20:46)
[GCC 4.6.3] on linux2
Type "copyright", "credits" or "license()" for more information.
>>> a='a string'
>>> a
'a string'
>>> print a
a string
>>> b='another string'
>>> print a+b
a stringanother string
>>>
```

```
Python 2.7.3 (default, Jan 13 2013, 11:20:46)
[GCC 4.6.3] on linux2
Type "copyright", "credits" or "license()" for more information.
>>> a='a string'
>>> a
'a string'
>>> print a
a string
>>> b='another string'
>>> print a+b
a stringanother string
>>> print a+' '+b
a string another string
>>> c=a+' '+b
>>> print c
a string another string
>>>
```

TIPS

Why does print remove quotes?

print is a good way to see the value of a variable. You can use it to show a user the result of a calculation, and you can also use it while debugging to see "inside" the variables in your code. When you print a string, you do not usually want to see the quotes around it, so print removes them.

Can I do other arithmetic with strings?

No. The + operation is unique, and somewhat misleading. You cannot use *, -, or / on strings. You can split strings, find common letters in strings, and perform other complex string operations. But the Python commands for these operations look nothing like arithmetic. For details, see the next section, "Split Strings."

Split Strings

You can split strings into smaller strings. In Python, strings are stored as a list of *characters* — letters, spaces, punctuation, and other symbols. You can count from the beginning of the list using an *index*, which starts at 0, to tell Python which character or range of characters to select.

To use string splitting, add square brackets ([]) to the end of a string and include a number for the index. You can tell Python to include all the characters before an index by putting a colon (:) before it, or all the characters after an index with a colon after it.

Split Strings

1 Launch the desktop and IDLE, if they are not already open.

2 Type a='one two three' and press **Enter**.

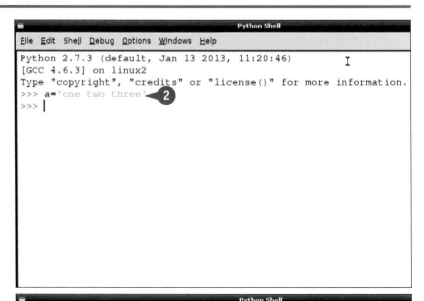

3 Type a[0] and press **Enter**.

A Python displays 'o', which is the first character in the string.

Note: The number in square brackets is called the *index*. The index starts from 0, not from 1.

4 Type a[3] and press **Enter**.

B Python displays ' ', which is the fourth character in the string.

5 Type a [:3] and press
[Enter].

c Python displays all the
characters before the third,
counting from 0.

6 Type a [3:] and press
[Enter].

d Python displays all the
characters including and
after the third, counting
from 0.

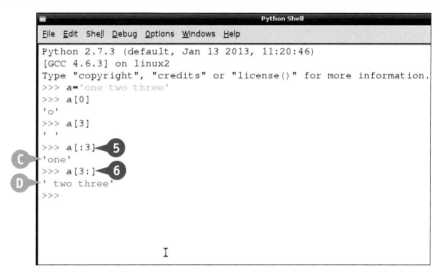

7 Type a [4:7] and press
[Enter].

e Python displays the
characters with an index
range of 4:7.

8 Type a [4:100] and press
[Enter].

f Python displays all the
characters from the fifth to
the end of the string.

Note: Usually, Python reports an
error if an index goes outside
the end of a string. This
example is a rare exception.

TIPS

Can I use a negative index?
Yes, but Python does something unexpected — it counts the
index from the end instead of the start, and begins at the last
characters. So [-5] gives the fifth character from the end.
You can use indexes elsewhere in Python to count items in
lists instead of individual characters, and negative indexes
can be useful when you do that.

**Can I step through a string picking just
some of the characters?**
Yes. You can add an extra step number
between square brackets. For example,
a [::3] picks every third character in the
string, from the first.

Pick Words from Strings

You can pick words out of strings in two ways. You can search a string for a character sequence to find its index. You can also split a string into a *list* — a collection of items arranged in order — and select items from the list.

To search a string, use the `find` feature — `astring.find('wordtofind')`. `find` returns the index at the beginning of the word if it finds it, or `-1` if it does not. To split a string, use `astring.split(' ')`. The result is a list of items. You can select items using an index.

Pick Words from Strings

1 Launch the desktop and IDLE, if they are not already open.

2 Type `a='one two three'` and press **Enter**.

3 Type `a.find('one')` and press **Enter**.

Ⓐ Python displays 0, which is the index where the string `'one'` begins.

4 Type `a.find('two')` and press **Enter**.

Ⓑ Python displays 4, which is the index where the string `'two'` begins.

Note: In Python, a word after a period is called a *method*, and does something to a variable. Each variable type has many different methods you can use.

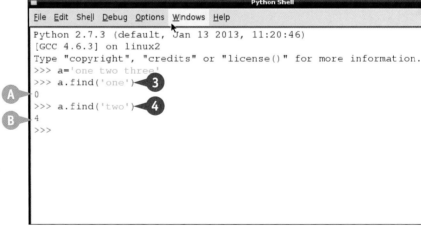

5 Type `a.find('beer')` and press `Enter`.

C Python displays `-1`.

Note: The find method returns `-1` if it cannot find the string you are searching for.

```
                              Python Shell
File  Edit  Shell  Debug  Options  Windows  Help
Python 2.7.3 (default, Jan 13 2013, 11:20:46)
[GCC 4.6.3] on linux2
Type "copyright", "credits" or "license()" for more information.
>>> a='one two three'
>>> a.find('one')
0
>>> a.find('two')
4
>>> a.find('beer')
-1
>>>
```

6 Type `b=a.split(' ')` and press `Enter`.

7 Type `b` and press `Enter`.

D Python displays `b`, which holds the words in `a` separated into a list.

Note: `split` looks for the character in the round brackets and creates a new list item when it finds it. This example splits on spaces. You can split with any character.

8 Type `b[1]` and press `Enter`.

E Python displays the word at index 1 in the list, that is, the second word.

```
                              Python Shell
File  Edit  Shell  Debug  Options  Windows  Help
Python 2.7.3 (default, Jan 13 2013, 11:20:46)
[GCC 4.6.3] on linux2
Type "copyright", "credits" or "license()" for more information.
>>> a='one two three'
>>> a.find('one')
0
>>> a.find('two')
4
>>> a.find('beer')
-1
>>> b=a.split(' ')
>>> b
['one', 'two', 'three']
>>> b[1]
'two'
>>> |
```

TIPS

How can I split text on more than one line?
Like many programming languages, Python uses *escape characters* — special characters that control how text is laid out. The escape character between lines of text is called a *newline*, and is represented by \n. So `astring.split("\n")` puts each line in `astring` into a separate string.

Where can I find out more about methods?
The definitive guide to methods for each variable type is the Python Standard Library at http://docs.python. org/2/library/index.html. The details are technical, and you do not need to remember most of them. Often, you can look up information when you need it. For example, the full list of string methods is at http://docs.python. org/2/library/stdtypes.html - string-methods.

Convert Strings and Numbers

You can convert strings and numbers into each other. For example, you can convert a string like '1000' into the number 1000. This feature only works if a string contains numerals, and not for pure text like "a thousand."

You can use template strings to control how numbers are displayed. A *template string* controls how many decimal digits a number has and whether it includes a sign. This example shows some basic options.

Convert Strings and Numbers

1 Launch the desktop and IDLE, if they are not already open.

2 Type a='1000' and press Enter.

3 Type float(a) and press Enter.

A Python converts the string to a floating point number.

4 Type int(a) and press Enter.

B Python converts the string to an integer and prints it.

Note: You can use the results in calculations just like numbers.

5 Type a='abc 123' and press Enter.

6 Type float(a) and press Enter.

C Python can only convert strings of digits. It cannot convert any other kind of text.

7 Type `a=10` and press `Enter`.

Note: a is now an integer.

8 Type `str(a)` and press `Enter`.

D Python converts the value of a into a string.

Note: This string is just like any other string. You cannot perform arithmetic on it, but you can perform any string operation.

9 Type `a=123.45678` and press `Enter`.

10 Type `('%.1f'%a)` and press `Enter`.

E Python converts a into a string with 1 digit after the decimal point.

Note: The symbols between the quotes are the format string.

11 Type `(' %+.2f'% a)` and press `Enter`.

Note: The characters between brackets are the template and define the format of the string. The % sign means "the variable I am formatting," not a percentage.

F Python converts a into a string with a leading space, a sign, and two digits after the decimal point.

```
>>> float(a)
1000.0
>>> int(a)
1000
>>> a='abc 123'
>>> float(a)

Traceback (most recent call last):
  File "<pyshell#4>", line 1, in <module>
    float(a)
ValueError: could not convert string to float: abc 123
>>> a=10
>>> str(a)
'10'
>>> |
```

```
>>> float(a)
1000.0
>>> int(a)
1000
>>> a='abc 123'
>>> float(a)

Traceback (most recent call last):
  File "<pyshell#4>", line 1, in <module>
    float(a)
ValueError: could not convert string to float: abc 123
>>> a=10
>>> str(a)
'10'
>>> a=123.45678
>>> ('%.1f' % a)
'123.5'
>>> (' %+.2f' % a)
' +123.46'
>>>
```

TIPS

Why do I need template strings?
You can use template strings to give your users key information without confusing them with extra detail. For example, if you are working out a currency exchange rate, answers should show two decimal digits for cents (pence). A temperature sensor project may only need one decimal digit.

Where can I learn more about template strings?
Template strings are powerful, but cryptic. You can see more examples in the official Python documentation, at http://docs.python.org/2/library/string.html. Note that in addition to template strings, Python also includes format strings, which are even more powerful and even more cryptic.

Work with Files

You can use files to save information and read it back. A *file* holds information permanently. If you do not save variables to a file before you quit an application, the information is lost.

To use a file you must open it, access it, and then close it to fix the information. You can write (that is, *save*) and read text only. You can read, write, or *append* — save information to the end of — files. To save numbers and other kinds of information, convert the numbers to text with `str()`. Convert them back after reading.

Work with Files

1 Launch the desktop and IDLE, if they are not already open.

2 Type `afilename='afile.txt'` and press Enter.

Note: You must save information to a named file. The filename must be a string.

3 Type `afile=open (afilename, 'w')` and press Enter.

Note: `afile` is a *file object*. You can apply various methods to make a file object do useful things.

Note: w means "create a file if it does not exist, delete everything in it if it does."

4 Type `b=123.45678` and press Enter.

5 Type `afile.write(str(b))` and press Enter.

6 Type `afile.close()` and press Enter.

Python writes the value of b as a string to afile.txt.

Note: Python creates files in your /home/pi directory. You can make files in other directories.

```
                              Python Shell
File  Edit  Shell  Debug  Options  Windows  Help
Python 2.7.3 (default, Jan 13 2013, 11:20:46)
[GCC 4.6.3] on linux2
Type "copyright", "credits" or "license()" for more information.
>>> afilename='afile.txt'   2
>>> afile=open(afilename, 'w')   3
>>>
```

```
                              Python Shell
File  Edit  Shell  Debug  Options  Windows  Help
Python 2.7.3 (default, Jan 13 2013, 11:20:46)
[GCC 4.6.3] on linux2
Type "copyright", "credits" or "license()" for more information.
>>> afilename='afile.txt'
>>> afile=open(afilename, 'w')
>>> b=123.45678   4
>>> afile.write(str(b))   5
>>> afile.close()   6
>>>
```

7 Click the **File Manager** icon (█).

Ⓐ Linux opens the File Manager and displays your /home/pi directory.

8 Double-click **afile.txt**.

Ⓑ Linux loads the file into LeafPad.

Ⓒ The file holds a text string with the value you wrote in steps **4** to **6**.

9 Click the Python Shell window and type `afile=open (afilename, 'r')` and press `Enter`.

10 Type `b=afile.read()` and press `Enter`.

11 Type `b` and press `Enter`.

Ⓓ b holds the contents of the file as a string.

Note: You can convert b to a number with `float(b)`.

12 Type `afile.close()` and press `Enter`.

Note: You must always close a file after opening it. If you do not, the file contents may become corrupted.

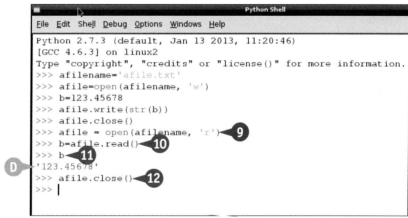

TIPS

What is the difference between appending and writing?
If you open a file with the w option, all the information in it disappears as soon as you write to it. If you use a+, old information is kept and new information is written after it. Use w to store a single variable that changes. Use a+ to collect information — for example, to create a list of measurements from a sensor.

Why can I not open a file with the rw option?
You can only use the r option if a file already exists. If you try to use r before you create a file, Python displays an error message.

Create and Run a Python Script

You can use IDLE to create, run, and save a Python script. When you create a script, you can save it to a file with a .py extension. You can load the script back into IDLE to edit it or run it again. You can also run the script from the Linux command line and see the results appear after the command prompt.

This example creates a simple script that counts the number of times you run it. It saves the count to a file and uses `print` to display the count. Because it is a very simple example, you must create the count file and set it up by hand.

Create and Run a Python Script

Note: You can find the code used in this section on this book's website, www.wiley.com/go/tyvraspberrypi.

1. At the command prompt or in LXTerminal, type `nano count.txt` and press **Enter**.

Ⓐ Linux creates a new file called count.txt and opens it in `nano`.

2. Type 0.

3. Press **Ctrl**+**O**, **Enter**, and **Ctrl**+**X** to save the file and close the editor.

Note: Steps 1 to 3 create a file named count.txt with 0 as the initial count.

4. Launch the desktop with `startx` if it is not already open, and double-click IDLE to launch it.

5. Click **File**.

6. Click **New Window**.

Ⓑ Python creates a new window for your script.

7. Type the code shown into the window.

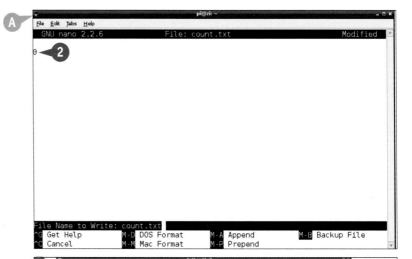

8 Click **File**.

9 Click **Save As**.

The Save As dialog box appears.

10 Type **count.py** into the File Name field.

11 Click **Save**.

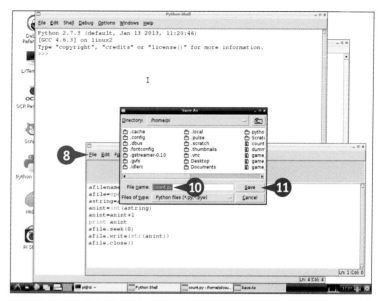

12 Click **Run**.

13 Click **Run Module**.

Note: Alternatively, press `F5`.

C Python runs your script and prints its output to the Python Shell window.

Note: You can repeat step **13**.

14 Double-click LXTerminal to open it.

15 Type `python count.py` and press `Enter` at the prompt.

D Python runs the script and prints the output to the command line.

TIPS

What does RESTART mean?
When you run a script in IDLE, Python is reset to its default values. The =====RESTART===== message reminds you about this. Usually, you can ignore it.

What does afile.seek(0) do?
When you open a file with `r+` you can read and write to it. Python does not delete the existing contents, and it also positions the write pointer at the end of the file. So if you write a number, Python puts it after whatever is already there. `seek(0)` moves the write pointer to the start of the file. When you write a number, it overwrites the numbers already there. Try deleting this line and running the code to see the difference.

## CHAPTER 11

Organizing Information with Python

Python has powerful tools for organizing information and making decisions.
For example, you can save time by creating reusable blocks of code.

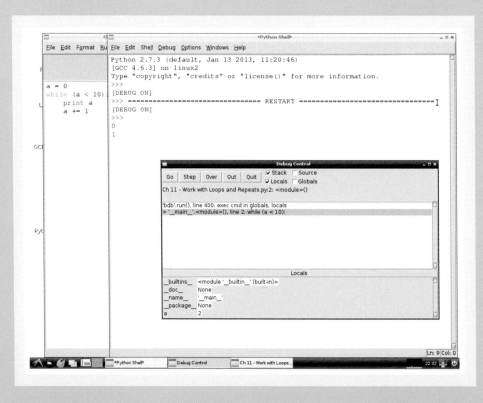

Get Started with Lists

You can use a *list* to collect information of more than one type. Lists can hold numbers, strings, and the more complex types of data introduced later in this chapter. You can select an item by its index or by its value.

To create a list, place the elements in square brackets — [ ] — and put commas between each element. Lists are *mutable*, which means you can change their elements and even perform in-place arithmetic on one list element without changing the others.

Get Started with Lists

1 Launch the desktop and IDLE if they are not already open.

2 Type alist = [1, 2, 3, 'one', 'two', 'three'] and press Enter.

3 Type alist and press Enter.

Ⓐ Python displays the items in the list, surrounded by square brackets.

```
                          Python Shell
File  Edit  Shell  Debug  Options  Windows  Help
Python 2.7.3 (default, Jan 13 2013, 11:20:46)
[GCC 4.6.3] on linux2
Type "copyright", "credits" or "license()" for more information.
>>> alist = [1,2,3,'one','two','three']       2
>>> alist       3
[1, 2, 3, 'one', 'two', 'three']
>>> |
```

4 Type alist[0] and press Enter.

Ⓑ Python displays the first item in the list.

5 Type alist[4] and press Enter.

Ⓒ Python displays the fifth item in the list.

```
                          Python Shell
File  Edit  Shell  Debug  Options  Windows  Help
Python 2.7.3 (default, Jan 13 2013, 11:20:46)
[GCC 4.6.3] on linux2
Type "copyright", "credits" or "license()" for more information.
>>> alist = [1,2,3,'one','two','three']
>>> alist
[1, 2, 3, 'one', 'two', 'three']
>>> alist[0]       4
1
>>> alist[4]       5
'two'
>>>
```

6 Type `alist[1] = alist[1]+10` and press **Enter**.

7 Type `alist` and press **Enter**.

D The second element changes.

```
                        Python Shell
File  Edit  Shell  Debug  Options  Windows  Help
Python 2.7.3 (default, Jan 13 2013, 11:20:46)
[GCC 4.6.3] on linux2
Type "copyright", "credits" or "license()" for more information.
>>> alist = [1,2,3,'one','two','three']
>>> alist
[1, 2, 3, 'one', 'two', 'three']
>>> alist[0]
1
>>> alist[4]
'two'
>>> alist[1]=alist[1]+10          ◄ 6
>>> alist     ◄ 7
[1, 12, 3, 'one', 'two', 'three']
>>> |
              D
```

8 Type `alist = alist+alist` and press **Enter**.

9 Type `alist` and press **Enter**.

E The + operation adds one list to the end of another.

Note: This is called concatenation.

```
                        Python Shell
File  Edit  Shell  Debug  Options  Windows  Help
Python 2.7.3 (default, Jan 13 2013, 11:20:46)
[GCC 4.6.3] on linux2
Type "copyright", "credits" or "license()" for more information.
>>> alist = [1,2,3,'one','two','three']
>>> alist
[1, 2, 3, 'one', 'two', 'three']
>>> alist[0]
1
>>> alist[4]
'two'
>>> alist[1]=alist[1]+10
>>> alist
[1, 12, 3, 'one', 'two', 'three']
>>> alist=alist+alist          ◄ 8
>>> alist     ◄ 9
[1, 12, 3, 'one', 'two', 'three', 1, 12, 3, 'one', 'two', 'three']  ◄ E
>>> |
```

TIPS

Can I use arithmetic symbols to change every element in a list?

No. If `a` is a list of *ints*, or integers, `a+10` gives an error. To modify every element, use a `for` loop. See the section "Work with Loops and Repeats" later in this chapter.

Can a list include another list?

Yes. You can include a list as an item in another list. This is called nesting. Lists can include lists of lists, to as many levels as you need.

Using List Methods

You can use *list methods* to work with lists in more complex ways. The methods are a small library of built-in list processing tools. You can use them to count list items, join lists together, and modify them in various useful ways.

List methods save you the extra work needed to reinvent the wheel. You can use them to save time by adding useful features to your code without having to add them from scratch.

Using List Methods

1 Launch the desktop and IDLE if they are not already open.

2 Type `alist = [1, 2, 3, 'one', 'two', 'three']` and press `Enter`.

3 Type `alist.append('four')` and press `Enter`.

4 Type `alist` and press `Enter`.

A The `append()` method adds a single item to the end of a list.

5 Type `alist.insert(3, 4)` and press `Enter`.

6 Type `alist` and press `Enter`.

B The `insert()` method adds 4 at the fourth index.

```
                                          Python Shell
File  Edit  Shell  Debug  Options  Windows  Help
Python 2.7.3 (default, Jan 13 2013, 11:20:46)
[GCC 4.6.3] on linux2
Type "copyright", "credits" or "license()" for more information.
>>> alist=[1,2,3,'one','two','three']     2
>>> alist.append('four')     3
>>> alist     4
[1, 2, 3, 'one', 'two', 'three', 'four']
>>> |
```

A

```
                                          Python Shell
File  Edit  Shell  Debug  Options  Windows  Help
Python 2.7.3 (default, Jan 13 2013, 11:20:46)
[GCC 4.6.3] on linux2
Type "copyright", "credits" or "license()" for more information.
>>> alist=[1,2,3,'one','two','three']
>>> alist.append('four')
>>> alist
[1, 2, 3, 'one', 'two', 'three', 'four']
>>> alist.insert(3,4)     5
>>> alist     6
[1, 2, 3, 4, 'one', 'two', 'three', 'four']
>>> |
```

B

7 Type `alist.remove(4)` and press `Enter`.

8 Type `alist` and press `Enter`.

C The `remove()` method removes an item by name/value instead of by index.

Note: Only the first matching item is removed. If there are further matching items, this method does not remove them.

```
                          Python Shell
File  Edit  Shell  Debug  Options  Windows  Help
Python 2.7.3 (default, Jan 13 2013, 11:20:46)
[GCC 4.6.3] on linux2
Type "copyright", "credits" or "license()" for more information.
>>> alist=[1,2,3,'one','two','three']
>>> alist.append('four')
>>> alist
[1, 2, 3, 'one', 'two', 'three', 'four']
>>> alist.insert(3,4)
>>> alist
[1, 2, 3, 4, 'one', 'two', 'three', 'four']
>>> alist.remove(4)         7
>>> alist         8
[1, 2, 3, 'one', 'two', 'three', 'four']
>>> |
```

9 Type `alist.reverse()` and press `Enter`.

10 Type `alist` and press `Enter`.

D The method reverses the list order.

11 Type `alist.sort()` and press `Enter`.

12 Type `alist` and press `Enter`.

E The method sorts the list.

Note: `sort()` always places numbers before strings. Strings are sorted alphabetically.

```
Type "copyright", "credits" or "license()" for more informatio
>>> alist=[1,2,3,'one','two','three']
>>> alist.append('four')
>>> alist
[1, 2, 3, 'one', 'two', 'three', 'four']
>>> alist.insert(3,4)
>>> alist
[1, 2, 3, 4, 'one', 'two', 'three', 'four']
>>> alist.remove(4)
>>> alist
[1, 2, 3, 'one', 'two', 'three', 'four']
>>> alist.reverse()        9
>>> alist         10
['four', 'three', 'two', 'one', 3, 2, 1]
>>> alist.sort()        11
>>> alist         12
[1, 2, 3, 'four', 'one', 'three', 'two']
>>>
```

TIPS

Where can I find more information about list methods?
There is a complete list of list methods, with examples at http://docs.python.org/2/tutorial/datastructures. html#more-on-lists. You can also type a period after a list and a single letter. A floating menu appears with all the list methods. This is an example of the IDLE's *code completion*. Many objects have methods. With code completion, you can select them from the menu without having to type them.

What is a stack?
A stack is like a pile of items. You can use `append()` to add items to the top of the pile, and a method called `pop()` to remove items from the top of the pile. A stack is a good way to add a backtrack feature to a game, or a multilevel undo feature to an editing application.

Explore Tuples

You can use a tuple for fixed information. You cannot add or remove elements from a tuple. The contents are fixed, or *immutable*. However, you can access all the elements in the usual ways. You can also check if an element is in a tuple. Tuples are faster and more efficient than lists. Use them when you have a list of elements that never changes.

Tuples are enclosed in round brackets — () — and tuple items are separated by commas. To avoid confusion with other Python features, a single item in a tuple always has a comma after it.

Explore Tuples

1 Launch the desktop and IDLE if they are not already open.

2 Type `atuple = (1, 2, 3, 'one', 'two', 'three')` and press **Enter**.

3 Type `atuple` and press **Enter**.

A Python displays the contents of the tuple.

```
                          Python Shell
File  Edit  Shell  Debug  Options  Windows  Help
Python 2.7.3 (default, Jan 13 2013, 11:20:46)
[GCC 4.6.3] on linux2
Type "copyright", "credits" or "license()" for more information.
>>> atuple = (1, 2, 3, 'one', 'two', 'three')
>>> atuple
(1, 2, 3, 'one', 'two', 'three')
>>> |
```

4 Type `atuple.append('four')` and press **Enter**.

B Python displays an error message.

Note: You cannot use any of the list editing methods to change a tuple.

```
                          Python Shell
File  Edit  Shell  Debug  Options  Windows  Help
Python 2.7.3 (default, Jan 13 2013, 11:20:46)
[GCC 4.6.3] on linux2
Type "copyright", "credits" or "license()" for more information.
>>> atuple = (1, 2, 3, 'one', 'two', 'three')
>>> atuple
(1, 2, 3, 'one', 'two', 'three')
>>> atuple.append('four')

Traceback (most recent call last):
  File "<pyshell#2>", line 1, in <module>
    atuple.append('four')
AttributeError: 'tuple' object has no attribute 'append'
>>> |
```

5 Type `1 in atuple` and press `Enter`.

6 Type `'one' in atuple` and press `Enter`.

7 Type `'four' in atuple` and press `Enter`.

D Python returns `True` or `False` when you use `in` to check if an item is in a tuple.

```
(1, 2, 3, 'one', 'two', 'three')
>>> atuple.append('four')

Traceback (most recent call last):
  File "<pyshell#2>", line 1, in <module>
    atuple.append('four')
AttributeError: 'tuple' object has no attribute 'append'
>>> 1 in atuple          ◄─ 5
True                     D
>>> 'one' in atuple      ◄─ 6
True                     D
>>> 'four' in atuple     ◄─ 7
False                    D
>>> |
```

8 Type `anothertuple = atuple + atuple` and press `Enter`.

9 Type `anothertuple` and press `Enter`.

E Python joins two tuples to create a third tuple.

Note: You cannot change individual tuples, but you can join them together to create a new tuple.

10 Type `anothertuple[-1]` and press `Enter`.

F Python displays the last element of the new tuple.

```
(1, 2, 3, 'one', 'two', 'three')
>>> atuple.append('four')

Traceback (most recent call last):
  File "<pyshell#2>", line 1, in <module>
    atuple.append('four')
AttributeError: 'tuple' object has no attribute 'append'
>>> 1 in atuple
True
>>> 'one' in atuple
True
>>> 'four' in atuple
False
>>> anothertuple = atuple + atuple   ◄─ 8
>>> anothertuple                     ◄─ 9
(1, 2, 3, 'one', 'two', 'three', 1, 2, 3, 'one', 'two', 'three')
>>> anothertuple[-1]                 ◄─ 10
'three'
>>> |
```

TIPS

Can I convert a tuple to a list?
Yes. Use the `list` method: `list(tuple)` creates a new list from a tuple. Predictably, `tuple(list)` creates a new tuple from a list. Conversion is slow and inefficient, so avoid it if you can. Treat tuples as read-only information you define once, not as broken lists.

How can I tell whether round brackets hold a tuple?
If the brackets are preceded by an equals sign (=), you have a tuple. Python uses round brackets elsewhere. Methods often have round brackets immediately after their name. Sometimes the brackets hold items separated by commas. However, if the brackets are preceded by a word, you have a function, not a tuple. Functions are described later in this chapter.

Work with Dictionaries

You can use *dictionaries* to organize information in pairs. Where arrays use an index to access an item, dictionaries use a key. The *key* can be any string or number. You can also use a tuple as a key. The item linked to the key is the *value*.

Dictionaries are *associative*, which means they link one item of information with another. Use a dictionary when you want an easy and quick way to look up a value given a key. Unlike an array or list, you can pull a value out of a dictionary without having to search the contents in order.

Work with Dictionaries

1 Launch the desktop and IDLE if they are not already open.

2 Create a dictionary by typing a variable name, pressing ⬜, and typing some paired keys and values separated by colons, between curly braces.

Note: Separate keys and values with colons, and key/value pairs with commas. Include quote marks around strings.

3 Type the name of your dictionary and press Enter.

Ⓐ Python displays the paired keys and values you typed.

4 Type your dictionary name and one of the keys between square brackets.

Ⓑ Python uses the key like an index and displays the corresponding value.

5 Type your dictionary name and one of the values between square brackets.

Ⓒ Python displays an error message.

```
                                    Python Shell
 File  Edit  Shell  Debug  Options  Windows  Help
 Python 2.7.3 (default, Jan 13 2013, 11:20:46)
 [GCC 4.6.3] on linux2
 Type "copyright", "credits" or "license()" for more information.
 >>> adictionary = {'alice': 1001, 'bob': 2002, 'hieronymous': 301}
 >>> adictionary
 {'bob': 2002, 'alice': 1001, 'hieronymous': 301}
 >>> |
```

```
                                    Python Shell
 File  Edit  Shell  Debug  Options  Windows  Help
 Python 2.7.3 (default, Jan 13 2013, 11:20:46)
 [GCC 4.6.3] on linux2
 Type "copyright", "credits" or "license()" for more information.
 >>> adictionary = {'alice': 1001, 'bob': 2002, 'hieronymous': 301}
 >>> adictionary
 {'bob': 2002, 'alice': 1001, 'hieronymous': 301}
 >>> adictionary['bob']
 2002
 >>> adictionary[2002]

 Traceback (most recent call last):
   File "<pyshell#3>", line 1, in <module>
     adictionary[2002]
 KeyError: 2002
 >>>
```

6 Type your dictionary name followed by .keys() and press `Enter`.

D Python displays the keys in the dictionary as a list.

7 Type your dictionary name followed by `.values()` and press `Enter`.

E Python displays the values in the dictionary as a list.

Note: You can use these methods to extract keys or values from a dictionary.

8 Type your dictionary name followed by `.has_key('akeyname')` and press `Enter`.

F If akeyname is in the dictionary Python prints True, otherwise it prints False.

9 Type your dictionary name followed by `.items()` and press `Enter`.

G Python creates a list of all the items in the dictionary. Each element is a tuple with a key and its value.

```
>>> adictionary
{'bob': 2002, 'alice': 1001, 'hieronymous': 301}
>>> adictionary['bob']
2002
>>> adictionary[2002]

Traceback (most recent call last):
  File "<pyshell#3>", line 1, in <module>
    adictionary[2002]
KeyError: 2002
>>> adictionary.keys()          6
['bob', 'alice', 'hieronymous']
>>> adictionary.values()        7
[2002, 1001, 301]
>>>
```

```
>>> adictionary
{'bob': 2002, 'alice': 1001, 'hieronymous': 301}
>>> adictionary['bob']
2002
>>> adictionary[2002]

Traceback (most recent call last):
  File "<pyshell#3>", line 1, in <module>
    adictionary[2002]
KeyError: 2002
>>> adictionary.keys()
['bob', 'alice', 'hieronymous']
>>> adictionary.values()
[2002, 1001, 301]
>>> adictionary.has_key('bob')    8
True
>>> adictionary.items()           9
[('bob', 2002), ('alice', 1001), ('hieronymous', 301)]
>>>
```

TIPS

When would I use a dictionary?
An example is a text dictionary, where each word (key) is linked to a description (value.) You can also use a tuple to define a standard set of keys and use the keys in multiple dictionaries to store records in a standard format.

Does the order of keys and values matter?
No. Unlike an array, where items are stored in strict sequence, dictionaries are not organized in a strict order. If you step through every key/value pair in a dictionary using the looping and repeat tools described in the next few sections, you cannot rely on a set order.

Understanding Repeats and Decisions

All computer languages, including Python, include many options for repeating code and for making decisions. You can use these features to make "smart" applications that can make decisions. For example, you can create an application that looks at a frame from a webcam and turns on a light when it gets dark. Repeats and decisions are often described with *pseudocode*, which is easy to understand because it looks more like English than real Python code. The illustrations in this section use pseudocode. You can find the equivalent practical Python code in the following sections.

Understanding Python Code Windows

To make use of repeats and decisions, you must write Python code over multiple lines. Rather like a Linux script, The Python shell works through each line in turn. You cannot write multiline code directly into the Python shell window. You must open another window, write the Python instructions into it, and save the file. To run the program, press F5. Results appear in the Python shell window.

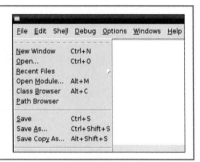

Understanding if Statements

You can use an `if` statement to test for some condition and do something only if the result is true. You can add an optional `else` statement, which does something else if the result is not true. Python also includes a further test statement called `elif`. You can chain various possible tests between `elif` statements, and Python will keep testing them until it finds one that returns true.

```
if (test condition)
    do something...
else
    do something else...
```

Understanding Loops

You often need to write code that does something a set number of times. For example, you may want to write code that steps through every item in a list, or that repeats until some test becomes true. Python includes various tools for creating loops and controlling when they end. The two simplest and most useful options are `for` and `while` statements.

```
code...
loop start
    do something over and over
more code...
```

Understanding for Statements

You can use a `for` statement to count through a collection of items or values, usually so you can do something to each one. With an `in` statement you can count through an array, list, or tuple. To count numerically, you can use the `range` statement to define a range of numbers. By default, range counts up from 0. But you can add extra information to set the start of the count and the count step. You can even count backward.

```
for (range) repeats
    do something

for each item in a list/tuple/dictionary
    do something
```

Understanding while Statements

You can use a `while` statement to keep looping through code until the results of a test become true. `while` is useful when you do not know how often you need to repeat the loop, or do not know how much information you need to work through. In a game, you can use `while` to wait for key presses or mouse clicks.

```
while (a test is true)
    do something...
then continue as normal
```

Understanding break

Sometimes your code needs to break out of a loop — for example, when you do not need to finish the rest of the loop code because it is no longer relevant. You can use `break` to "break out" of a loop or an `if` statement, skipping past the rest of the code.

```
while (a test is true)
    do something...
    if (another test is true)
        break out of the while test
then continue as normal
```

Understanding Indentation

When you use `while`, `if`, `for`, and so on, you must tell Python which of the following lines belong to the decision or `loop` statement, and which are normal code. You do this by *indenting* the lines with Tab. IDLE automatically adds four spaces (it does not insert tabs). Python understands that all indented lines belong to the `conditional` or `loop` statement, while all unindented lines are normal code. Note that you can nest a `conditional` or `loop` within another, and you must add further indentation whenever you do.

```
test or loop
    indented code
    belongs to the test/loop
continue as normal
```

Make Decisions

You can use an `if` statement to include a test and select different code if the result is `true` or `false`. To use an `if` statement, include code for the test between round brackets, followed by a colon. When you press [Enter], the Python shell automatically indents the next line. Indented code "belongs to" the test and only runs if the test is `true`.

To continue with normal code, press [Backspace] to remove the indentation. Unindented code is not part of the test and runs normally. Optionally, you can include an `else` statement that only runs if the test fails.

Make Decisions

1 Launch the desktop and IDLE if they are not already open.

2 Click **File**.

3 Click **New Window**.

A Python opens a new window for your code.

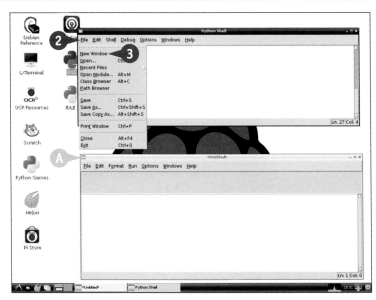

4 Type `a = 3` and press [Enter].

5 Type `if (a == 3):` and press [Enter].

B Python automatically indents the cursor ready for the next line.

Note: Remember to include the colon at the end of the `if` statement.

Note: You must use `==` not `=` to test for equality.

6 Type `print 'A is 3'` and press **Enter**.

7 Press **F5**.

The Save Before Run or Check dialog box appears.

8 Press **Enter** or click **OK**.

The File Save dialog box appears.

9 Type a filename including the .py extension.

10 Click **OK** to save the file.

C Python opens a new shell window.

D The window displays the results of your code.

Note: In this example, `A is 3` so the test passes and Python runs the code under the `if` line. To see what happens when `A is not 3`, change the first line.

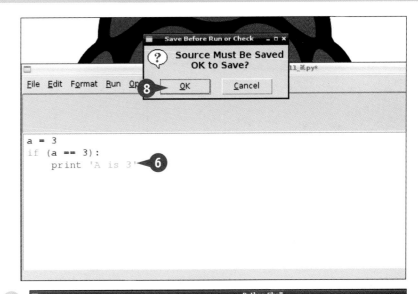

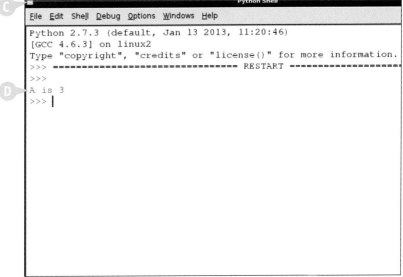

TIPS

What should I type between the brackets?

To compare two values, choose from `>`, `>=`, `==`, `<=`, and `<` — greater than, greater than or equal, equal, less than or equal, and less than, respectively. You can also specify `True` or `False` as a test value.

How do I use else?

To add an `else` statement, press **Backspace** to unindent the code by one level, type `else:` — you must include the colon — and press **Enter**. Python indents the next line. Add as many lines of `else` code as you need. Press **Backspace** when done to unindent and continue with normal code. You can find an extended example using `else` on this book's website, www.wiley.com/go/tyvraspberrypi.

Work with Loops and Repeats

You can use a `for` statement to repeat a block of code a number of times, and set by a range function. The last number in the range is not included, so `range(0,10)` counts from 0 to 9, not 0 to 10, as you might expect.

To keep repeating code until something happens or a test becomes `true`, use `while`, followed by the test, and a colon. `while` is useful when you do not know how many times you need to repeat something or when your code is waiting for something to happen — for example, for the user to press a key.

Work with Loops and Repeats

1 Launch the desktop and IDLE if they are not already open.

2 Click **File**.

3 Click **New Window**.

Python opens a new window for your code.

4 Type `for a in range (0,10):` and press Enter.

5 Type `print a` and press Enter.

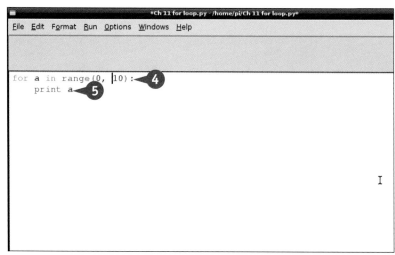

6 Press F5.

The Save Before Run or Check dialog box appears.

7 Press Enter or click **OK**.

The File Save dialog box appears.

8 Type a filename including the .py extension.

9 Click **OK** to save the file.

A Python opens a new shell window and counts from 0 to 9.

Note: The last item in a range is the `stop` value. The loop does not include the `stop` value. In this example, the count stops at 9, not 10.

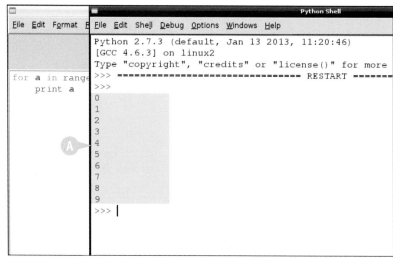

10 Select all the code and press Delete.

The code is deleted.

11 Type a = 0 and press Enter.

12 Type while (a < 10): and press Enter.

Python indents the code after the colon.

13 Type print a and press Enter.

14 Type a += 1 and press Enter.

Note: a += 1 is shorthand for a = a + 1.

15 Press F5 and save the file with a .py extension.

Ⓑ Python counts from 0 to 9 again, using a while statement instead of a for statement.

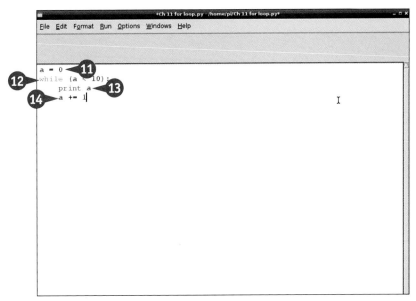

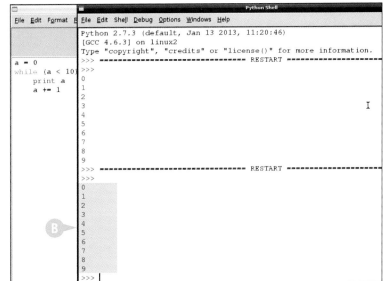

How can I step through an array?

You can use range() to step through each item in turn, using the output of range() as a numerical index. But enumeration is faster and simpler. Type for temporaryVariable in array:. Python selects each item from the array in turn, and assigns it to the temporary variable. You do not need to specify the length of the array. Enumeration loops until it runs out of items and then it stops automatically.

Is enumeration limited to arrays?

No, it also works with tuples, lists, and dictionaries. To read values and keys from a dictionary, use two temporary variables instead of one. You can find an example of both kinds of enumeration on this book's website, www.wiley.com/go/tyvraspberrypi.

Understanding Functions and Objects

You can prepackage and reuse code using some of Python's more advanced features. *Functions* make it easy to reuse code. Objects make it easy to package information and create a collection of tools.

Understanding Functions

In complex projects, you often need to perform the same steps over and over on different information. For example, in a game you might want to check

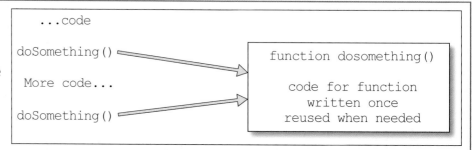

if any of the game objects have collided with any other game objects. Instead of copying and pasting the code and making minor changes every time you use it, you can package it into a function. The code in the function is kept in one place. You can use the function as a premade tool, passing information to it, and getting a result from it.

Understanding Parameter Passing

Some functions work as-is and do not need further data. For example, a function that returns the date and time does not need any input.

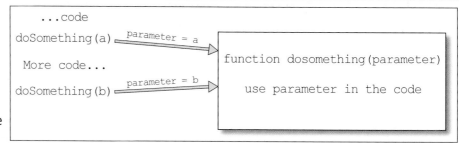

Other functions work on information you pass to them. This is called *parameter passing*. Each item of information you send to the function is a separate parameter. Functions can take any number of parameters, but you do not usually pass more than a few. For conciseness and clarity, you can pass complex information into a single list, tuple, or array, and pass the array as a parameter.

Understanding Scope

When you define a parameter, it is valid for all the code inside the function. Even if you use the same name elsewhere, Python automatically keeps the names separate. Similarly, if you use variables inside a function, their names are "private" to the function. You cannot access them outside it. This separation is called *variable scope*. It helps keep code uncomplicated, because you do not have to think of a new name for every variable in your code.

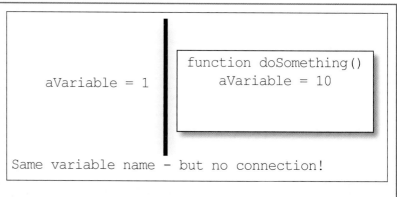

Understanding Return Values

Functions usually return a result. (You can write functions that do not return a result, but functions that do are usually easier to work with and more useful.)

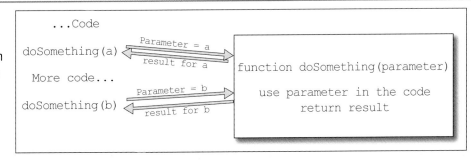

```
...Code

doSomething(a)        Parameter = a
                      result for a        function doSomething(parameter)
  More code...                              use parameter in the code
doSomething(b)        Parameter = b              return result
                      result for b
```

Use `return` to specify the value or variable you want to return from a function.

Understanding Function Definitions

To create a function, type `def` followed by a name, add round brackets with a colon, place parameters between the brackets, and add indented code after the colon. When Python finds a `return` it ends the function, even if there is more code after it.

```
def functionName(parameters):
    code...
    return value
```

Understanding Classes

You can package code even more neatly by creating a class. A class is like a mould. It includes a list of variables you can access, and a list of methods, which are functions that are built in to the class. Classes are useful when you want to create a lot of similar objects and define what information they hold and what they do. For example, you might use a class to define a game tile, storing information about its position and color, and adding a library of methods to create the tile, remove it, and perhaps to move it from one location to another.

```
class className(parameters):
    Variables...
    methods...
```

Understanding Instances

You use class followed by a class name and a colon to define a class. You can then define variables and functions — technically *attributes*. After you define a class, you can create instances of it. Each instance is an *object* made from the class mould with the same attributes. You give each object a standard variable name when you create it, so you can tell the instances apart. Python uses dot notation to access object attributes. For example, if you create an object called `myTile` with position attributes called x and y, you can access them with `myTile.x` and `myTile.y`.

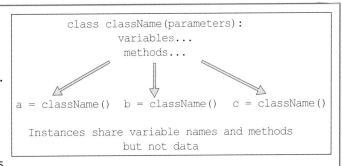

```
class className(parameters):
    variables...
    methods...

a = className()  b = className()  c = className()

Instances share variable names and methods
but not data
```

Create a Function

You can use the `def` keyword to define a new function. Follow it with the name of the function, and zero or more parameters between round brackets. End the first line of the definition with a colon.

You can use the function by referring to its name. If you defined any parameters, include them between the round brackets. If you include a `return` statement the function returns a value. Otherwise, it returns a special value called `none`. This example creates a simple function that doubles a number.

Create a Function

1 Launch the desktop and IDLE if they are not already open.

2 Click **File**.

3 Click **New Window**.

Python opens a new window for your code.

4 Type `def double (aValue) :` and press Enter.

A Python indents the next line ready for the function code.

5 Type `return 2*aValue` and press Enter.

B Python automatically ends the function and cancels indentation after a `return`.

6 Press Enter, type `a=4`, and press Enter.

Note: The first Enter is not essential, but adding an extra space makes the code easier to read.

7 Type `print double(a)` and press Enter.

Note: If you create any variables inside a function, they only exist inside the function. You cannot use them elsewhere. Technically, they are only *in scope* inside the function.

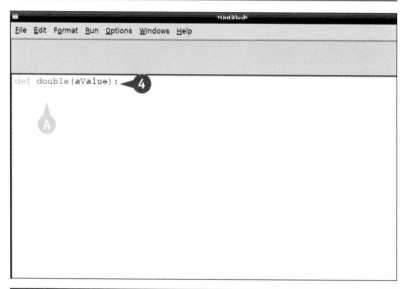

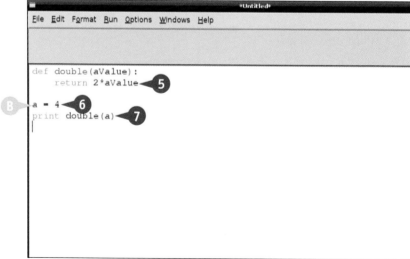

210

8 Press F5.

The Save Before Run or Check dialog box appears.

9 Press Enter or click **OK**.

The File Save dialog box appears.

10 Type a filename including the .py extension.

11 Click **OK** to save the file.

ⓒ Python opens a new shell window and prints the doubled value returned by the function.

12 Replace a = 4 with a = 'string'.

13 Repeat steps **8** to **11** to save the file.

ⓓ Python runs the function on a string. The double operation duplicates the string.

Note: Functions process information exactly as normal Python code does. In this example, doubling a string makes sense. A function with different code might only work on numbers and returns an error with a string.

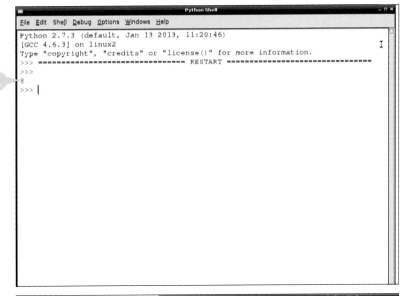

TIPS

Have previous examples used functions?
Yes. Whenever you see a pair of round brackets, Python refers to a function. (The one exception to this is tuples.) For example, the list methods introduced earlier in this chapter in the section "Using List Methods" are functions.

Can a function return more than one item?
No. Python only supports a single return item. But the item can be a simple variable or string, or an array, list, or tuple, or an instance of a class. So you can pack a lot of information into the one item.

Define a Class

You can use class to create your own classes. To create a useful class, include a selection of variables and methods. After defining a class, you can create as many instances of it as you need. Each instance holds its own data.

Classes often include a special function called __init__ which runs automatically when you create an instance of it. You can use this method to set values for all the variables used in your class, or to return a useful value. Class definitions often refer to self, which is a short way of saying "this instance."

Define a Class

1 Launch the desktop and IDLE, if they are not already open.

2 Click **File**.

3 Click **New Window**.

Python opens a new window for your code.

4 Type class myClass: and press Enter.

A Python indents the code after the colon.

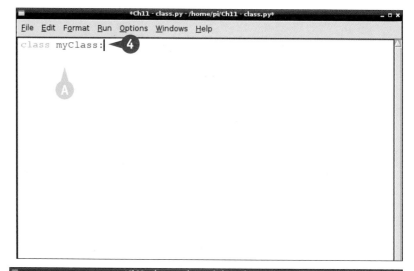

5 Type aVariable = 0 and press Enter.

Note: This line creates a variable for the class called aVariable and sets it to 0.

6 Type def __init__ (self): and press Enter.

Note: This lines creates the special __init__ method. You must include (self) if you define an __init__ method.

Note: __ is two underscore characters.

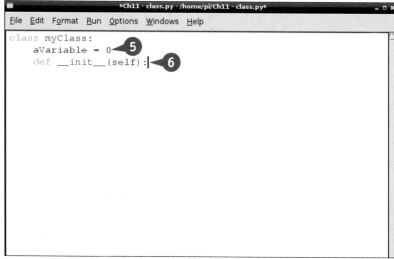

B Python indents the code again after the colon.

7 Type `self.myName = 'A new instance'` and press `Enter`.

Note: You can add as much code as you need to any method in a class. This simple one-line example creates a variable called `myName` and sets its value to a string.

8 Press `Backspace` to cancel one level of indentation.

9 Type `def changeName(self, newName):` and press `Enter`.

10 Type `self.myName = newName` and press `Enter`.

Note: These two lines create a new method that allows you to set `myName` to a new value.

11 Repeat steps **8** to **11** from the previous section, "Create a Function," to save the file.

Python creates your class without errors. The code does not print any output.

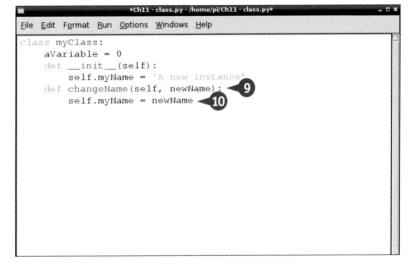

TIPS

Can I pass parameters to __init__?
Yes. Add a list of parameters separated by commas after `self`. You can then pass them to `__init__` when you create the class by including values between the round brackets. You do not need to define a value for `self` when you create an instance — Python does that for you.

Is there a difference between creating a variable inside and outside __init__?
If you create a variable outside `__init__` you can only give it a fixed value. If you create it inside `__init__` you can pass parameters to it, and the code in `__init__` can use them in a calculation before setting up an initial value. If you have a game tile, use `__init__` to create a variable called `area`, setting its value automatically when you create a tile with a given width and height.

Using a Class

To use a class, define a variable using the class name followed by round brackets. If you defined an __init__ method for the class, include the parameter values between the brackets. If your __init__ method includes a return statement, the variable takes the returned value. Otherwise, it is set to a special value called none.

After creating an instance, you can access the variables and methods you defined with dot notation. If the methods you define take a parameter, include it between round brackets. You do not need to specify a value for self because Python includes it automatically.

Using a Class

1 Continue from the end of the previous section, "Define a Class," or repeat the steps in that section to create a class and open the shell window.

2 In the shell window, type anInstance = myClass() and press **Enter**.

Python creates a new instance of the class.

Note: Python does not display any messages when you create an instance.

3 Type print anInstance.aVariable and press **Enter**.

Ⓐ Python prints 0, which is the default value your class code sets for aVariable.

4 Type print anInstance.myName and press **Enter**.

Ⓑ Python prints A new instance, which is the default value your class code sets for myName.

```
                              Python Shell
File  Edit  Shell  Debug  Options  Windows  Help
Python 2.7.3 (default, Jan 13 2013, 11:20:46)
[GCC 4.6.3] on linux2
Type "copyright", "credits" or "license()" for more information.
>>> ================================ RESTART ================================
===
>>>
>>> anInstance = myClass()  ◀2
>>> |
```

```
                              Python Shell
File  Edit  Shell  Debug  Options  Windows  Help
Python 2.7.3 (default, Jan 13 2013, 11:20:46)
[GCC 4.6.3] on linux2
Type "copyright", "credits" or "license()" for more information.
>>> ================================ RESTART ================================
===
>>>
>>> anInstance = myClass()
>>> print anInstance.aVariable  ◀3
0
>>> print anInstance.myName  ◀4
A new instance
>>> |
```

Note: Creating this class preassigns these variables. If you try to print a variable not defined in your class, Python displays an error.

5 Type `anInstance.`
`aVariable = 10` and press
`Enter`.

6 Type `print`
`anInstance.aVariable`
and press `Enter`.

C Python prints 10, because you have changed the value of `aVariable`.

7 Type `anInstance.`
`changeName('Something`
`else')` and press `Enter`
`Enter`.

Python runs the
`changeName` method you
defined, using `Something`
`else` as the parameter.

8 Type `print anInstance.`
`myName` and press `Enter`.

D Python prints the new changed value of the `myName` variable in `anInstance`.

```
Python Shell
File  Edit  Shell  Debug  Options  Windows  Help
Python 2.7.3 (default, Jan 13 2013, 11:20:46)
[GCC 4.6.3] on linux2
Type "copyright", "credits" or "license()" for more information.
>>> =============================== RESTART ===============
===
>>>
>>> anInstance = myClass()
>>> print anInstance.aVariable
0
>>> print anInstance.myName
A new instance
>>> anInstance.aVariable = 10
>>> print anInstance.aVariable
10
>>> |
```

```
Python Shell
File  Edit  Shell  Debug  Options  Windows  Help
[GCC 4.6.3] on linux2
Type "copyright", "credits" or "license()" for more information.
>>> =============================== RESTART ===============
>>>
>>> anInstance = myClass()
>>> print anInstance.aVariable
0
>>> print anInstance.myName
A new instance
>>> anInstance.aVariable = 10
>>> print anInstance.aVariable
10
>>> anInstance.changeName('Something else')
>>> print anInstance.myName
Something else
>>> |
```

TIPS

Are instances unique?
Yes. When you create a new instance of a class, it runs the `__init__` code and sets up the variables you define, so all instances are identical when they are created. But from then on, they are independent. If you change one instance of a class, the other instances are unaffected.

Can I delete an instance?
Yes. But you do not need to worry about deleting instances for small projects. If you create a complex class and create many instances of it, you can save memory by deleting instances with the `del` keyword.

Load Modules

You can use modules to package and reuse code, and to extend Python's features. Modules are prewritten blocks of Python code. Many features of Python are only available if you import them from a module before you try to use them. `import` typically goes at the start of your code.

To use features from a module, import it by name and access its features with dot notation. For example, if you `import math`, you can use any of the features in the `math` module by putting math in front of the name. You can also selectively import specific features using `from`.

Load Modules

1 Launch the desktop and IDLE if they are not already open.

2 Type `math.factorial` `(10)` and press **Enter**.

Ⓐ Python displays an error message.

Note: You must `import math` before you can use the `factorial` method. This feature is not available until you do.

Note: `factorial` multiplies a number by itself, decreasing by 1 on each repeat: for example, 10 × 9 × 8 ×...2 × 1. It is often used in statistics.

3 Type `import math` and press **Enter**.

Python imports the `math` module. It does not display a confirmation message.

4 Type `math.` `factorial(10)` and press **Enter**.

Ⓑ The `factorial` method runs correctly.

Python Shell

File Edit Shell Debug Options Windows Help

```
Python 2.7.3 (default, Jan 13 2013, 11:20:46)
[GCC 4.6.3] on linux2
Type "copyright", "credits" or "license()" for more information.
>>> math.factorial(10)

Traceback (most recent call last):
  File "<pyshell#0>", line 1, in <module>
    math.factorial(10)
NameError: name 'math' is not defined
>>> |
```

Python Shell

File Edit Shell Debug Options Windows Help

```
Python 2.7.3 (default, Jan 13 2013, 11:20:46)
[GCC 4.6.3] on linux2
Type "copyright", "credits" or "license()" for more information.
>>> math.factorial(10)

Traceback (most recent call last):
  File "<pyshell#0>", line 1, in <module>
    math.factorial(10)
NameError: name 'math' is not defined
>>> import math
>>> math.factorial(10)
3628800
>>>
```

5 Type `from decimal import *` and press `Enter`.

Python imports all methods from the `decimal` (special arithmetic) module.

6 Type `1.0/81` and press `Enter`.

C Python displays the result using the built-in Python arithmetic library, which has limited precision.

7 Type `getcontext().prec = 100` and press `Enter`.

Note: This line sets up the imported `decimal` module to give results to 100 decimal places. Details are in the online Python documentation.

8 Type `Decimal(1) / Decimal (81)` and press `Enter`.

D Python uses the `decimal` module to perform the calculation to 100 places, using and returning special "Decimal" numbers, which can calculate results with as much precision as you set.

```
Type "copyright", "credits" or "license()" for more information.
>>> math.factorial(10)

Traceback (most recent call last):
  File "<pyshell#0>", line 1, in <module>
    math.factorial(10)
NameError: name 'math' is not defined
>>> import math
>>> math.factorial(10)
3628800
>>> from decimal import *
>>> 1.0/81
0.012345679012345678
>>>
```

```
Type "copyright", "credits" or "license()" for more information.
>>> math.factorial(10)

Traceback (most recent call last):
  File "<pyshell#0>", line 1, in <module>
    math.factorial(10)
NameError: name 'math' is not defined
>>> import math
>>> math.factorial(10)
3628800
>>> from decimal import *
>>> 1.0/81
0.012345679012345678
>>> getcontext().prec = 100
>>> Decimal(1)/Decimal(81)
Decimal('0.0123456790123456790123456790123456790123456790123456790123456790123456790123456790123456790123456791')
>>> |
```

TIPS

Where can I find a list of modules?

You can read the definitive list at http://docs.python.org/2/library. A shorter list of the most useful modules with selected examples is at http://docs.python.org/2/tutorial/stdlib.html. Note that Pygame, the game add-on for Python described in the next Chapters 12 and 13, is also a module.

When would I use from?

Using `from` saves memory and also means your code starts more quickly. It takes time to import a module, and if you import a lot of modules, Python makes you wait before your code runs. You can minimize this time by importing only the features you need. For a few modules, `from [module name] import *` imports extra features that `import` alone does not load.

Work with pickle

You can use `pickle` to save and load class instances, arrays, tuples, lists, and other complex information. Technically, the pickle process is called *serialization*. It converts complex information into a simple format that can be saved and read from the hard drive. Without `pickle`, you have to read, save, load, and reassign all the variables separately.

You must import the `pickle` module before you can use it. `pickle` is easy to use. For basic use, the code for loading and saving information is very simple.

Work with pickle

1 Launch the desktop and IDLE if they are not already open.

2 Type `import pickle` and press Enter.

Python loads the `pickle` module, but does not generate a message.

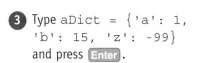

```
                              Python Shell
File  Edit  Shell  Debug  Options  Windows  Help
Python 2.7.3 (default, Jan 13 2013, 11:20:46)
[GCC 4.6.3] on linux2
Type "copyright", "credits" or "license()" for more information.
>>> import pickle ◄━2
>>> |
```

3 Type `aDict = {'a': 1, 'b': 15, 'z': -99}` and press Enter.

Note: This line creates a dictionary to give `pickle` something to save.

4 Type `pickle.dump(aDict, open("aDict.pickle", "wb"))` and press Enter.

Python saves the dictionary to your /home folder, but does not generate a message.

```
                              Python Shell
File  Edit  Shell  Debug  Options  Windows  Help
Python 2.7.3 (default, Jan 13 2013, 11:20:46)
[GCC 4.6.3] on linux2
Type "copyright", "credits" or "license()" for more information.
>>> import pickle
>>> aDict = {'a': 1, 'b': 15, 'z': -99} ◄━3
>>> pickle.dump(aDict, open("aDict.pickle", "wb")) ◄━4
>>> |
```

5 Click the **File Manager** icon (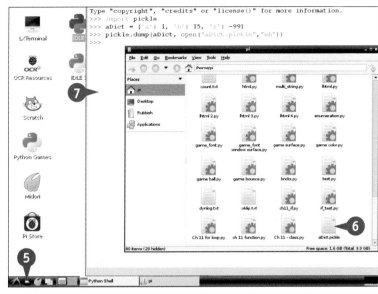).

6 Scroll down to check that the file exists in your /home directory.

Note: "wb" means "write binary." You cannot open the file in a text editor such as Leafpad because it contains binary code, not text.

7 Click the shell window to reselect it and hide File Manager.

8 Type aDict = "".

Note: This line creates an empty dictionary.

9 Type aDict =pickle. load(open("aDict. pickle", "rb")) and press Enter.

10 Type aDict and press Enter.

Ⓐ pickle reloads the contents of the dictionary.

Note: "rb" is short for "read binary" — the opposite of "write binary." If you use "b" while writing, you must use it while reading.

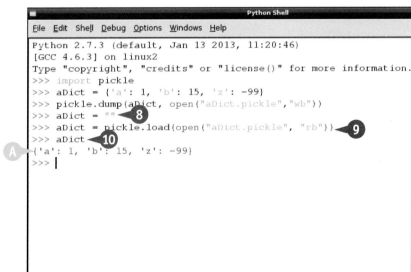

TIPS

What happens if I change a class after saving it?

pickle assumes the structure of the information has not changed. If the structure does change, it can make some educated guesses about what to do. But for the most reliable results, do not change the way you structure information after you save it with pickle.

What is cPickle?

cPickle is a faster, but less intelligent and less robust, alternative to pickle. Consider cPickle if you are saving huge volumes of data. For simple projects, pickle is good enough and fast enough. Note that cPickle cannot work with foreign text or strings with unusual symbols. pickle can. To use cPickle, type import cPickle as pickle at the top of your code.

Using the Debugger

In computing, a *bug* is an error that keeps your code from working as it should. You can use IDLE's debugger to step through code one line at a time, viewing variables and checking the contents of class instances.

The debugger is easy to use, but not very sophisticated. To load it, click **Debug** and then **Debugger** from the main IDLE menu. You can now use five buttons to control the debugger. Variable values appear in the lower part of the window.

Using the Debugger

1 Launch the desktop and IDLE if they are not already open.

2 Click **Debug**.

3 Click **Debugger**.

Ⓐ Python prints a [DEBUG ON] message.

Ⓑ A Debug Control window appears.

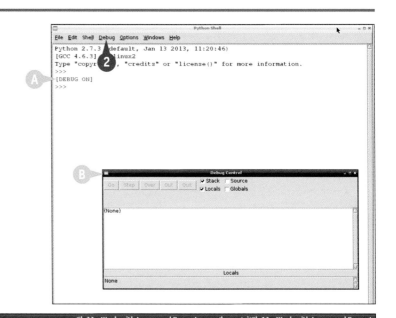

4 Either click **File** and then **New** and press Enter and save the code from the section "Work with Loops and Repeats," or reload the file if you saved it.

5 Press F5 to run the code.

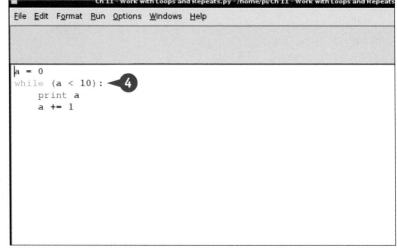

Python loads the code but stops at the first line.

6 Click **Over** repeatedly to step through the code line by line.

The current line appears in the main window.

Variables and their current values appear at the bottom of the window.

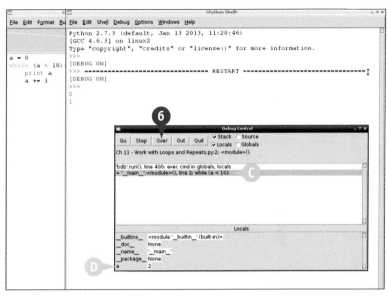

Note: This example has a single variable. In a more typical Python project, many variables appear in the window.

7 Click the **Source** check box (☐ changes to ☑).

8 Click **Over** repeatedly.

Python highlights the current line in your original code, so you can see where you are in the code and what it is doing.

Note: Python locks you out of the shell window while your code runs.

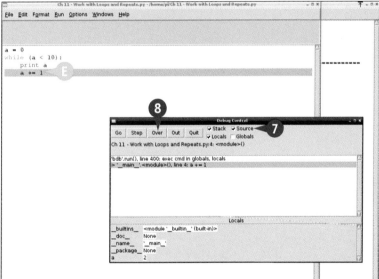

TIPS

What are globals and locals?
Globals and locals are types of variables. Global variables are defined for your Python project as a whole, and every function can see and edit them. Local variables are only defined for the current function or method in a class and are "hidden" from the rest of the code. Technically, local variables are *in scope*. See the section "Create a Function" for more information about scope. If there are no local variables, the Debug Control window leaves the Locals section empty.

What do the other buttons do?
Go runs the code without stopping. Step steps into a function or method. It steps through Python's internals, which are hard to follow and not usually relevant or interesting. Out runs the code to the end of a function, loop, or method.

## CHAPTER 12

Getting Started with Pygame

Pygame adds a selection of game-ready modules to Python and makes it easy to create games without having to reinvent code that has already been written. Pygame is as easy to use as Python, but includes some unexpectedly powerful features.

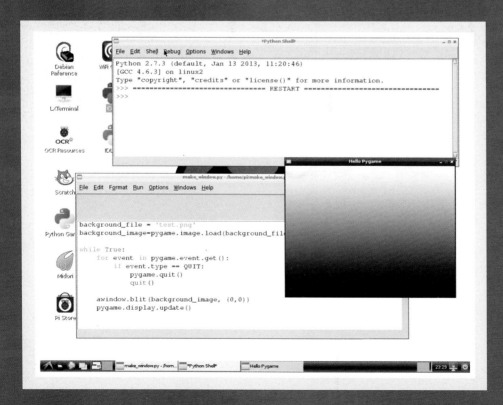

Introducing Pygame

You can use a module called Pygame with Python to develop games. Pygame is a game toolkit with many useful features. Pygame makes it easy to create a window on the screen, draw a background, fill it with action, and respond to mouse and keyboard events.

Understanding Computer Games

Almost all computer games draw graphics in a window, check for collisions between graphic objects and for keyboard/mouse events, make decisions about what to do next, and then redraw the graphics. Game code repeats this loop many times a second to give the illusion of smooth movement.

Understanding Games with Pygame

With Pygame, you can create games without having to reinvent the wheel. The basic features of game play — drawing, collision testing, and event handling — are sketched out for you. You can assemble a game skeleton with the features in Pygame and then add your own custom code for scoring and optional special effects.

Understanding Pygame and Scratch

You can think of Pygame as a grown-up version of Scratch. Instead of joining blocks, you have to create custom code, and Pygame is much more complex and powerful than Scratch. But some of the elements, including basic sprite drawing and collision testing, are very similar.

Understanding Sprites and Graphics

On the screen, a *sprite* is a graphic that moves or responds as the player interacts with the game. Sprites are collected into *groups*. You can make all the sprites in a group react or respond together. Sprites also have a custom *behavior* — a method that controls the sprite. The method code can include collision tests, responses to collisions, and position updates. Pygame includes support for more complex graphics and effects, but sprites are easy to work with and powerful enough for simple games.

Understanding Events

In Pygame, an *event* includes user actions such as key taps and mouse clicks. It also includes window events. For example, when the user clicks the Close icon on a window, Pygame receives a QUIT event. Events are also created when a user drags the side of a window to resize it. Pygame queues events, so they are not lost. Your code can create events to simulate user actions.

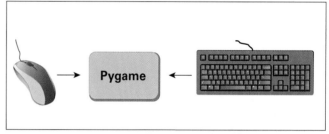

Understanding Pygame on the Pi

Some Pygame features do not work on the Pi. For example, music and MIDI (Musical Instrument Digital Interface) support is limited because the Pi does not include a preinstalled sound synthesizer. The Pi is not as powerful as a PC or Mac, so games with complex graphics can run slowly. And while it is possible to connect game buttons and joysticks, setting them up is much harder than on a larger computer. However, you can still create interesting games with Pygame and learn a lot about game programming.

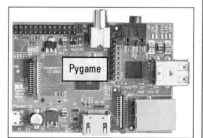

Create a Window

Pygame is a module and is preinstalled on the Pi. You can use it by importing it at the start of your game. Once you import it you can import its local variables to use them in your code.

You can create a window with a submodule called `pygame.display.set_mode()`. Pass it two numbers to set the width and height of the window. Optionally, you can use a submodule called `pygame.display.set_caption()` to set the text that appears in the window's title bar.

Create a Window

1 If the desktop is not running, launch it with `startx` and double-click **IDLE** to launch it.

2 Click **File**.

3 Click **New Window** to create a new Python module.

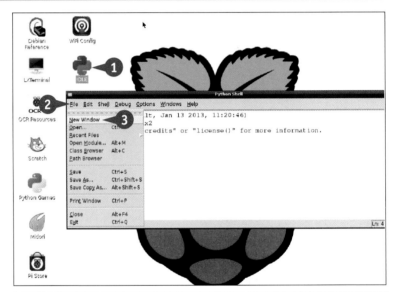

4 Type `import pygame`.

5 Type `from pygame.locals import *`.

6 Type `pygame.init()`.

Note: This boilerplate code imports Pygame, makes its variables accessible, and launches it.

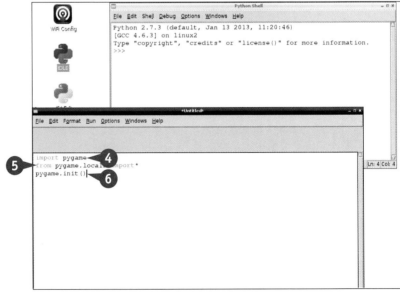

7 Type `awindow=pygame.display.set_mode((400, 300))`.

Note: The two numbers set the width and height of the window.

8 Type `pygame.display.set_caption('Hello Pygame')`.

9 Click **File**.

10 Click **Save As**.

11 Type **make_window.py** in the File Name field.

12 Click **Save**.

13 Click **Run**.

14 Click **Run Module**.

Note: Alternatively, press F5.

A Python and Pygame create an empty game window with the title you set in step **8**.

Note: To end the program, click **File** and **Exit** in the Python Shell window.

Note: Clicking the Close button (✖) at the top right of the game window does nothing.

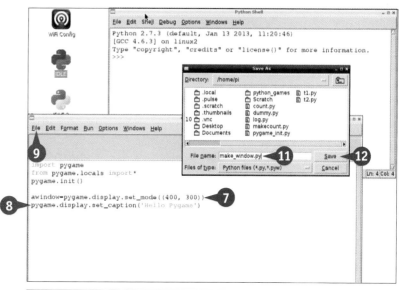

TIPS

Why are there two brackets in step 7?
The extra bracket leaves space for you to set an optional display mode and bit depth as two numbers. The *display mode* settings add extra features — for example, you can make the display resizable. You can ignore the bit depth because Pygame always picks the best possible setting. For technical details, see www.pygame.org/docs/ref/display.html. (Note that *surface* means "display.")

Is there a better way to quit?
Yes. You can add code that checks if the user has clicked the Close button on the game window. See the next section, "Close a Window," for details.

Close a Window

Y̶ou can use an *event loop* to check when the user clicks the window Close button. Almost all games include an event loop to check for other events, including mouse clicks and key presses. The loop repeats as long as the game is running. It includes code to check for and respond to different kinds of events.

This example adds an event loop and checks for the QUIT event, which is generated when the user clicks the window Close button. The code quits Pygame and then quits the Python shell, closing the shell window as well.

Close a Window

1 If the desktop is not running, launch it with startx and double-click **IDLE** to launch it.

2 Click **File**.

3 Click **Open** and load the make_window.py file from the previous section, "Create a Window."

Ⓐ Python loads the file.

4 Type import sys.

Note: Step **4** imports the sys module, which includes the quit() submodule.

5 Type while True:.

IDLE indents the next line automatically.

6 Type for event in pygame.event.get():.

Note: Steps **5** and **6** create a loop that repeats forever and checks to see if there are any events on every repeat.

7 Type if event.type == QUIT:.

8 Type pygame.quit().

9 Type quit().

Note: Steps **7** to **9** check for QUIT events. When a QUIT event arrives, the code stops Pygame and then quits Python.

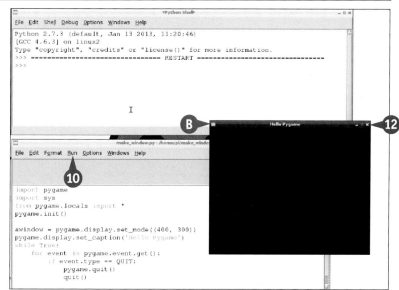

```
import pygame
import sys
from pygame.locals import *
pygame.init()

awindow = pygame.display.set_mode((400, 300))
pygame.display.set_caption('Hello Pygame')
while True:
    for event in pygame.event.get():
        if event.type == QUIT:
            pygame.quit()
            quit()
```

10 Click **Run**.

11 Click **Run Module**.

Note: Alternatively, press F5 to run the code.

B Pygame creates a window.

12 Click the **Close** button (☒) to close the window.

The window closes.

Note: A dialog box also appears. If you click **OK**, the Python Shell window also closes.

TIPS

Why does this code close the Python shell window?
Typically, you run a game from the command line with the python command. IDLE is only used to code games, not to run them, and closing windows in IDLE is messy and complex. If you run the code from the command line, it closes the window cleanly with no dialog boxes or other issues.

Why does the game max out the processor?
When you include an event loop in your code, it cycles as quickly as it can. This looping uses all the available processor power. Games typically use an event timer or a pause within the loop instead of a simple event loop. For details, see the section "Create a Timed Loop."

Load a Background Image

You can use the `pygame.image.load` submodule to load and prepare a background image for a game. Python can load images in any of the popular image formats — JPEG, GIF, and PNG. You can create a suitable image in any graphics editor such as Photoshop, GIMP, and so on. This example uses a file with a simple gradient fill.

To make the image appear in the background you must *blit* it, which means to copy it to the display and then tell Pygame to update the display. Games typically redraw everything in the display window, starting with the background, on every repeat of the main event loop.

Load a Background Image

Note: You can find the code used in this section on this book's website, www.wiley.com/go/tyvraspberrypi.

① If the desktop is not running, launch it with `startx` and double-click **IDLE** to launch it.

② Load the make_window.py file you created in the section "Create a Window."

③ Type `background_file = 'test.png'`.

④ Type `background_image = pygame.image.load(background_file).convert()`.

Note: You must create a file called test.png in an editor of your choice and place it in your Pygame folder before continuing.

⑤ Type `awindow.blit(background_image,(0,0))`.

⑥ Type `pygame.display.update()`.

```
make_window.py - /home/pi/make_window.py
File  Edit  Format  Run  Options  Windows  Help
                                    ②

awindow = pygame.display.set_mode((400, 300))
pygame.display.set_caption('Hello Pygame')

background_file = 'test.png'  ③
background_image=pygame.image.load(background_file).convert()  ④

while True:
    for event in pygame.event.get():
        if event.type == QUIT:
            pygame.quit()
            quit()
```

```
make_window.py - /home/pi/make_window.py
File  Edit  Format  Run  Options  Windows  Help

background_file = 'test.png'
background_image=pygame.image.load(background_file).convert()

while True:
    for event in pygame.event.get():
        if event.type == QUIT:
            pygame.quit()
            quit()

    awindow.blit(background_image, (0,0))  ⑤
    pygame.display.update()  ⑥
```

Note: Steps **3** and **4** select a background image file and load it, converting it so it works correctly on the display.

Note: Step **5** gets Pygame ready to copy the image from the file to the top-left corner of the display.

Note: You must include the line from step **6** in every game. If you do not include it, Pygame ignores all drawing commands.

7 Click **Run**.

8 Click **Run Module**.

Note: Alternatively, press F5 to run the code.

A Pygame loads the background image and displays it in the window.

TIPS

Should the background image be the same size as the game window?

Yes. For maximum speed and efficiency, load a file that has the same dimensions as the window. Pygame does not stretch files that are too small or squeeze files that are too large. The content of the file makes no difference to speed. You can use a photo, a custom graphic, or any other image file.

Can I change (0,0) before blitting?

In Pygame, (0,0) is the top-left corner of the display, using X and Y coordinates. If you blit to some other point, such as (20,20), Pygame draws the background offset from the top left. This is not usually what you want. However, if you are blitting a larger image, you can use negative offsets to select the area visible in the window.

Read the Mouse

You can use `pygame.mouse.get_pos()` to read the current mouse x and y positions as a tuple. To split the tuple, simply assign it to two variables. (See Chapter 11 for more about tuples.) If you read the mouse position in the main game event loop, you can use the x and y positions to control what happens on the screen.

You can use `pygame.mouse.get_pressed()` to read the status of the mouse buttons as a Boolean (that is, a 1 means the button is pressed). The mouse also generates up/down/motion events, which you can read with `pygame.event.get()`. The best way to read mouse information depends on your application.

Read the Mouse

1 If the desktop is not running, launch it with `startx` and double-click **IDLE** to launch it.

2 Load the make_window.py file you created in the section "Create a Window."

3 Type `mouse_x, mouse_y = pygame.mouse.get_pos()`.

4 Type `print mouse_x, mouse_y`.

5 Click **Run**.

6 Click **Run Module**.

Note: Alternatively, press F5 to run the code.

Ⓐ Pygame reads the mouse position. Your code shows the x and y positions in the Python Shell window.

Note: This example uses `print` to show the x and y positions. This slows down the game; a real game would not output text from the event loop.

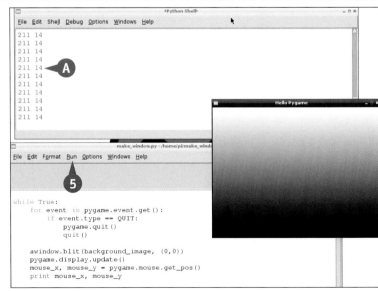

7 Type `left_button,`
`mid_button,`
`right_button =`
`pygame.mouse.`
`get_pressed().`

8 Type `if`
`right_button:.`

Note: This is a quick way to say
`if right_button ==`
`True:.`

9 Type `pygame.quit()` to
quit Pygame.

10 Type `quit()` to quit the
application.

11 Click **Run**.

12 Click **Run Module**.

Note: Alternatively, press F5 to
run the code.

13 Click the right mouse button.

B When you click the right
button, the game quits.

Note: You can find the code used
in this section on this book's
website, www.wiley.com/go/
tyvraspberrypi.

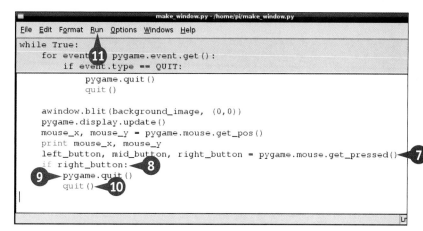

TIPS

What does pygame.mouse.get_rel() do?
Where `get_pos()` gets the absolute mouse
position, `get_rel()` gets the x and y distance
the mouse has moved since the last time you
checked its position. You can use it to estimate the
speed of the mouse — the bigger the numbers, the
faster the user is moving the mouse.

Why would I read mouse events?
Waiting for mouse motion events or mouse click
events can be more efficient than checking the
status of the mouse in an event loop. But reading
mouse information directly can make your code
simpler and easier to follow. Either option works. The
"right" option depends on your specific application.

Respond to Keyboard Events

You can respond to the keyboard by waiting for keyboard events. When the user presses a key, Python creates a KEYDOWN event. You can wait for this event in the game's event loop, and process it to discover which key was pressed.

A KEYDOWN event returns useful information about each keypress. You can use event.key to return a key number, and event.unicode to return the key as a single text character. The character takes into account the state of the modified keys, including Shift, Caps lock, and so on.

Respond to Keyboard Events

Note: You can find the code used in this section on this book's website, www.wiley.com/go/tyvraspberrypi.

1. If the desktop is not running, launch it with startx and double-click **IDLE** to launch it.

2. Load the make_window.py file you created in the section "Create a Window."

3. In the event loop, type if event.type == KEYDOWN:.

4. Type print event.key, event.unicode.

5. Save the file as game_keys.py.

6. Click **Run**.

7. Click **Run Module**.

    Note: Alternatively, press F5 to run the code.

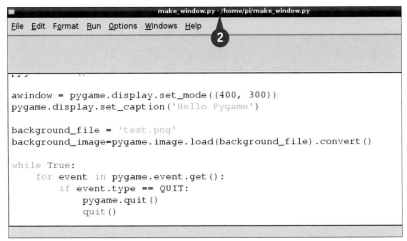

```
make_window.py - /home/pi/make_window.py
File  Edit  Format  Run  Options  Windows  Help

awindow = pygame.display.set_mode((400, 300))
pygame.display.set_caption('Hello Pygame')

background_file = 'test.png'
background_image=pygame.image.load(background_file).convert()

while True:
    for event in pygame.event.get():
        if event.type == QUIT:
            pygame.quit()
            quit()
```

```
game_keys1.py - /home/pi/game_keys1.py
File  Edit  Format  Run  Options  Windows  Help

awindow = pygame.display.set_mode((400, 300))
pygame.display.set_caption('Hello Pygame')

while True:
    for event in pygame.event.get():
        if event.type == KEYDOWN:
            print event.key, event.unicode

        if event.type == QUIT:
            pygame.quit()
            quit()
```

8 Press K E Y S and Spacebar on the keyboard.

A Pygame prints the key code and the key character for each key you press.

Note: The space character does not appear on-screen.

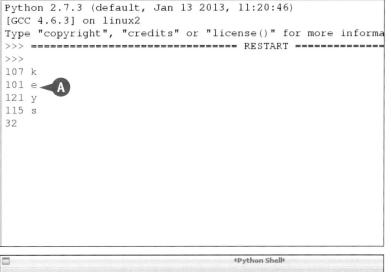

9 Press Caps lock.

B Pygame prints the code for the Caps Lock key.

10 Press letter keys.

C Pygame prints a code to indicate Caps Lock, followed by a capitalized key.

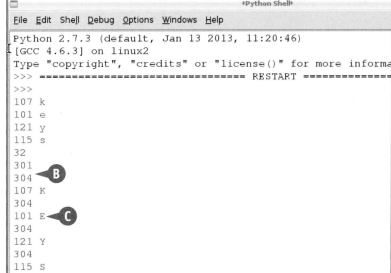

TIPS

What are keyboard constants?

The documentation for pygame.key at www.pygame.org/docs/ref/key.html has a long list of *keyboard constants*, or text identifiers, for each key. Key numbers can vary between computers. If you use the keyboard constants, your code should work on any computer. For example, to check if the up arrow key is pressed, use if event.type == K_UP:.

Is there a KEYUP event?

Yes. You can use it in a similar way, but it is less useful than KEYDOWN. You can use KEYDOWN and KEYUP together to manage a list of which keys are pressed. But there is a better way to do this. For details, see the next section, "Scan the Keyboard."

Scan the Keyboard

You can scan the keyboard with `pygame.key.get_pressed()`, which returns a long list of 0 (up) and 1 (pressed) values. Enumerate the list to find the state of each key. Each key has a *key number*, which is the same as `event.key` in the previous section, "Respond to Keyboard Events." Use `pygame.key.name(key_number)` to convert the number into a keycap name.

Note that the keycap names are not the same as the characters returned by the KEYDOWN event. For example, pressing any of the special keys such as (Insert), (Delete), (F1) through (F12), and so on, returns a useful keycap name, but an empty character. Keycap names ignore the modifier keys.

Scan the Keyboard

Note: You can find the code used in this section on this book's website, www.wiley.com/go/tyvraspberrypi.

1 If the desktop is not running, launch it with `startx` and double-click **IDLE** to launch it.

2 Load the game_keys.py file you created in the previous section, "Respond to Keyboard Events."

3 In the event loop, type `pressed_keys = pygame.key.get_pressed()`.

4 Type code to read each key in turn from the keyboard list.

5 Type `if pressed:` to check if a key is pressed.

6 Type code to convert a key number into a keycap name.

game_keys.py - /home/pi/game_keys.py

File Edit Format Run Options Windows Help

2

```
background_file = 'test.png'
background_image=pygame.image.load(background_file).convert()

while True:
    for event in pygame.event.get():
        if event.type == QUIT:
            pygame.quit()
            quit()
        if event.type == KEYDOWN:
            print event.key, event.unicode
```

game_keys.py - /home/pi/game_keys.py

File Edit Format Run Options Windows Help

```
while True:
    for event in pygame.event.get():
        if event.type == QUIT:
            pygame.quit()
            quit()
        if event.type == KEYDOWN:
            print event.key, event.unicode

        pressed_keys = pygame.key.get_pressed()    3
        for this_key, pressed in enumerate(pressed_keys):    4
            if pressed:    5
                key_name = pygame.key.name(this_key)    6
```

7 Type code to filter out the Caps Lock and Num Lock keys.

8 Type code to print the key number and keycap name.

9 Save the file as game_keys_scanned.py.

10 Click **Run**.

11 Click **Run Module**.

Note: Alternatively, press F5 to run the code.

12 Press keys on the keyboard.

A Pygame lists the key number and the keycap name.

Note: The key number is the same as the number returned by a key event. The keycap name describes a key and is not the same as a key character.

```
game_keys_scanned.py - /home/pi/game_keys_scanned.py
File  Edit  Format  Run  Options  Windows  Help

while True:
    for event in pygame.event.get():
        if event.type == QUIT:
            quit()
        if event.type == KEYDOWN:
            print event.key, event.unicode

    pressed_keys = pygame.key.get_pressed()
    for this_key, pressed in enumerate(pressed_keys):
        if pressed:
            key_name = pygame.key.name(this_key)
            if ((key_name != "numlock") & (key_name != "caps lock")):
                print "pressed:", this_key, key_name
```

```
*Python Shell*
File  Edit  Shell  Debug  Options  Windows  Help
Python 2.7.3 (default, Jan 13 2013, 11:20:46)
[GCC 4.6.3] on linux2
Type "copyright", "credits" or "license()" for more information.
>>> ========================= RESTART =========================
>>>
107 k
pressed: 107 k
101 e
pressed: 101 e
pressed: 101 e
121 y
pressed: 121 y
116 t
101 e
pressed: 101 e
115 s
pressed: 115 s
116 t
pressed: 116 t
280
pressed: 280 page up
265 9
pressed: 265 [9]
273
pressed: 273 up
296
pressed: 296 f15
9
pressed: 9 tab
27
pressed: 27 escape
```

TIPS

Why does the code filter the Num Lock and Caps Lock keys?

As their names suggest, Caps lock and Num lock are locking keys. If you do not filter them, they appear on every repeat of the event loop, cluttering up the output from the code, and making it hard to see other keys.

What is the difference between reading events and scanning keys?

Events happen once, when the user presses a key. Use key events to trigger a one-off game event, such as firing a weapon. Key scanning reports keys that are locked or held down. Use it for events that can repeat — for example, to allow the user to move or rotate a sprite for as long as a key is pressed. Key scanning can miss keys. Use events if you need to guarantee key input.

Create a Timed Loop

You can use the Pygame clock to control how often Pygame repeats the event loop. Without a clock, Pygame repeats the loop as quickly as it can. This uses all available processor power and makes the Pi board run hot.

Use `pygame.time.Clock()` to create a clock, and `clock.tick(number)` to set the update rate. 60 and 30 are good numbers to use. 60 uses more processor power and creates smoother motion. 30 uses less power, but game movement is less smooth.

Create a Timed Loop

Note: You can find the code used in this section on this book's website, www.wiley.com/go/tyvraspberrypi.

1 If the desktop is not running, launch it with `startx` and double-click **IDLE** to launch it.

2 Load the make_window.py file you created in the section "Create a Window."

3 Click **Run**.

4 Click **Run Module**.

Note: Alternatively, press F5 to run the code.

Ⓐ Note that the processor graph is always at 100 percent while your game is running.

5 Click the **Close** button (✖) to quit the game.

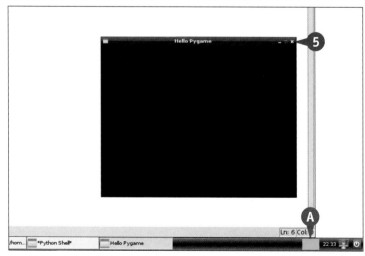

```
make_window.py - /home/pi/make_window.py
File  Edit  Format  Run  Options  Windows  Help

awindow = pygame.display.set_mode((400, 300))
pygame.display.set_caption('Hello Pygame')

background_file = 'test.png'
background_image=pygame.image.load(background_file).convert()

while True:
    for event in pygame.event.get():
        if event.type == QUIT:
            pygame.quit()
            quit()
```

⑥ Type `clock = pygame.time.Clock()`.

Note: Step **6** sets up the clock/timer.

⑦ Type `clock.tick(30)`.

Note: Step **7** waits for the next clock tick.

Note: You must place this line inside the event loop.

⑧ Save the file as game_clock.py.

⑨ Click **Run**.

⑩ Click **Run Module**.

Note: Alternatively, press F5 to run the code.

Ⓑ The processor now runs at around 30 percent instead of 100 percent.

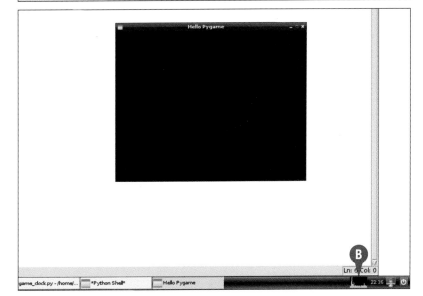

TIPS

What is the refresh rate?
The clock tick time sets how often the game tries to update the display. This is called the *refresh rate*. If your game is doing a lot of work, it may need two or three ticks to draw a new screen. The true update rate is measured in frames per second (fps.) You can check it with `pygame.time.Clock.get_fps()`.

Do clock ticks set the processor use percentage?
No. In this example, the clock ticks and processor use percentage happen to be similar. This is a coincidence. There is no direct relationship.

## CHAPTER 13

Creating Graphics with Pygame

You can combine Pygame's basic features with the standard features of Python to create simple games.

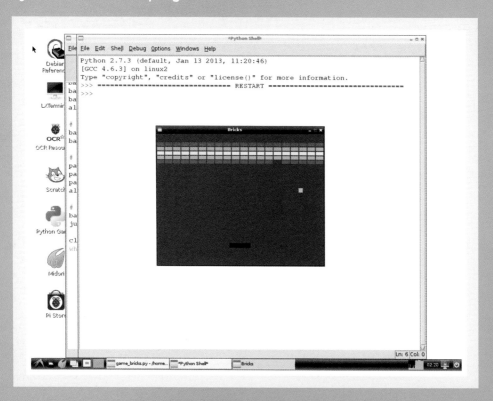

Understanding Graphics and Animation

Pygame is designed to make graphics and animation easy. Most games spend most of their time responding to user events, drawing a screen full of graphics, and repeating this loop over and over. Each repeat redraws everything on the screen from scratch.

Understanding Surfaces

A *surface* is an area of memory into which you can draw. When you create a window on the screen, it comes with a "free" surface you can use for graphics. You can also create your own surfaces. The contents of a surface are invisible unless you *blit*, or copy, them to the window's surface.

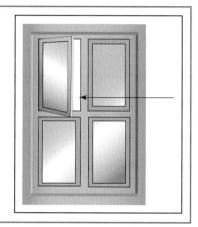

Understanding Blitting

Blitting copies some or all of one surface to another. (The word is a short form of Block Image Transfer.) Pygame supports blit effects that can combine the source and destination surface in complex ways. Most blit operations simply overwrite the destination with the source. But you can subtract the destination from the source to create special effects.

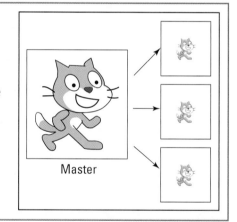

Master

Understanding Colors

Pygame defines colors as a mix of red, green, and blue — a system known as *RGB*. You can make colors transparent by setting an optional value called *alpha*, in *RGBA*. You can vary the brightness of each color between 0 and 255. (255,255,255) is white, (255,0,0) is red, and (0,0,0) is black. If you set alpha to 128, the color is partly transparent.

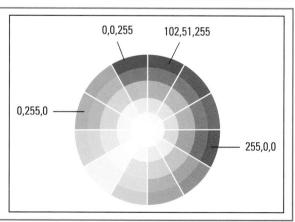

Understanding Shapes

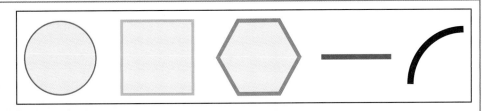

Pygame includes a set of functions for basic shapes, including circles, boxes, polygons, lines, ellipses, and arcs. You can also draw *antialised* lines, which are deliberately blurred slightly to appear smoother on the screen. When you draw a shape, you can specify a width parameter that *strokes*, or draws a line, around the outside of the shape. If you set the stroke width to 0, Pygame fills the shape with a single color.

Understanding Fonts

Fonts are letter shapes. Linux on the Raspberry Pi includes a small library of predefined fonts such as Droid Sans, Déjà Vu Serif, Liberation Sans, and Free Sans. You can use these fonts to add text to your game — for example, to show a score. Fonts are handled like other shapes. You cannot print text to a Pygame window. You must create a surface, pick letters of a certain size and style by creating a font object, *render* text using the font object to draw it, and then blit the text surface to the main window.

AntiqueOliveStd
BaskervilleCyrLTStd
CaflischScriptWebPro
DanteMTStd
EurostileLTStd

Understanding Game Graphics

All games cycle around a loop. The code checks whether the user has clicked a button or moved the mouse. Next, it checks for collisions and other game events and uses this information to calculate the positions of all the visible graphics in the game. Finally, it uses the new position information to draw and display the game graphics. The loop then begins again. The loop typically repeats 30 or 60 times a second to create smooth movement.

Understanding Sprites and Images

Pygame includes special classes to simplify game coding. You can use image files to make your games look more interesting, and sprites to simplify drawing and collision testing.

Understanding Images

An image is a rectangular grid of dots, or *pixels*. Each pixel is a single color, defined by the brightness of separate red, green, and blue values, with an optional alpha (transparency) value. In Pygame, images are always stored in a surface.

Understanding Image Formats in Pygame

Saving an image grid creates large files and is inefficient. Images are typically compressed to remove duplicated and unnecessary information. *Lossy* compression degrades image detail. When you save an image with lossy compression, some of the detail is gone forever. *Lossless* compression keeps all the detail. The main lossless formats Pygame can work with have a PNG, GIF, or TIF extension. The main lossy format is JPG. Pygame supports other formats such as TGA, BMP, and LBM, but these are old and rarely used.

Understanding Rects

A *rect,* short for rectangle, defines a rectangular area with an x, y position referenced to the top-left corner, a width, and a height. Sprites use rects to check for collisions. Pygame also includes a `pygame.Rect()` class with many methods for defining, copying, and combining rects, and checking if rects overlap. Most methods create a new rect. *In place* methods have a `_ip()` suffix and modify the original rect.

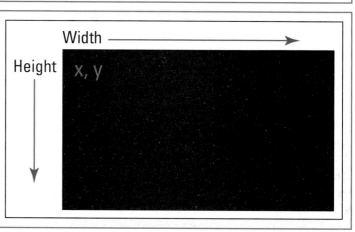

Understanding Sprites

A *sprite* is an object that stores an image and includes useful methods for grouping objects and checking if they have collided. By default, a sprite stores a surface and its dimensions. You can fill the surface by loading an image from a file or by using Pygame's draw methods. Sprites are stored in groups. Sprite methods can draw all sprites in a group with one line of code.

Understanding Vectors

You can use vector math in games to control the speed and direction of a sprite. Pygame does not include a vector class, so you must create your own code to manage movement. The simplest technique is to use separate x and y velocities to control the x and y speed of a game object. A more advanced, but slower, technique is to define a speed and direction and to calculate the
x and y speeds with a polar-rectangular conversion. You only need to perform the conversion once when the speed changes.

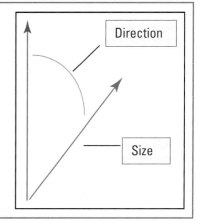

Understanding Collisions and Bounces

Most game events are collisions between on-screen objects. Pygame includes special features that manage collisions. You can test a sprite group for collisions with a single line of code. The test checks all the sprites in a group for overlap with a single sprite you specify. Optionally, you can force the test to delete colliding sprites automatically. You can also create manual test code, which checks for collisions by comparing the position and size of two sprites and checking for an overlap. Sprites often bounce on collision. To create a bounce, invert the x or y velocity, depending on the bounce direction.

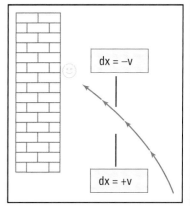

Get Started with Surfaces

You can use a surface to draw graphics. With Pygame, you cannot draw directly into a window. Instead, you can use `pygame.display.get_surface()` to find the window's surface and then fill or draw to the surface. You can also create your own surface objects and draw into them. Use `pygame.Surface()` with a width and a height to create a surface.

The surface object has many options. You can read and set individual pixels and areas, fill a surface with a color, and set a *clipping area* that limits drawing and copying operations to just part of the surface. You do not need these options in a simple game.

Get Started with Surfaces

1 Launch the desktop and IDLE if they are not already open.

2 Click **File**.

3 Click **New Window** to open a new code window.

4 Type `import pygame, sys` and press **Enter**.

5 Type `from pygame. locals import *` and press **Enter**.

6 Type `pygame.init()` and press **Enter**.

Note: Steps **5** and **6** load the Pygame module and set it up.

7 Type `awindow = pygame.display. set_mode((400, 300))` and press **Enter**.

8 Type `pygame.display. set_caption('Hello Pygame')` and press **Enter**.

Note: Steps **7** and **8** create a window and set the title.

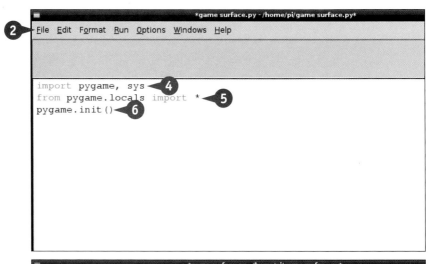

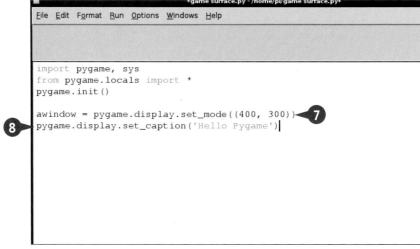

9 Type `surface = pygame.display.get_surface()` and press `Enter`.

10 Type `surface.fill((255, 255, 255))` and press `Enter`.

Note: Steps **9** and **10** get the surface used in the window, and fill the surface with black.

```
import pygame, sys
from pygame.locals import *
pygame.init()

awindow = pygame.display.set_mode((400, 300))
pygame.display.set_caption('Hello Pygame')

surface = pygame.display.get_surface()      ◄9
surface.fill((255, 255, 255))    ◄10
```

11 Press `F5` and save the file as game surface.py.

A The code creates a window and fills its surface with black.

TIPS

Does a surface have to be visible?
No. A surface is only visible if you blit its contents to a visible window. If you do not blit the contents, they remain hidden. You can use this option to create complex multilayered graphics off-screen before blitting the mix of layers to the screen.

What is double buffering?
If you create a window with the FULLSCREEN, DOUBLEBUF, and HWSURFACE flags set, Pygame creates two surfaces. At any time, Pygame displays one surface, and you draw into the other one, which is hidden. `pygame.display.update()` flips the surfaces and the process repeats. You can use this technique to create smoother animation, but it only works when you use the FULLSCREEN to make a window that fills the screen.

Define Colors

You can use the `pygame.Color` object to predefine colors as a list of red, green, and blue brightness values between 0 and 255. Optionally, you can specify a fourth *alpha value* to set the transparency of the color.

You can use `pygame.Color()` in two ways. You can create named color variables and insert them whenever a method requires a color. Or, as a shortcut, you can leave out `pygame.Color()` and place RGB values as a list between double round brackets.

Define Colors

Note: You can find the code used in this section on this book's website, www.wiley.com/go/tyvraspberrypi.

1 Launch the desktop and IDLE if they are not already open.

2 Add code to import and set up Pygame.

3 Add code to create a window and find its surface.

4 Add code to set up three variables named r, g, b to control color.

5 Add code to create a timed loop.

6 Add code to quit when the user clicks the Close box on the game window.

```
                        *game color.py - /home/pi/game color.py*
File  Edit  Format  Run  Options  Windows  Help

import pygame, sys
from pygame.locals import *   ◄─ 2
pygame.init()

awindow = pygame.display.set_mode((400, 300))
pygame.display.set_caption('Hello Pygame')        ◄─ 3
surface = pygame.display.get_surface()                        I

r = 0
g = 0   ◄─ 4
b = 0

|
```

```
import pygame, sys
from pygame.locals import *
pygame.init()

awindow = pygame.display.set_mode((400, 300))
pygame.display.set_caption('Hello Pygame')
surface = pygame.display.get_surface()

r = 0
g = 0
b = 0

clock = pygame.time.Clock()
while True:                           ◄─ 5
    clock.tick(30)
    for event in pygame.event.get():
        if event.type == QUIT:
            pygame.quit()             ◄─ 6
            quit()
```

7 Add code to create a color object using the values of r, g, and b.

Note: The % module division forces the values into the range 0 to 255.

8 Add code to update the values of r, g, and b.

Note: Step **8** makes the color change slowly.

9 Add code to fill the surface with the color and update the display.

Note: For more information about steps **2** to **9**, see Chapter 12.

10 Press **F5** and save the file as game color.py.

Ⓐ The code creates a window and fills its surface with cycling colors.

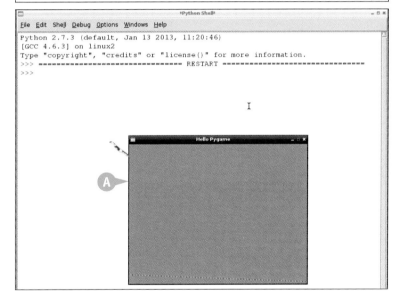

```
r = 0
g = 0
b = 0

clock = pygame.time.Clock()
while True:
    clock.tick(30)
    for event in pygame.event.get():
        if event.type == QUIT:
            pygame.quit()
            quit()

    color = pygame.Color(r % 255, g % 255 ,b % 255)  ◄7
    r = r + 1
    b = b + 2   ◄8
    g = g + 3

    surface.fill(color)
    pygame.display.update()  ◄9
```

```
*Python Shell*
File  Edit  Shell  Debug  Options  Windows  Help
Python 2.7.3 (default, Jan 13 2013, 11:20:46)
[GCC 4.6.3] on linux2
Type "copyright", "credits" or "license()" for more information.
>>> ============================= RESTART =============================
>>>
```

TIPS

Does Pygame include predefined colors?

Yes, but they are not easy to find. You can see a list of color swatches (preview blocks) at http://sites.google.com/site/meticulosslacker/pygame-thecolors. To see the name of each swatch, hover your mouse over it. You can also create your own custom colors and save them as a module.

How can I use alpha values?

You can create two effects with alpha values. Instead of making game elements appear or disappear suddenly, you can fade them in or out by changing the alpha value over time. You can also use an alpha mask to create game elements with complex edges. Without a mask, shapes must be rectangular or elliptical. With a mask, shape edges can be as complex as you like.

Draw Shapes

You can use `pygame.draw()` methods to draw simple shapes to a surface. The methods can draw rectangles, polygons, circles, ellipses, arcs, and lines, either individually or as a connected sequence. For example, `pygame.draw.circle()` draws a circle.

If you do not specify a line width, pygame *fills* the shape with the color you select. Otherwise, pygame *strokes* the shape, or draws a line around the edge. You cannot stroke and fill in different colors. However, you can draw the same shape twice with slightly different dimensions and colors to create a similar effect. This example uses `randint` to create randomly colored and sized rectangles.

Draw Shapes

Note: You can find the code used in this section on this book's website, www.wiley.com/go/tyvraspberrypi.

1. Launch the desktop and IDLE if they are not already open.

2. Add code to import and set up Pygame.

3. Include an extra line to import and set up `randint`.

Note: `randint` is a random number generator.

4. Add code to create a window and find its surface.

5. Add code to create a game clock loop to check for QUIT events.

6. Add code to fill the surface with white.

7. Add code to pick random values for `r`, `g`, and `b` variables.

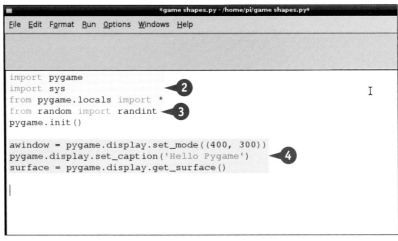

```
import pygame
import sys                        ◀2
from pygame.locals import *
from random import randint        ◀3
pygame.init()

awindow = pygame.display.set_mode((400, 300))
pygame.display.set_caption('Hello Pygame')    ◀4
surface = pygame.display.get_surface()
```

```
from random import randint
pygame.init()

awindow = pygame.display.set_mode((400, 300))
pygame.display.set_caption('Hello Pygame')
surface = pygame.display.get_surface()

clock = pygame.time.Clock()

while True:
    clock.tick(30)
    for event in pygame.event.get():          ◀5
        if event.type == QUIT:
            pygame.quit()
            quit()
    surface.fill((255, 255, 255))             ◀6
    r = randint(0, 255)
    g = randint(0, 255)                       ◀7
    b = randint(0, 255)
```

8 Add code to convert r, g, and b into a color object.

9 Add code to draw a rectangle with the random color, with a random position and dimensions.

10 Add code to update the display.

11 Press F5 and save the file as game shapes.py.

A Python creates a window with a randomly colored and positioned rectangle.

Note: Because the window is set to white on every game loop before a rectangle is drawn, the random rectangles flash once. They do not fill up the window.

```
while True:
    clock.tick(30)
    for event in pygame.event.get():
        if event.type == QUIT:
            pygame.quit()
            quit()
    surface.fill((255, 255, 255))
    r = randint(0, 255)
    g = randint(0, 255)
    b = randint(0, 255)
    color = pygame.Color(r, g, b)      8
    pygame.draw.rect(surface, color, (randint(0, 400),
                                       randint(0, 300),
                                       randint(10, 100),     9
                                       randint(10, 100)),
                                       0)

    pygame.display.update()      10
```

```
                              *Python Shell*
File  Edit  Shell  Debug  Options  Windows  Help
Python 2.7.3 (default, Jan 13 2013, 11:20:46)
[GCC 4.6.3] on linux2
Type "copyright", "credits" or "license()" for more information.
================================ RESTART ================================
>>>
>>>
>>> ================================
>>>
```

TIPS

What does surface locking do?
You can lock a surface before drawing to it with the `pygame.surface.lock()` method. Locking a surface speeds up drawing and makes your game more efficient. Use `pygame.surface.unlock()` to unlock the surface immediately after drawing. You can include more than one drawing method `lock()` and `unlock()`. Note that you must unlock a surface before you can blit it.

What is antialiasing?
Antialiasing is a trick used by graphics software to make lines and shapes appear smoother. Without antialiasing, shapes and lines have hard edges. With antialiasing, the edges are softened slightly. This makes them look less jagged. The `pygame.draw.aalines()` method draws antialiased lines. Unfortunately, there is no antialiasing option for the other shape methods.

Animate an Object

You can animate an object by changing one or more of its properties over time. The simplest form of animation is movement. To move an object, use x and y variables to store its position. If you change x and y on each game loop and redraw the object, it appears to move.

Game objects often move at a fixed speed and angle. To control the speed, use an extra pair of variables to control how quickly x and y change. These variables are often called dx and dy (short for delta, which is a change in value). Add dx and dy to x and y on each game loop.

Animate an Object

Note: You can find the code used in this section on this book's website, www.wiley.com/go/tyvraspberrypi.

1. Launch the desktop and IDLE if they are not already open.

2. Add code to import and set up Pygame.

3. Add code to create a window with a title, and get its surface.

4. Add code to create a gray color.

5. Add animation variables to set the size, position, and two-axis speed of a square ball.

Note: ball_dx and ball_dy hold the horizontal and vertical speed of the ball.

6. Add code to create a timed loop, and to check for QUIT events.

```
                              *game ball.py - /home/pi/game ball.py*
File  Edit  Format  Run  Options  Windows  Help


import pygame
import sys
from pygame.locals import *        ◀ 2
pygame.init()

awindow = pygame.display.set_mode((400, 300))
pygame.display.set_caption('Hello Pygame')    ◀ 3
surface=pygame.display.get_surface()
```

```
surface=pygame.display.get_surface()

color_gray = pygame.Color(100,100,100) ◀ 4

ball_x = 0
ball_y = 0
ball_dx = 1.5        ◀ 5
ball_dy = 1.5
ball_width = 10
ball_height = 10

clock = pygame.time.Clock()

while True:
    clock.tick(30)
    for event in pygame.event.get():   ◀ 6
        if event.type == QUIT:
            pygame.quit()
            quit()
```

7 Add code to fill the window with white.

8 Add code to draw the ball as a rect.

9 Add code to update the display.

10 Add code to calculate the next ball position.

```
awindow = pygame.display.set_mode((400, 300))
pygame.display.set_caption('Hello Pygame')
surface=pygame.display.get_surface()

color_gray = pygame.Color(100,100,100)

ball_x = 0
ball_y = 0
ball_dx = 1.5
ball_dy = 1.5
ball_width = 10
ball_height = 10

clock = pygame.time.Clock()

while True:
    clock.tick(30)
    for event in pygame.event.get():
        if event.type == QUIT:
            pygame.quit()
            quit()
    surface.fill((255,255,255))
    pygame.draw.rect(surface, color_gray, (ball_x, ball_y, ball_width, ball_heig
    awindow.blit(surface, (0,0))
    pygame.display.update()
    ball_x += ball_dx
    ball_y += ball_dy
```

Ln: 1 Col: 0

11 Press **F5** and save the file as ball game.py.

A Pygame creates a window, paints it white, and animates a ball moving from the top left.

Note: The ball does not include code for bounces, so it moves off the bottom of the window.

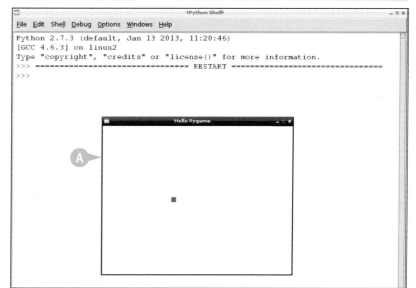

TIPS

How can I animate other properties?

You can animate any property in the same way you animate position — use a variable, or variables, to hold the current value, and corresponding variables to set how much the property changes on each loop repeat.

How can I create more complex animations?

Commercial games create complex effects in two ways. *AI* (artificial intelligence) makes game elements respond to their surroundings and to other events. For example, one object can track or follow another. A *physics engine* models complex effects such as gravitational acceleration, friction, and so on. Physics engines use relatively simple math to create these effects. You can find more information about both options online.

Bounce a Shape

You can bounce an object off the side of your window with some simple tests and basic arithmetic. To check if an item has collided with the window edges, test if the x and y positions are outside the window.

For example if your game window is 400 pixels wide and the x position of your ball is greater than or equal to 400, the ball has collided with the right-hand edge. To make an object bounce, multiply dx or dy by −1, depending on the edge. This makes the object move in the opposite direction.

Bounce a Shape

1 Launch the desktop and IDLE if they are not already open.

2 Load game ball.py from the previous section, "Animate an Object."

3 Change `ball_dx` and `ball_dy` to 3 so the ball moves faster.

```
screen_width = 300
screen_height = 400

awindow = pygame.display.set_mode((screen_height, screen_width))
pygame.display.set_caption('Hello Pygame')
surface=pygame.display.get_surface()

color_gray = pygame.Color(100,100,100)

ball_x = 0
ball_y = 0
ball_dx = 3
ball_dy = 3
ball_width = 10
ball_height = 10

clock = pygame.time.Clock()

while True:
```

4 Add code to check if the left corner of the ball is outside the left window edge.

5 Add code to move the ball to the edge if it is outside it.

Note: Step **5** avoids some subtle animation errors.

6 Add code to reverse the horizontal speed of the ball at the left edge.

7 Repeat the code in steps **4** to **6**, changing x to y for the top edge of the ball and window.

```
while True:
    clock.tick(30)
    for event in pygame.event.get():
        if event.type == QUIT:
            pygame.quit()
            quit()
    surface.fill((255,255,255))
    pygame.draw.rect(surface, color_gray, (ball_x, ball_y, ball
    awindow.blit(surface, (0,0))
    pygame.display.update()
    ball_x += ball_dx
    ball_y += ball_dy
    if (ball_x <= 0):
        ball_x = 0
        ball_dx = -ball_dx
    if (ball_y <= 0):
        ball_y = 0
        ball_dy = -ball_dy
```

8 Repeat the previous code making changes for the right window edge and ball corner.

9 Repeat the code from step **7** making changes for the bottom of the screen.

Note: The ball should bounce from the bottom right edge, but the ball is drawn from the top left. You must offset the test by the width and height of the ball to compensate.

10 Press **F5** and save the file as game bounce.py.

A The ball bounces off the edges of the window.

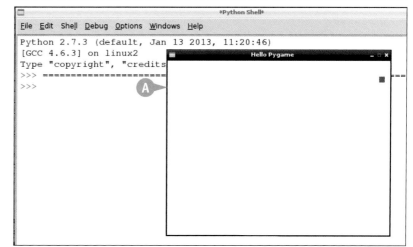

```
            quit()
    surface.fill((255,255,255))
    pygame.draw.rect(surface, color_gray, (ball_x, ball_y, ball
    awindow.blit(surface, (0,0))
    pygame.display.update()
    ball_x += ball_dx
    ball_y += ball_dy
    if (ball_x <= 0):
        ball_x = 0
        ball_dx = -ball_dx
    if (ball_y <= 0):
        ball_y = 0
        ball_dy = -ball_dy
    if (ball_x >= screen_height - ball_height):
        ball_x = screen_height-ball_height        8
        ball_dx = -ball_dx
    if (ball_y > screen_width - ball_width):
        ball_y = screen_width-ball_width          9
        ball_dy = -ball_dy
```

TIPS

Why does the object seem to bounce past the edge?

Most objects have a width and height. To create a realistic bounce, allow for the width and height when checking for bounces: test for the bottom of the screen with the screen height less the object height. Likewise for the right edge. Top and left bounces are relative to the top-left corner of the object, so you do not need to include an adjustment.

How can I randomize a bounce?

Some games include variable bounces. For example, a paddle game may bounce objects at different angles depending on the speed of the paddle or on the bounce position. To simulate this, multiply both dx and dy by some factor other than -1; select values from a list, or use a random number in a set range.

Draw Text with Fonts

You must call `pygame.font.init()` before working with fonts. You can then use `pygame.font.get_fonts()` to show a list of fonts on the Pi, and `pygame.font.SysFont()` to load a font from the list. The method takes the name of the font as a string and a size in pixels (not points) as an integer.

To write text to a surface, use the `render()` method on the loaded font object. This creates a surface that holds an image of the text. You can then blit the surface to your main game window to display it. Optionally, `text.get_rect()` returns the rect size of the text.

Draw Text with Fonts

Note: You can find the code used in this section on this book's website, www.wiley.com/go/tyvraspberrypi.

1 Launch the desktop and IDLE if they are not already open.

2 Add code to import and set up Pygame.

3 Add code to create a window, find its surface, and fill it with white.

4 Add code to create a timed event list and blit the surface contents back to the window.

5 Add code to initialize the font module.

6 Add code to get a list of available fonts.

7 Add code to print the list of fonts.

Note: Steps **5** to **7** are instructional so you can see a font list. You do not need it to load and display a font, unless you want to check if a specific font is available.

```
import pygame
import sys
from pygame.locals import *      2
pygame.init()

awindow = pygame.display.set_mode((400, 300))
pygame.display.set_caption('Hello Pygame')
surface = pygame.Surface(awindow.get_size())      3
surface.fill((255,255,255))

clock = pygame.time.Clock()
while True:
    clock.tick(30)
    for event in pygame.event.get():
        if event.type == QUIT:
            pygame.quit()      4
            quit()
    awindow.blit(surface, (0,0))
    pygame.display.update()
```

game_font.py - /home/pi/game_font.py

File   Edit   Format   Run   Options   Windows   Help

```
import pygame
import sys
from pygame.locals import *
pygame.init()

awindow = pygame.display.set_mode((400, 300))
pygame.display.set_caption('Hello Pygame')
surface = pygame.Surface(awindow.get_size())
surface.fill((255,255,255))

pygame.font.init()      5
fonts = pygame.font.get_fonts()      6
print fonts      7
```

8 Add code to load the `droidsans` font, which is preinstalled on Raspbian.

9 Add code to render font text to a surface.

10 Add code to center the text.

Note: In Python, you can work out a result in brackets to pass it as a parameter.

11 Add code to blit the text surface to the window surface at the position.

12 Press **F5** and save the file as game font.py.

A Python displays a list of preinstalled fonts.

B Python displays the text centered on the top line of the window using the font you selected.

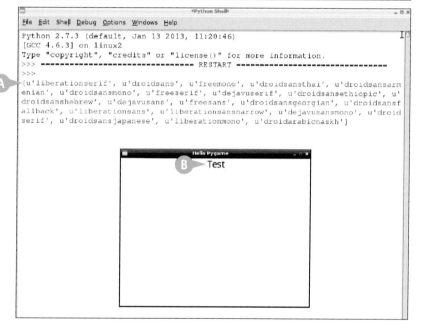

```
import pygame
import sys
from pygame.locals import *
pygame.init()

awindow = pygame.display.set_mode((400, 300))
pygame.display.set_caption('Hello Pygame')
surface = pygame.Surface(awindow.get_size())
surface.fill((255,255,255))

pygame.font.init()
fonts = pygame.font.get_fonts()
print fonts
dfont = pygame.font.SysFont('droidsans', 20)    ◀8
text = dfont.render('Test', 1, (0,0,0))    ◀9
textpos = text.get_rect(centerx = surface.get_width()/2)    ◀10
surface.blit(text, textpos)    ◀11

clock = pygame.time.Clock()
while True:
```

```
*Python Shell*                                         _ □ X
File  Edit  Shell  Debug  Options  Windows  Help
Python 2.7.3 (default, Jan 13 2013, 11:20:46)          I
[GCC 4.6.3] on linux2
Type "copyright", "credits" or "license()" for more information.
>>> ============================ RESTART ============================
>>>
[u'liberationserif', u'droidsans', u'freemono', u'droidsansthai', u'droidsansarm
enian', u'droidsansmono', u'freeserif', u'dejavuserif', u'droidsansethiopic', u'
droidsanshebrew', u'dejavusans', u'freesans', u'droidsansgeorgian', u'droidsansf
allback', u'liberationsans', u'liberationsansnarrow', u'dejavusansmono', u'droid
serif', u'droidsansjapanese', u'liberationmono', u'droidarabicnaskh']
```

```
Hello Pygame            _ □ X
        B  Test
```

TIPS

Can I use a nonstandard font?
Yes. Instead of `pygame.font.Sysfont()`, use `pygame.font.Font()` and pass the path of your font file as one of the parameters. You can then use the `font` object to render text.

Can I apply text effects?
Yes. You can apply bold, underline, and italic effects with `pygame.font.Font()`, and bold and italic effects with `pygame.font.SysFont()`. See the `pygame.font()` documentation at www.pygame.org/docs/ref/font.html for details.

Load and Show an Image

You can use the `pygame.image.load()` method to load an image from a file. Pygame does a good job of guessing the file type, but you can add an optional name hint to specify the type explicitly. The method automatically creates a surface. You can blit the surface to your window's surface in the usual way.

You may need to use optional methods to optimize the date before blitting. Use `surface.convert()` to optimize the image for the display, and the `convert_alpha()` method to load .png files with alpha transparency.

Load and Show an Image

Note: You can find the code used in this section on this book's website, www.wiley.com/go/tyvraspberrypi.

1 Launch the desktop and IDLE if they are not already open.

2 Add code to import and set up Pygame.

3 Add code to create a window.

4 Add code to set the window title.

Note: Step 4 is optional.

5 Add code to create a timed game loop and to check for `QUIT` events.

```
import pygame
import sys
from pygame.locals import *
pygame.init()
```

(step 2)

```
import pygame
import sys
from pygame.locals import *
pygame.init()

awindow = pygame.display.set_mode((400, 300))
pygame.display.set_caption('Hello Pygame')

while True:
    for event in pygame.event.get():
        if event.type == QUIT:
            pygame.quit()
            quit()
```

(steps 3, 4, 5)

6 Add code to define a file path.

Note: If you do not set a file path, Python looks in your home directory.

7 Add code to load an image from the file.

Note: `.convert()` makes the image format compatible with the current display.

8 Add code to blit the background image to the display surface.

Note: Change `(0,0)` to control the position of the image in the window.

9 Add code to update the display.

10 Press `F5` and save the file as game image.py.

Ⓐ Python loads the file and displays it in the window.

Note: In this example, the file is a game background with a white-to-black gradient fill. You can use any compatible image file.

Note: If the image does not fit into the window, it is clipped automatically.

```python
import sys
from pygame.locals import *
pygame.init()

awindow = pygame.display.set_mode((400, 300))
pygame.display.set_caption('Hello Pygame')

background_file = 'test.png'          ⟵ 6
background_image = pygame.image.load(background_file).convert()   ⟵ 7

while True:
    for event in pygame.event.get():
        if event.type == QUIT:
            pygame.quit()
            quit()

    awindow.blit(background_image, (0,0))   ⟵ 8
    pygame.display.update()                 ⟵ 9
```

TIPS

What are the image string methods?
In Pygame, you can convert image data to strings, and vice versa. You can edit the string content using any of Python's features. This option is slow and inefficient, but you can use it to create filter effects such as blurring and sharpening, or to save image data to a text file for data analysis and processing.

Can I save image data?
Yes. You can use `pygame.image.save()` to save data from a surface to a filename as a BMP, TGA, PNG, or JPEG file. The BMP and TGA formats are uncompressed and lossless. The PNG format is compressed and lossless. The JPEG format is compressed and lossy.

Create a Sprite Class

You can use your own version of the `sprite` class to create custom sprites. The sprite must include a custom method called `__init__` to set up the sprite. Your code must define a rect for the sprite. If you want the sprite to be visible, it must include an image property.

Sprites are often collected into groups. Use `pygame.sprite.Group.add()` to add a sprite to a group. You can draw all the sprites in a group with `pygame.sprite.Group.draw()`. Games often include an "all sprites" group for drawing, and subgroups to check for game events and collisions.

Create a Sprite Class

1 Launch the desktop and IDLE if they are not already open.

2 Add the code introduced in previous sections to load and set up Pygame, create a window and get its surface, and create a timed game loop.

3 Add code to import the `randint` module from random.

4 Add code to create a class called `Block` with an `__init__` method that takes a color, height, and width.

```
import pygame
import sys                                    ◀2
from pygame.locals import *
from random import randint  ◀3
pygame.init()

class Block(pygame.sprite.Sprite):
    def __init__(self, color, width, height):   ◀4

awindow = pygame.display.set_mode((400, 300))
surface = pygame.display.get_surface()
surface.fill((255, 255, 255))
pygame.display.set_caption('Sprites')

clock = pygame.time.Clock()                     ◀2

while True:
    clock.tick(30)
    for event in pygame.event.get():
        if event.type == QUIT:
            pygame.quit()
            quit()
        pygame.display.update()
```

5 Add code to the `__init__` method to create a sprite.

6 Add code to link the sprite's image contents with a new surface.

7 Add code to fill the image with a color, and to set the sprite's height and width to match the height and width of the image.

Note: The `image.lock()` and `image.unlock()` methods speed up the `fill()` function.

8 Add code to create two sprite groups — one for block sprites and one for all sprites.

```
                         *game_sprite.py - /home/pi/game_sprite.py*
File  Edit  Format  Run  Options  Windows  Help


from random import randint
pygame.init()

class Block(pygame.sprite.Sprite):
    def __init__(self, color, width, height):
        pygame.sprite.Sprite.__init__(self)      ◀5
    ◀6 self.image = pygame.Surface([width, height])
        self.image.lock()
        self.image.fill(color)     ◀7
        self.image.unlock()
        self.rect = self.image.get_rect()  ◀8

awindow = pygame.display.set_mode((400, 300))
surface = pygame.display.get_surface()
surface.fill((255, 255, 255))
pygame.display.set_caption('Sprites')

blockSprites = pygame.sprite.Group()
allSprites = pygame.sprite.Group()
```

9 Add a `for` loop to create ten instances of the `Block` class with random width, height, color, and position.

10 Add code to add the blocks to both sprite groups.

11 Add code to draw the all sprites group in the main game loop.

Note: Including a group for all sprites means you can draw them in the main loop with this one line of code.

12 Press `F5` and save the file as game sprites.py.

A The code draws ten block sprites with random colors and positions.

Note: The code does not include position updates, so the sprites do not move.

Note: You can find the code used in this section on this book's website, www.wiley.com/go/tyvraspberrypi.

```
clock = pygame.time.Clock()

for block in range(0,10):
        thisWidth = randint(10, 100)
        thisHeight = randint(10, 100)
        thisColor = pygame.Color(randint(0, 255),
                                 randint(0, 255),
                                 randint(0, 255))
        block = Block(thisColor, thisWidth, thisHeight)
        block.rect.x = randint(0, 400)
        block.rect.y = randint(0, 300)
        allSprites.add(block)
        blockSprites.add(block)

while True:
    clock.tick(30)
    for event in pygame.event.get():
        if event.type == QUIT:
            pygame.quit()
            quit()
    allSprites.draw(surface)
    pygame.display.update()
```

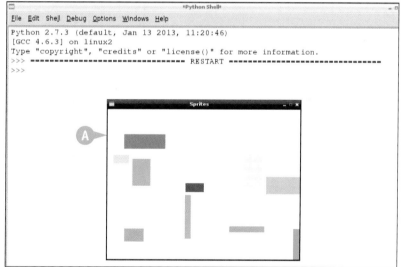

Python Shell
File Edit Shell Debug Options Windows Help
Python 2.7.3 (default, Jan 13 2013, 11:20:46)
[GCC 4.6.3] on linux2
Type "copyright", "credits" or "license()" for more information.
>>> ============================= RESTART =============================
>>>

TIPS

What is a dirty sprite?
Pygame includes a `pygame.sprite.DirtySprite` class, with more features than a standard sprite. A *dirty flag* sets whether the sprite should be repainted on each game loop. A visible flag can be set to 1 or 0 to control sprite visibility. You can also set a blit *blendmode*, which combines the sprite image rect with the destination surface.

What are sprite layers?
More complex games include sprites on multiple layers — for example, to create *parallax scrolling*, where a front, middle, and background layer scroll at different speeds to create an illusion of depth. You can use the `pygame.sprite.LayeredUpdates()` group to work with sprite layers, as described in www.pygame.org/docs/ref/sprite.html.

Check for Sprite Collisions

You can use various `pygame.sprite.collide()` methods to check if two sprites overlap. Collision testing is a key component of many games, and Pygame's collision options can handle most requirements. With the collision testing methods, you can check entire sprite groups with a few lines of simple code.

This example uses the simple `spritecollide()` method to check if a moving ball sprite is touching a group of random block sprites. The method returns a list of sprites. You can decide to delete sprites automatically on collision. This code leaves the sprites where they are, and prints the x y location of all sprites overlapping the ball.

Check for Sprite Collisions

1 Launch the desktop and IDLE if they are not already open.

2 Either open or create the game sprites.py file from the previous section, "Create a Sprite Class."

3 Add code to fill the display window with white at the beginning of the game loop.

Note: This line ensures the window has no content left over from the previous update.

4 Add code to create a new `Block` sprite with a gray color and 10-pixel sides.

5 Add code to add the ball to the `allSprites` group, so it is drawn with the other sprites.

6 Add code to set the starting position and speed of the ball.

7 Add code to the main loop to move the ball's position.

```
        thisHeight = randint(10, 100)
        thisColor = pygame.Color(randint(0, 255),
                                 randint(0, 255),
                                 randint(0, 255))
        block = Block(thisColor, thisWidth, thisHeight)
        block.rect.x = randint(0, 400)
        block.rect.y = randint(0, 300)
        blockSprites.add(block)
        allSprites.add(block)

while True:
    clock.tick(30)
    for event in pygame.event.get():
        if event.type == QUIT:
            pygame.quit()
            quit()

    surface.fill((255, 255, 255))      ◄─ 3
    allSprites.draw(surface)
    pygame.display.update()
```

```
ball = Block(pygame.Color(25, 25, 25), 10, 10) ◄─ 4
allSprites.add(ball) ◄─ 5

ball.rect.x = 0
ball.rect.y = 0      ◄─ 6
ball_dx = 1
ball_dy = 1

while True:
    clock.tick(30)
    for event in pygame.event.get():
        if event.type == QUIT:
            pygame.quit()
            quit()

    ball.rect.x += ball_dx
    ball.rect.y += ball_dy      ◄─ 7

    surface.fill((255, 255, 255))
```

8 Add code for the main loop to get a collision list with all the block sprites colliding with the ball.

Note: If you change `False` to `True`, sprites are deleted as soon as they collide.

9 Add code to check if the collision list is empty.

10 Add code to step through the sprites in a nonempty list.

11 Add code to print the x and y position of each sprite.

12 Press `F5` and save the file as sprite collisions.py.

A The code animates a ball passing through randomly positioned rectangles.

B The code prints the position of the sprites overlapping the ball on every game loop.

Note: You can find the code used in this section on this book's website, www.wiley.com/go/tyvraspberrypi.

```
ball = Block(pygame.Color(25, 25, 25), 10, 10)
allSprites.add(ball)

ball.rect.x = 0
ball.rect.y = 0
ball_dx = 1
ball_dy = 1

while True:
    clock.tick(30)
    for event in pygame.event.get():
        if event.type == QUIT:
            pygame.quit()
            quit()

    ball.rect.x += ball_dx
    ball.rect.y += ball_dy

    collisionList = pygame.sprite.spritecollide(ball, blockSprites, False)
    if (collisionList):
        for sprite in collisionList:
            print "Collided with sprite at: ", sprite.rect.x, sprite.rect.y

    surface.fill((255, 255, 255))
    allSprites.draw(surface)
    pygame.display.update()
```

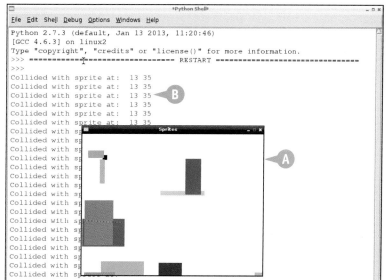

TIPS

What does the collide_mask() method do?
The default sprite collision methods test for collisions along the center lines of all sprites. You can use the `collide_mask()` method to find the exact point where sprites collide. This is useful for more advanced collision testing — for example, you can make a game element respond differently to collisions on each side. The method creates a *mask*, which is usually a rect. You can create a custom mask for more complex shapes.

Can I check for collisions between other shapes?
Yes. A collision mask can be any shape. You can also use the `collide_circle()` method to check for overlapping circles. The method uses the radius and center of each sprite for the collision test instead of a rect.

Create a Breakout Game

You can use the techniques you learned in this chapter and in Chapter 12 to create a simple video game with a wall of blocks, a ball, and a paddle, controlled from the keyboard that returns the ball. The ball removes a brick when it collides with it.

This example is a minimal version you can extend with your own enhancements. It uses sprites and code from previous sections for all the game elements. A key enhancement over previous examples is that the window size and other settings are stored in variables, so you can modify them with a single edit.

Create a Breakout Game

Note: You can find the code used in this section on this book's website, www.wiley.com/go/tyvraspberrypi.

1 Launch the desktop and IDLE if they are not already open and create a new file. Add code to import and set up Pygame.

2 Add code to create a sprite class.

3 Add code to define variables to set the window size, number of blocks, ball size, paddle dimensions, and paddle speed.

4 Add code to create and set up a window and surface using variable values instead of integers.

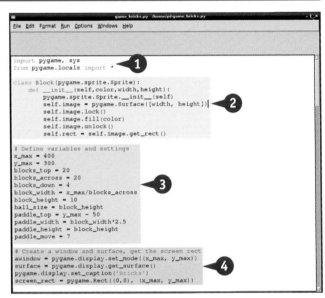

5 Add code to define the colors used in the game, and make a list of block colors.

Note: See the section "Define Colors" for details.

6 Add code to create two sprite groups — one to manage screen redraws and one to hold the block list.

7 Add two `for` loops to create a row of blocks for each color, and columns of blocks in each row.

Note: The block size calculation allows some space between the blocks so they do not form a single long row.

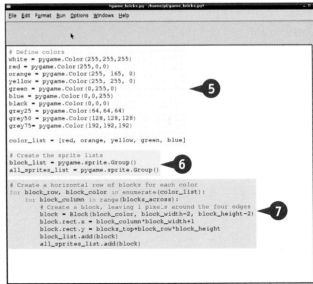

8 Add code to create a ball sprite and add it to the main sprite list.

9 Add code to set the ball speed.

Note: Increasing these numbers makes the ball move more quickly. The horizontal and vertical speeds are kept separate to simplify bounce calculations.

10 Add code to create a sprite for the game paddle.

Note: The `rect.x` calculation sets the width of the paddle.

11 Add two *flags* — True/False values — to manage the status of the ball.

12 Add code to create a game loop.

13 Add code to fill the window with a medium gray color.

Note: You can also use white or a lighter gray.

14 Add code to check for a `QUIT` event.

15 Add code to control the paddle from the keyboard.

Note: The code checks if 🔜 or 🔙 are pressed, and updates the paddle position and direction if they are.

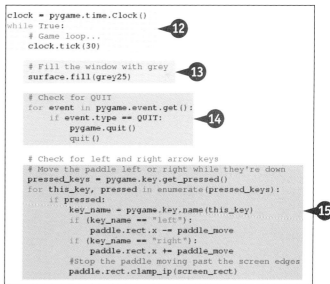

```
# Create a ball sprite
ball = Block(grey75, ball_size, ball_size)      8
ball.rect.x = (x_max - ball_size)/2
ball.rect.y = paddle_top - ball_size
all_sprites_list.add(ball)

# Set the initial ball speed              9
ball_dx = 3
ball_dy = 5

# Create a paddle sprite
paddle = Block(black, paddle_width, paddle_height)
paddle.rect.x = (x_max - paddle_width)/2        10
paddle.rect.y = paddle_top
all_sprites_list.add(paddle)

# A couple of 'flags' (Boolean values)
ball_in_play = True                             11
just_bounced = False
```

```
clock = pygame.time.Clock()
while True:                                      12
    # Game loop...
    clock.tick(30)

    # Fill the window with grey
    surface.fill(grey25)                         13

    # Check for QUIT
    for event in pygame.event.get():
        if event.type == QUIT:                   14
            pygame.quit()
            quit()

    # Check for left and right arrow keys
    # Move the paddle left or right while they're down
    pressed_keys = pygame.key.get_pressed()
    for this_key, pressed in enumerate(pressed_keys):
        if pressed:
            key_name = pygame.key.name(this_key)   15
            if (key_name == "left"):
                paddle.rect.x -= paddle_move
            if (key_name == "right"):
                paddle.rect.x += paddle_move
            #Stop the paddle moving past the screen edges
            paddle.rect.clamp_ip(screen_rect)
```

TIPS

Does this example include scoring?
No. This example is very simple and does not include code for scoring or for resetting the game when the ball drops out of play beneath the paddle. Try adding these features if you want to experiment further with Pygame.

How can I make the graphics more interesting?
This example uses a traditional 8-bit vintage game look with single-color block graphics. For a more complex look, add a simple image loader to the sprite `__init__` function and modify the nested `for` loops to load the images for each block row instead of selecting colors. The rest of the code should work without changes.

continued ▶

Create a Breakout Game (continued)

A fter setting up the game graphics, you can use simple code to manage ball bounces and sprite collisions. Because the ball can only bounce off the paddle, you do not need to include code to check for bounces off the bottom of the screen.

This example uses a version of the code from the section "Bounce a Shape" to control the bounces, and the section "Check for Sprite Collisions" code to manage collisions between the ball and the blocks. It includes an extra test to check for collisions between the paddle and ball.

Create a Breakout Game (continued)

Note: Red lines beginning with # are comments. Python ignores them.

16 Add code to update the ball position.

17 Add code to check if the ball has collided with the paddle.

18 Add code to bounce the ball off the screen edges.

Note: An alternative and simpler way to check for edge bounces is to create "invisible" sprites off the sides of the screen and use sprite collision methods to check for bounces.

19 Add code to check if the ball bounced off the paddle, using sprite collision detection.

20 Add code to change the vertical speed after a bounce.

21 Add code to check if the ball passed by the paddle and the game is over.

```python
if ball_in_play:

    # Move the ball
    ball.rect.x += ball_dx          # 16
    ball.rect.y += ball_dy

    # Check if it collided with the paddle
    if ball.rect.y < paddle_top:              # 17
        just_bounced = False

    # Bounce off the screen edges
    if (ball.rect.x <= 0):
        ball.rect.x = 0
        ball_dx = -ball_dx

    if (ball.rect.y <= 0):                      # 18
        ball.rect.y = 0
        ball_dy = -ball_dy

    if (ball.rect.x > x_max - ball_size):
        ball.rect.x = x_max - ball_size
        ball_dx = -ball_dx
```

```python
    if (ball.rect.y <= 0):
        ball.rect.y = 0
        ball_dy = -ball_dy

    if (ball.rect.x > x_max - ball_size):
        ball.rect.x = x_max - ball_size
        ball_dx = -ball_dx

    # No need to check for bounces at the screen bottom

    # Check if the ball bounced off the paddle
    if (pygame.sprite.collide_rect(ball, paddle) and not just_bounced):    # 19
        ball_dy = -ball_dy          # 20
        just_bounced = True
        # While ball and paddle are in contact, don't bounce again

    # Ball didn't - game over
    elif (ball.rect.y > paddle_top+ball_size/2):        # 21
        ball_in_play = False
        all_sprites_list.remove(ball)
```

266

22 Add code to check if the ball collided with a block.

Note: Setting `True` means blocks are deleted automatically when the ball bounces off them.

23 Add code to change the ball's vertical direction after a bounce.

24 Add code to draw all sprites and update the display.

```
        ball_dx = -ball_dx

    # No need to check for bounces at the screen bottom

    # Check if the ball bounced off the paddle
    if (pygame.sprite.collide_rect(ball, paddle) and not just_bounced):
        ball_dy = -ball_dy
        just_bounced = True
        # While ball and paddle are in contact, don't bounce again

    # Ball didn't - game over
    elif (ball.rect.y > paddle_top+ball_size/2):
        ball_in_play = False
        all_sprites_list.remove(ball)

    # Check if the ball bounced off a block
    blocks_hit_list = pygame.sprite.spritecollide(ball, block_list, True)    22
    if blocks_hit_list:
        ball_dy = -ball_dy    23
    # Change ball direction after a block bounce

    # Draw everything
    all_sprites_list.draw(surface)    24
    pygame.display.update()
```

25 Press **F5** and save the file as game bricks.py.

A The code draws the graphics for a bricks game with an animated ball and paddle, and collision detection for all elements.

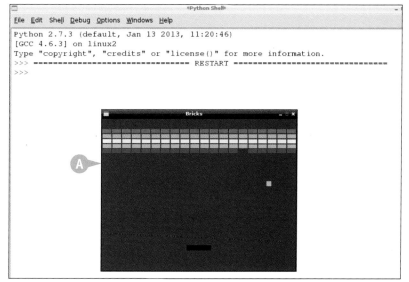

TIPS

Why is there extra code managing paddle/ball collisions?

Without the extra code, the ball bounces for as long as it overlaps the paddle. So it can get stuck and rebound in a zigzag as the vertical speed changes on each bounce. The extra code only counts the first bounce and keeps it from getting stuck.

Why is the game so predictable?

"Official" versions of the game include code that changes the ball direction depending on where it contacts the paddle and/or the speed of the paddle. This allows for "slices" and creates a more exciting game. Some versions also speed up the ball the longer it remains in play. This version simply bounces the ball in the same direction every time you play.

Share Your Games

You can share your games and download other games and apps at the official Raspberry Pi App Store. The store uses a special app called `pistore` that is preinstalled in the official release of Raspbian. You should update it to the most recent and most reliable version.

To share your games you must register as a developer with Indie City, the Pi App Store's official distribution partner. Registration is a complex multistage process. Clear instructions are available online, so this section indicates where to find them without taking you through every step.

Share Your Games

1 At the command prompt or in LXTerminal type `sudo apt-get update && sudo apt-get install pistore` and press **Enter**.

Linux checks if a more recent version of `pistore` is available, and downloads and installs it.

Note: If there is no updated version, this command does not install new software.

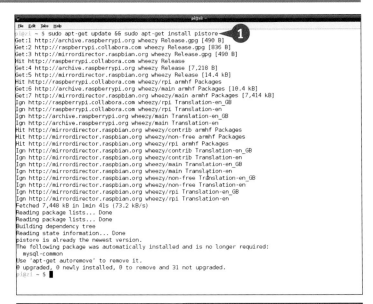

2 In LXTerminal, type `pistore` and press **Enter**.

The Pi App Store loads in its own window.

3 If you have not yet registered, click **Register** and follow the steps.

4 If you have registered, type your e-mail address and password and click **Log In**.

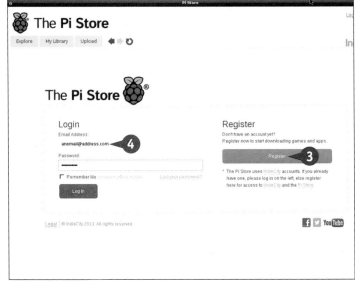

5 Click **Upload**.

6 Click **How to upload content to the Pi Store**.

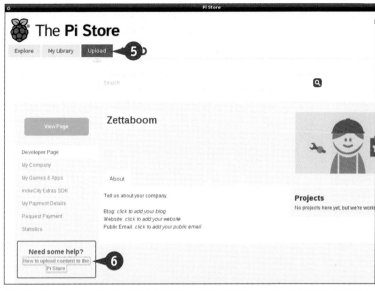

Detailed instructions appear.

7 Follow the instructions to set up a developer account.

Note: You may need to package some applications if they work with `sudo apt-get install`. Search online for "Debian Package Maker" for details.

TIPS

How do I download files from the store?
The `pistore` app makes it easy to install games and other code. To install a free item, click the **Explore** tab and find items labeled Free. Click **Free Download** to download and install the item. The downloader runs a shell script to download, unpack, and install the item in your library. Click **My Library** and then **Launch** on the new item to launch it. The steps for paid games and apps are similar, but include an extra payment stage.

Is there an easier way to share games?
Python files are self-contained text files, so you can easily send game code in e-mail as an attachment, include it as a downloadable link on a web page, and so on.

## CHAPTER 14

Adding Custom Hardware

In this chapter, you use everything you learned in previous chapters to begin using your Pi for small projects that combine electronic add-ons, Linux, Python, and a web server.

Understanding Electronics

To expand your Pi with add-on boards and components, you need a basic understanding of electronics. Professional electronic design is complex, but you can do a lot with a handful of components and a very basic understanding of what they do.

Understanding Volts and Amps

Electronic circuits work with two units called volts and amps. *Volts* (V) measure how much of a kick the electricity has. Small batteries produce a few volts. A household main supply produces hundreds of volts. *Amps* (A) measure the volume, or flow, of electricity. A car battery produces tens of amps. A small battery produces less than 1 amp. When you connect two circuits or components, one circuit must be able to produce the correct volts and amps to drive the other. If it does not, your design does not work. Volts are measured across a component. Amps are measured through it.

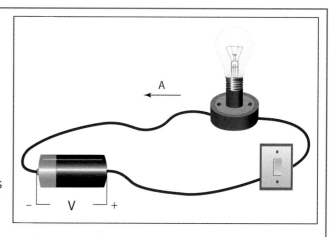

Understanding Decimal Notation

Circuit components and measurements are often labeled with abbreviated powers of 10. You should know the following: m (milli) is 1/1000, u or μ (micro) is 1 millionth, and n (nano) is 1 billionth. So 500mV is 0.5V. K or k (kilo) is thousand, and M is million. The abbreviation often replaces the decimal point, so 4k7 means 4700. Resistors use a special R multiplier, which means 1. 330R means 300 resistance units (called *ohms* — the official Ω symbol and the word are often left out).

M	1,000,000
K	1,000
R	1
m	0.001
u	0.000001
n	0.000000001

Understanding Components

All electronic circuits use the same few kinds of components. Each component does something to the flow of electricity. A *resistor* partially blocks the flow, or the electronic equivalent of a pinched pipe. A *capacitor* acts like a tiny reservoir of

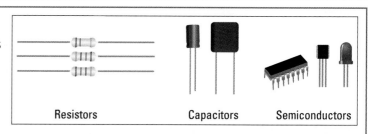

Resistors   Capacitors   Semiconductors

electricity. A *diode* only allows electricity to pass in one direction. An *LED* (Light Emitting Diode) is a diode that can light up. A *transistor* works like a valve or switch. *Relays* are part-mechanical switches. You can use them to switch big and powerful circuits, such as heaters and cookers, from a small control source, like the Pi. *Integrated Circuits* (ICs) include many components, and are building blocks designed to perform a complex task.

Understanding Digital Logic

There are two kinds of electronic circuits. *Analog* circuits work with any value. *Digital* circuits work with two voltages. One represents 0/off/false, and a different voltage represents 1/on/true. Unfortunately, the voltages used are not standardized. Two popular options are 0V/3V, and 0V/5V on. The Pi works with 3V logic, but many popular relays and switches use 5V logic. You must include a buffer or level shifter circuit to make the two kinds of logic work together.

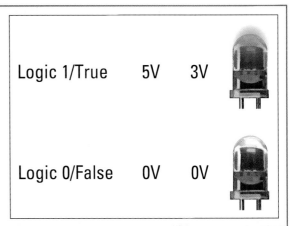

Logic 1/True	5V	3V
Logic 0/False	0V	0V

Understanding Breadboards

A *breadboard* is a plastic board with holes that cover internal metal tracks. You can use a breadboard to *prototype*, or plug together, a circuit without having to use a soldering iron. You plug the components directly between lines on the breadboard. You can use jumper cables to link the circuit to your Pi. Jumper cable ends are either *male*, with a pin you can plug into a breadboard, or *female*, with a socket you can place onto a GPIO, or General Purpose Input Output, pin. The most useful cables are male/female.

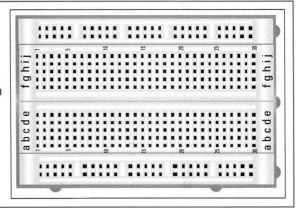

Understanding Pi Expansion Pins

The Pi includes a built-in connector with *expansion pins*, also known as GPIO (General Purpose Input Output) pins. The pins use 0V/3V logic, and you can set them up to read digital signals, to output digital signals, or some mix of both. The simplest way to control the pins with custom software is with a free Python module called RPi.GPIO, which is available online.

Understanding Tools and Kits

You can buy a component kit from a supplier such as Adafruit Industries (www.adafruit.com). Component kits include a breadboard and a selection of components with different values. They do not include a Pi board. You should also buy a digital multimeter so you can measure voltages and currents in your circuit. Basic models are available from $15 (£10). If you want to build a permanent circuit, you will need a soldering iron, and copper stripboard, which has component holes joined by strips of copper that can be soldered.

Using a Digital Multimeter

You can use a digital multimeter (DMM) to identify component values and check what is happening in a circuit. You can also check values visually by referring to an industry-standard color-code system, or by reading numbers and identification codes printed on each component and looking up its details online.

DMMs measure volts, amps, and ohms. Use a switch on the panel to select the measurement. Budget DMMs have *manual ranging*. You must guess an approximate range for the measurement using a switch on the panel. Expensive DMMs are *autoranging* and display the range automatically.

Using a Digital Multimeter

Note: This section assumes you have an introductory kit.

Ⓐ Most DMMS have one black probe, and one red probe, plugged into one black socket and one red socket.

Note: If your DMM has a 10A socket, ignore it.

❶ To measure a small voltage, turn the switch so it points to the 20V setting.

Note: The setting may be 10V or 5V on some models.

❷ If there is a DC/AC switch, switch it to DC.

❸ Turn on the power.

❹ Touch the black probe to any of the bare metal parts on the Pi board.

❺ Touch the red probe to one of the pins at the top left of the board.

❻ Read the value.

Note: BE VERY CAREFUL not to connect two pins together by accident with a probe. You may reset your Pi or damage it.

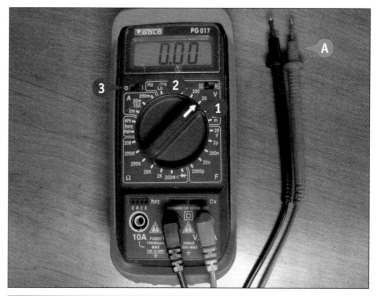

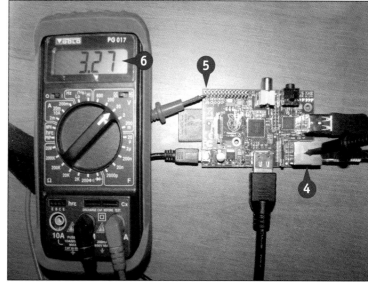

7 To measure a resistor value, move the switch to one of the settings in the ohm (Ω) section.

Note: 20K is a good starting setting.

8 Hold the probes in both hands across the resistor's leads.

9 Read the value. To work out the tens multiplier, assume the value is a fraction of the range setting.

Note: If the value is too big for the range, the display shows OL or INF. Select a bigger range. If the display shows 0.00, select a smaller range. Try again.

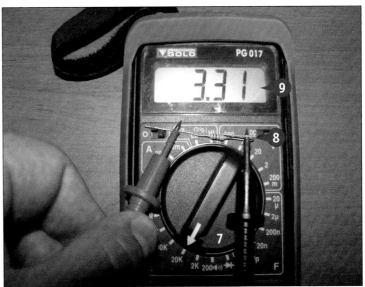

10 If your meter has a small speaker symbol, you can use it to test continuity, or connections. Select the continuity range.

11 Touch the tips of the probes together.

The meter makes a buzzing sound as long as there is a connection between the pins.

Note: You can use this feature to check if there is a break in a wire or cable, by checking if there is a connection between the ends of the wire.

Note: Not all meters have this feature.

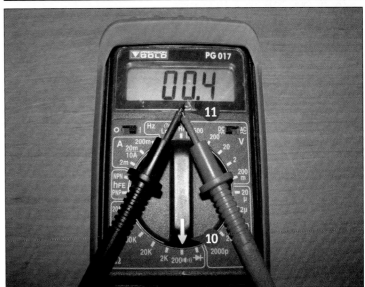

TIPS

What do the colored bands on a resistor mean?
Resistors are labeled with a standard resistor color code. If you know the code and the resistor is big enough to show the colored bands clearly, you can read its value directly without having to measure it. You can find more detailed explanations and free calculators by searching online for "resistor color code." Some capacitors use a similar code. Most do not, and have a printed value instead.

How do I measure amps?
You can measure amps by putting one probe on a pin and the other on the lead into which the electricity flows. However, you do not usually need to do this. You typically use a DMM to measure volts.

Set Up GPIO Control Software

You can use a free Python module called RPi.GPIO to control the GPIO pins from Python. RPi.GPIO is an unofficial user-led project and is not preinstalled on the Pi. You cannot install it with `apt-get install`. You must download it from a web site, and install it manually.

Installation from the command line is easy as long as you know the "magic word" commands. One minor complication is that the software is updated regularly. To find the latest version, visit the project website and make a note of the version number. Use that number in your commands.

Set Up GPIO Control Software

1 Launch the desktop and open the Midori web browser.

2 Type **https://pypi.python. org/pypi/RPi.GPIO** in the address bar.

3 Make a note of the current version number.

4 Click **Download**.

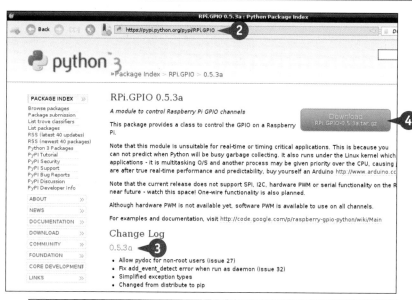

The Open or Download File dialog box appears.

5 Click **Save As**.

The Save File dialog box appears.

6 Select your home (Pi) directory.

7 Click **Save**.

Midori downloads and saves the file.

Note: If Midori does not work, open LX Terminal, type `wget http://pypi.python.org/packages/source/R/RPi.GPIO/RPi.GPIO-[versionnumber].tar.gz`, and press Enter.

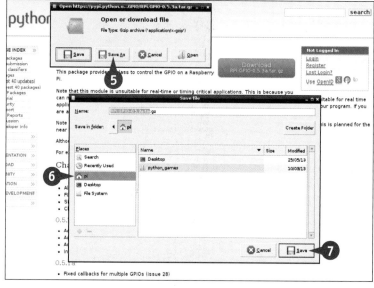

8 In LX Terminal, type `sudo apt-get install python-dev` and press Enter.

9 Type Y and press Enter at the prompt.

Linux downloads and installs the Python development tools.

Note: You must install these tools before you can build and install the RPi.GPIO module.

```
                               pi@pi: ~
File  Edit  Tabs  Help
pi@pi ~ $ sudo apt-get install python-dev     8
Reading package lists... Done
Building dependency tree
Reading state information... Done
The following extra packages will be installed:
  libexpat1-dev libssl-dev libssl-doc python2.7-dev
The following NEW packages will be installed:
  libexpat1-dev libssl-dev libssl-doc python-dev python2.7-dev
0 upgraded, 5 newly installed, 0 to remove and 0 not upgraded.
Need to get 31.6 MB of archives.
After this operation, 42.2 MB of additional disk space will be used.
Do you want to continue [Y/n]? Y     9
```

10 Type `tar zxf [the name of the downloaded file]` and press Enter.

Note: `tar` is the Linux equivalent of the Windows/Mac Unzip tool. It decompresses a compressed file into a directory.

11 Type `cd [the name of the downloaded file]` and press Enter.

12 Type `sudo python setup.py install` and press Enter.

Linux builds and installs the RPi.GPIO module. You can now use it in your Python projects.

```
Unpacking libexpat1-dev (from .../libexpat1-dev_2.1.0-1_armhf.deb) ..
Selecting previously unselected package libssl-dev.
Unpacking libssl-dev (from .../libssl-dev_1.0.1e-2+rpi1_armhf.deb) ..
Selecting previously unselected package libssl-doc.
Unpacking libssl-doc (from .../libssl-doc_1.0.1e-2+rpi1_all.deb) ...
Selecting previously unselected package python2.7-dev.
Unpacking python2.7-dev (from .../python2.7-dev_2.7.3-6_armhf.deb) ..
Selecting previously unselected package python-dev.
Unpacking python-dev (from .../python-dev_2.7.3-4_all.deb) ...
Processing triggers for man-db ...
Setting up libexpat1-dev (2.1.0-1) ...
Setting up libssl-dev (1.0.1e-2+rpi1) ...
Setting up libssl-doc (1.0.1e-2+rpi1) ...
Setting up python2.7-dev (2.7.3-6) ...
Setting up python-dev (2.7.3-4) ...
pi@pi ~ $ tar zxf RPi.GPIO-0.5.3a.tar.gz     10
pi@pi ~ $ cd RPi.GPIO-0.5.3a     11
pi@pi ~/RPi.GPIO-0.5.3a $ sudo python setup.py install     12
```

TIP

What does "build" mean?
You can install software in two ways. Consumer software is supplied as a *binary*, which is a ready-made file that you can download and use. Software developers often *build* software instead. This means taking raw computer code files written as text and running it through a set of tools that creates a finished binary. Building software is more work and takes longer, but you can see the instructions that make the software work, and you can change them to customize the software before you build a binary. You only need to build a binary once. From then on it works like any other binary. But you can change it and rebuild it at any time.

Control an LED with a Button

You can breadboard a simple circuit around the Pi to control an LED with a button or switch. Both components connect to the Pi's GPIO (general-purpose input output) pins. To light an LED, connect a GPIO pin to the LED, to a small resistor (220R to 470R) next, and finally to GND.

To use a switch, connect one end directly to GND. Connect the other end to a GPIO pin. You must add a *pull-up resistor* that "pulls" the pin to 3V3 — that is, logic one, when it is not connected to anything. Use a medium (4k7 to 10k) resistor.

Control an LED with a Button

Note: You can find the code used in this section on this book's website, www.wiley.com/go/tyvraspberrypi.

Note: These steps assume you have a breadboard with power lines on at least one side, and a collection of male-to-female jumper leads.

Note: On a breadboard, the holes are joined horizontally, except for the power lines on either or both sides, which are joined vertically.

1 Connect pin 1 (3V3) — the lower pin at the far left — to one power line.

2 Connect pin 6 (GND) — the third pin from the left on the top row — to another line.

Note: Use the diagram at www.modmypi.com/blog/raspberry-pi-gpio-cheat-sheet as a reference.

3 Connect pin 11 to a line on the breadboard.

4 Plug the long leg of the LED into the same line.

5 Plug the short leg of the LED into a lower line.

6 Join that line to the GND power line through a 330R resistor.

7 Place the switch into the breadboard so that the two switch connectors are over the break in the board.

8 Connect pin 13 to the top of the switch.

9 Connect pin 13 to the 3V3 power line via a 4k7 resistor.

Note: You can use any resistor from 4k7 to 10k.

10 Connect the other end of the switch directly to 0V.

Note: Use a male-to-male jumper lead. If you do not have one, cut the leg off a resistor and use that.

11 Launch the desktop and IDLE.

12 Type the code shown, and save it to a file called LED.py.

13 Open LXTerminal, type `sudo python LED.py`, and press Enter.

The LED lights when you push the switch.

Note: You must run the code as root with `sudo`. You cannot run it from IDLE.

Note: Press Ctrl, type `C exit()`, and press Enter to quit Python.

```
import RPi.GPIO as GPIO
import time

GPIO.setmode(GPIO.BCM)
GPIO.setup(17, GPIO.OUT)
GPIO.setup(27, GPIO.IN)
while True:
    readButton = GPIO.input(27)
    GPIO.output(17, (not readButton))
    time.sleep(0.1)
```

```
pi@pi ~ $ sudo python LED.py
```

TIPS

Can I use any LED?

There are hundreds of LEDs in every color. High-brightness LEDs are "tuned" to produce brighter light. A standard LED will work, but it may not be as bright. For more light, use a smaller resistor. Keep it bigger than 220R to avoid burning out the LED or your Pi.

My circuit does not work. What did I do wrong?

A common mistake is using the wrong GPIO pins. Double-check using the online diagram mentioned after step **2**. Next, check that the LED is the correct way around. Finally, check that you connected the LED to GND and not 3V3, and that the order of components is Pin, LED, Resistor, and GND.

Connect a Digital Temperature Sensor

You can use the Dallas D18B20 temperature sensor to measure temperatures with your Pi. Be sure to buy the D18B20, not the D18S20. You can buy the sensors as components on Amazon and eBay. You can also buy premade waterproof sensors.

The sensor is small, but sophisticated, and includes a simple microprocessor. It connects to the Pi's GPIO pins using a 1-wire bus. You can install simple free software on your Pi to set it up and read values. The readings appear as a file in a directory with a name that includes your sensor's unique serial number.

Connect a Digital Temperature Sensor

1 Plug a sensor across three breadboard lines, with the flat surface toward you.

Note: If you connect the sensor the wrong way, it does not work.

2 Use a jumper cable to connect the left pin on the sensor to the GND GPIO pin — the third pin from the left on the top row.

Note: Use the diagram at www.modmypi.com/blog/raspberry-pi-gpio-cheat-sheet as a reference for the GPIO pin layout.

3 Use a jumper cable to connect the right pin on the sensor to the 3V3 GPIO pin — the first pin from the left on the bottom row.

4 Use a jumper cable to connect the middle pin on the sensor to the GPIO 4 pin — the fourth pin from the left on the lower row.

5 Plug a 4k7 resistor between the middle and right sensor pins.

Note: Bend one leg to fit it into the small space. Be careful to keep the two legs separate.

6 In LXTerminal or at the command line, type sudo modprobe w1-gpio and press Enter.

7 Type sudo modprobe w1-therm and press Enter.

Note: Steps **6** and **7** load driver software for the sensor.

8 Type cd /sys/bus/w1/ devices and press Enter.

9 Type ls and press Enter.

Ⓐ You should see a directory named 28-xxxxxxxxxxxx, where the x's represent a unique serial number.

10 Type cd followed by the directory name and press Enter.

11 Type cat w1_slave and press Enter.

Ⓑ The driver displays the temperature data after t=. Divide by 1000 to get degrees Centigrade.

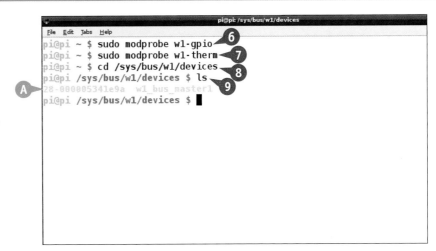

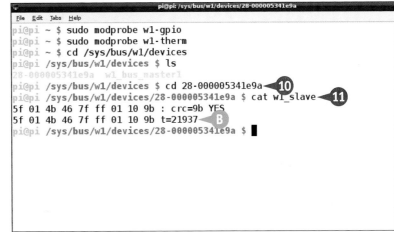

TIPS

Why does my circuit not work?
If you do not connect the circuit correctly, you will not see a 28-xxxxxxxxxxxxxxx directory. If you see a directory, your circuit is wired properly. The 1-wire interface is not completely reliable. If you see NO at the end of the first line in step **11**, the reading failed. Repeat step **11** to get a valid reading.

What is I2C?
Like 1-wire, I2C is a *bus* — an electronic system used to connect devices. I2C is more complicated than 1-wire, but works with a much wider selection of sensors. You can install various software add-ons that will make your Pi work with I2C. You can then modify the Python code in this section to work with those sensors. The tutorial at www.instructables. com/id/Raspberry-Pi-I2C-Python/?ALLSTEPS is a good introduction to I2C.

Log Sensor Readings to a File

You can use Python and `crontab` to log sensor readings to a file. This example uses the temperature sensor from the previous section. It logs readings to a file in the /var/www directory so they can be displayed by your Pi's web server, as discussed in the next section.

Because the sensors sometime return errors, this code checks if a reading is valid and rereads the sensor if it is not. If a sensor is permanently damaged, this code may get stuck in a loop and stop working. As an exercise, add code that stops checking after ten failures and writes an error message to the file.

Log Sensor Readings to a File

1 At the command prompt or in LXTerminal, type `nano .bashrc` and press **Enter**.

A Linux opens the .bashrc file.

2 Scroll to the end of the file.

3 Type `sudo modprobe w1-gpio` and press **Enter**. Type `sudo modprobe w1-therm` and press **Enter**.

4 Press **Ctrl**+**O**, and press **Enter**, and press **Ctrl**+**X** to save the file and quit.

Note: Making this edit tells your Pi to load the 1-wire driver for the sensor automatically when you log in.

5 Launch the desktop with `startx` if it is not already open, and double-click **IDLE** to launch it.

6 Click **File**.

7 Click **New Window**.

8 Add code as shown for a function that reads the time and returns a formatted date/time string.

9 Add code as shown to create a function that reads a temperature from the probe.

10 Add code that defines the unique ID for your sensor.

Note: Use the ID from the previous section, "Connect a Digital Temperature Sensor."

11 Add code that appends the current time and date created by the first function, and the temperature from the second function to a file called `temps.txt`.

12 Save the file to /var/www instead of your home directory.

13 Open LXTerminal.

14 Type `crontab -e` and press Enter.

15 Type `*/1 * * * * sudo python /var/www/log.py` on the first line.

16 Press Ctrl+O, press Enter, and press Ctrl+X to save and quit.

Your Pi appends a new temperature reading to the file once a minute.

Note: You can view the log with `sudo cat /var/www/temps.txt`.

Note: You can find the code used in this section on this book's website, www.wiley.com/go/tyvraspberrypi.

```
    # Now get the second line
    sline = thistext.split("\n")[1]
    # Get the 10th item on the line, which is the temperature rea
    tdata = sline.split(" ")[9]#
    # Get the temperature from the string as a number
    temp = float(tdata[2:])
    # Return it formatted with 2.1 digits and a sign as deg C
    return (" %+2.1f" % (temp/1000))


# Change this to match your sensor's serial number
sensor = "28-000005341e9a"    10

# Open the file in the web server directory
tfile = open("/var/www/temps.txt", "a+")
# Write the time, temperature, and a newline
tfile.write(dotime())
tfile.write(dotemp(sensor))               11
tfile.write("\n")
# Close the file to finish appending the reading
tfile.close()
```

```
                                              pi@pi: /sys/bus/w1/devices
File  Edit  Tabs  Help
  GNU nano 2.2.6                    File: /tmp/crontab.44NVSj/crontab

*/1 * * * * sudo python /var/www/log.py    15

# Edit this file to introduce tasks to be run by cron.
#
# Each task to run has to be defined through a single line
# indicating with different fields when the task will be run
# and what command to run for the task
#
# To define the time you can provide concrete values for
# minute (m), hour (h), day of month (dom), month (mon),
# and day of week (dow) or use '*' in these fields (for 'any').#
# Notice that tasks will be started based on the cron's system
# daemon's notion of time and timezones.
#
# Output of the crontab jobs (including errors) is sent through
# email to the user the crontab file belongs to (unless redirected)
```

TIPS

How can I use more than one sensor?
You can connect at least ten D18B20 sensors and their cabling to the same GPIO pins. You do not need to add more resistors. The driver software automatically creates a unique 28-xxxxxxxxxxxxxxxx directory for each sensor. You can extend the Python code easily by adding more sensors and using the `dotemp()` function to get a measurement from each one.

How long can I make the cabling?
The 1-wire interface is unexpectedly robust. If you use the right kind of cabling — look for twisted-pair wires that you can often strip out of an old Ethernet cable — the maximum range is approximately 300 feet (100 meters).

Graph Readings on a Web Page

You can use a free software tool called GNUPLOT to read a file of sensor readings and convert them into a graph. You can then embed the graph, and perhaps the sensor readings, into a web page, so you can view a set of readings from a web browser. GNUPLOT has many options, but you can ignore most of them and get good results with the default settings.

To use GNUPLOT, install it with `apt-get install`, and create a PLT file with your settings. This example includes PHP web server code to graph the most recent 300 readings whenever a page is loaded.

Graph Readings on a Web Page

Note: You can find the code used in this section on this book's website, www.wiley.com/go/tyvraspberrypi.

1. At the command line or LXTerminal, type `sudo apt-get install gnuplot` and press Enter.

2. Type Y and press Enter to confirm installation at the prompt.

Note: Some online tutorials mention gnuplot-x11. This is a different package. You cannot use it with the code in this section.

3. Type `sudo nano /var/www/index.php` and press Enter.

4. Type `<?php` and press Enter to start a block of PHP code.

5. Add a line to copy the last 300 entries in temps.txt to a file called 300.txt, and another to run GNUPLOT, taking settings from a file called 300.plt.

6. Type `?>` and press Enter to finish the PHP code.

Note: PHP's `exec` runs a one-line Linux command string.

7. Add a line of HTML to display an image called 300.png.

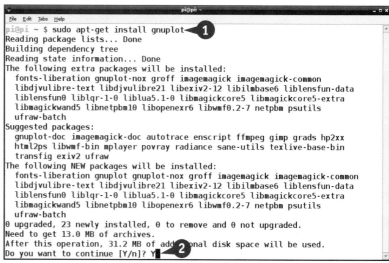

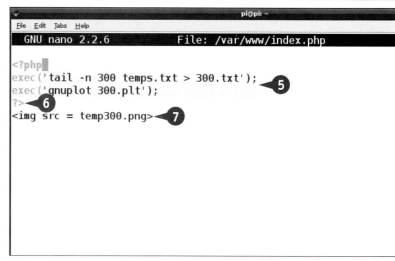

8 Press `Ctrl`+`O`, press `Enter`, and press `Ctrl`+`X` to save and quit.

9 Type `sudo nano /var/www/300.plt` and press `Enter` to create a settings file for GNUPLOT.

10 Add the code shown.

Note: You can find out more about these "magic word" commands on the GNUPLOT documentation page at www.gnuplot.info/documentation.html.

11 Double-click the **Midori** browser to open it.

12 Delete any existing contents in the address bar.

13 Type **http://127.0.0.1** in the address bar and press `Enter`.

Ⓐ The Pi displays a graph of the last 300 temperature readings.

Note: If your temps.txt file has fewer than 300 readings, the graph shows all the readings logged so far.

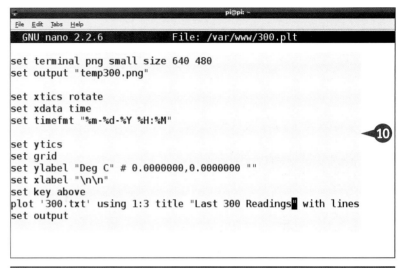

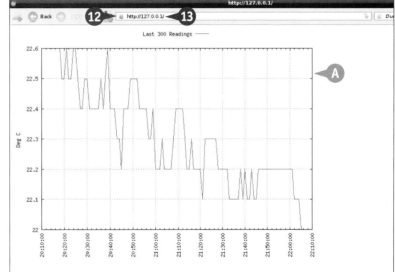

TIPS

Do I have to use GNUPLOT?
No. Alternatives to GNUPLOT are available, such as JpGraph and phpgraph. Although GNUPLOT does not look as polished as the alternatives, it works well on a Linux web server because you can run it as a command with `exec`. For beginners, the alternatives are harder to work with. GNUPLOT is also fast enough to generate a graph when you load the page — although on a busy public server, you would update the graph with `crontab` to avoid redrawing it every time.

How does GNUPLOT work out the scale on the axes?
GNUPLOT automatically scales both axes to fit the data. It rounds the x-axis to larger intervals, so you may see gaps at the left and right of the plot.

Connect a Real-Time Clock

You can connect a real-time clock card to your Pi. The Pi keeps good time while it is powered up and can access the Internet. However, if the power goes off and it cannot access the Internet when it reboots, its "fake hardware clock" time will be wrong.

This project uses a simple add-on clock board supplied by Hobbytronics (www.hobbytronics.co.uk) with the popular DS1302 clock chip. You can find similar boards from other suppliers of Pi add-ons. See the section "Understanding Further Options" for a list.

Connect a Real-Time Clock

Note: You can find the code used in this section on this book's website, www.wiley.com/go/tyvraspberrypi.

Note: This section uses a breadboard to link sets of male/female jumpers. If you use female-to-female jumpers, you do not need the breadboard.

1 Plug five jumpers onto the pins of the clock board.

2 Plug the jumpers into rows on the breadboard.

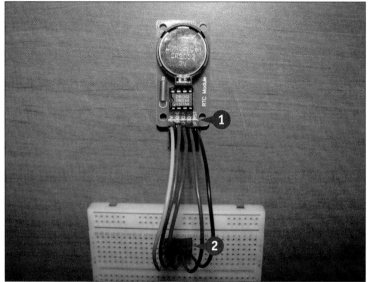

3 Plug another row of jumpers into the same lines.

4 Plug the jumpers into the GPIO pins on the Pi as follows, counting from the top: 3V3, GND, GPIO 27, GPIO 18, GPIO 17.

Note: These instructions assume you have a version 2 Pi board. For a version 1 board, use the instructions and software at www.hobbytronics.co.uk/tutorials-code/raspberry-pi-tutorials/raspberry-pi-real-time-clock.

5 Use Midori or `wget` to download the code for a software driver from this book's website to a directory named `rtc`.

6 Type `cd rtc` and press Enter if you are not already in `rtc`.

7 Type `cc rtc.c - o rtc` and press Enter to create a binary.

The source code builds a binary you can run from the command line.

Note: The source code is written in the C language. You can read it with `cat`, or edit it with `nano`.

8 Type `sudo sh -c "date +%Y%m%d%H%M%S | xargs -0 ./rtc"` and press Enter.

Note: This complex "magic word" command pipes a formatted date string to the clock driver as root to set the clock.

9 Type `sudo ./rtc` and press Enter.

Ⓐ The clock driver displays the time.

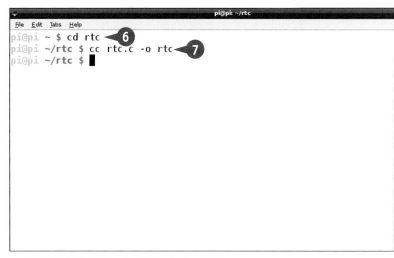

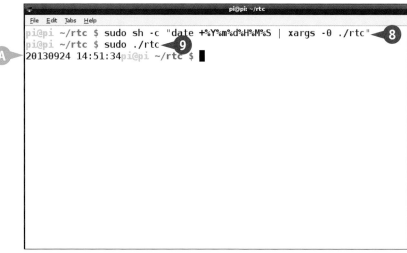

TIPS

How can I save and restore the time automatically?
You can set the clock manually with `sudo ./rtc`
`YYYYMMDDhhmmss`, replacing the letters with a date/time. To set the
Linux date, use `date -set "YYYYMMDD hh:mm:ss"`, including
the quotes and replacing the letters with the time/date. To read the date
in a format you can pass to the RTC, use `date +%Y%m%d%H%M%S`. You
can add commands that load/save the time to the .bashrc and .bash_
logout files. Adventurous readers can try modifying the `fake_hwclock`
and/or `hwclock.sh` scripts in /etc/init.d.

Is this clock better than others?
This clock is relatively easy to set up
and not too difficult to use. You can
share the GPIO power lines with
other add-ons. Other clock boards
need more complex software. Some
also use a special connector that
prevents pin sharing.

Create a Python Webcam

You can connect a standard USB webcam to your Pi and use it as a camera. Most recent USB cams are compatible with the Pi, although very cheap or very old cams may not be. If you have a webcam you can experiment with it to see if it works.

The Pi does not include webcam software. You can use the camera features in Pygame to create a simple still webcam, embedding a Python/Pygame script in a web page, and adding one line of HTML to make it refresh automatically.

Create a Python Webcam

Note: You can find the code used in this section on this book's website, www.wiley.com/go/tyvraspberrypi.

1. Connect a webcam to your Pi's USB hub and reboot.

2. Launch the desktop and IDLE.

3. Type #!/usr/bin/python and press **Enter**.

Note: Add this line to the start of a file when you want to create a Python script.

4. Add code to import pygame, sys, the pygame camera module, and the Python time module.

5. Add code to initialize Pygame and the Pygame camera module.

6. Add code to set the width and height of the image and to load the image from /dev/video0.

7. Add code to open the camera, capture an image, close the camera, and save the image to a file.

8. Save the file as webcam.py to /var/www.

Note: If you get an error, save the file to your home directory and use File Manager in root mode to copy it to /var/www.

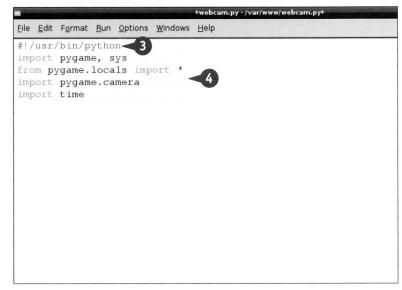

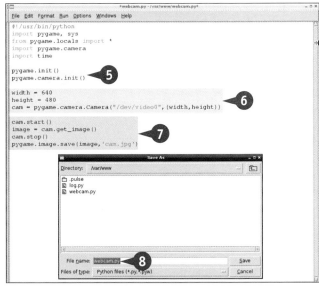

9 Launch LXTerminal.

10 Type `sudo chmod +x /var/www/webcam.py` and press `Enter`.

Note: Step **10** makes it possible for the web server to run the webcam script.

11 Type `sudo nano /var/www/cam.php` and press `Enter` to create a new PHP file.

12 Type `<META HTTP.EQUIV= Refresh CONTENT="3">` and press `Enter`.

Note: This line makes a webpage reload itself every 3 seconds.

13 Add code to run the webcam script using PHP's `exec` command.

14 Add a line to load and display the image created by the script.

15 Press `Ctrl`+`O`, press `Enter`, and press `Ctrl`+`X` to save and quit.

15 Open Midori at http://127.0.0.1/cam.php.

Note: On a networked computer, use `[your Pi's static address]/cam.php`.

The camera captures and displays stills every 3 seconds.

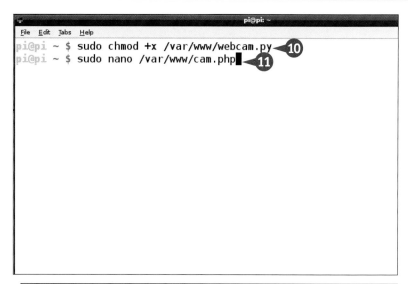

TIPS

Can I use the official Raspberry Pi camera?
Yes. The Raspberry Pi Foundation supplies an optional add-on camera that produces relatively good video and plugs into a special slot on the Pi board. You can use this camera instead of a USB webcam. Use the `raspistill` command to create an image instead of the Python script.

Can I make a live streaming webcam?
Not easily. Webcams are complex, and streaming video is even more complex. You can experiment with various tools and packages on the Pi, but none works reliably with all web browsers and webcam models. Investigate `motion`, `mjpg-streamer`, and `ffmpeg/fftsream` for some advanced possibilities.

Control a Relay

You can connect a relay to your Pi to switch power circuits. A *relay* is a logic-controlled switch. This example uses two relays controlled with 5V logic.

Because the Pi uses 3V logic you must use a level-converter board. The board in this example (supplied by Hobbytronics) has four lines with A (5V) and B (3V) connections. Each line works in either direction. The board is *through-hole plated*, which means there is metal through and around the holes on both sides. The holes work with jumper lead pins if you apply some side pressure to force a connection.

Control a Relay

1 Connect jumpers to the Vcc and the GND and a switch control pin on the relay board.

2 Plug the Vcc (5V) jumper into one of the breadboard power lines.

3 Plug the GND jumper into a track on the breadboard.

4 Place the level-converter board on the breadboard so the 0V hole lines up with GND.

Note: Use the diagram at www.modmypi. com/blog/raspberry-pi-gpio-cheat-sheet for steps **5** to **9**.

5 Connect your Pi's 5V power GPIO pins to the level converter and the power line.

6 Connect your Pi's 3V3 power GPIO pin to the level converter.

7 Connect GPIO pin 17 to one of the 3V3 B-side holes.

8 Connect the relay control from step **1** to the corresponding 5V A-side hole.

9 Insert a single jumper pin at the top or bottom of the converter board to force the holes to connect with the push pins inside them.

10 Boot your Pi, type `startx`, and press **Enter** to launch the desktop, and then launch IDLE.

11 Add code to load the GPIO and time modules, and set GPIO pin 17 as an output.

12 Add code to turn on GPIO 17, wait 4 seconds, and turn it off.

Note: If you use a different relay and/or converter, you may need to turn on your relay with logic 1 and turn it off with logic 0.

13 Save the file as relay.py.

14 In LXTerminal or at the command line, type `sudo python relay.py` and press **Enter**.

Your Pi switches the relay on, waits 4 seconds, and switches it off. The relay clicks when it switches. An LED indicates its state.

Note: You may need to repeat step **14** a couple of times until the circuit settles.

Note: You can now connect 12V lighting or some other circuit to the screw terminals on the relay. Modify the Python code as necessary.

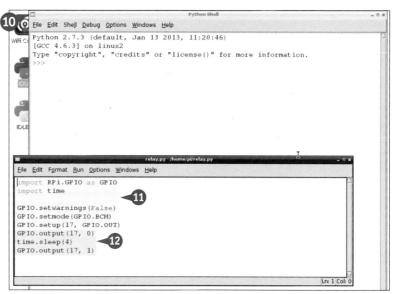

TIPS

Why do I need a relay?
Relays isolate power circuits from control systems like the Pi. You can use a relay to control 12V lighting circuits. You can also use it to switch a mains supply, but only if you have plenty of experience, life insurance, and legal indemnity cover. Mistakes with mains power can kill you and/or burn your house down. Work with it at your own risk.

Why are there no pins on the converter board?
Some add-on boards do not include jumper lead pins. You can either solder cables to them directly, or you can buy a breakaway header strip and add pins if you want them. Strips come in various *pitches*, or pin spacings. 0.1 inch is common. Make sure you buy the correct pitch for your board.

Learn to Solder

You can create long-lasting custom hardware by soldering components together. Many intermediate to advanced Pi kits require some soldering. You typically solder components to copper stripboard, which is described in the next section, "Create a Circuit on Stripboard," or to a premade circuit board.

Light your work area with a bright light, use a fine-tipped 15W or 25W soldering iron — available for $15 (£10) from electronics stores — and wait until the bit is hot before starting. Heat the joint for long enough to allow the solder to flow, and keep the joint still while the solder cools and sets.

Learn to Solder

1 Find or improvise a fireproof, melt-proof stand for the iron. Most kits include a basic stand.

2 If your kit does not include a sponge, find or improvise a wiper for the tip.

Note: You can use a wet pad of paper towels or toilet paper. Do not use a domestic dish scourer because the plastic will melt and damage your iron.

3 Plug in your soldering iron and wait for the tip to heat up.

Note: This can take a few minutes.

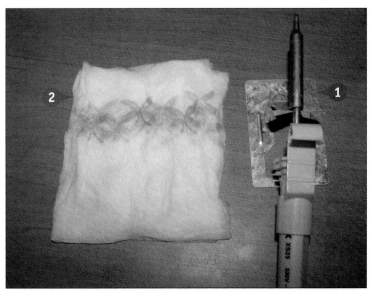

4 Hold a line of solder against the tip.

When the iron is ready to use, the solder melts instantly. If the iron is too cool, the solder does not melt.

Note: The first time you use an iron, "tin the bit" by melting solder on it, leaving it for a while, and wiping it clean. This conditions the bit and prolongs its life.

Note: Apply enough solder to cover the bit, but not so much that it splashes down the iron.

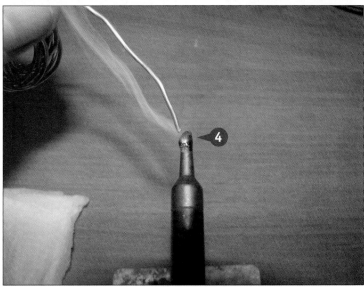

5 To solder a component to a board, insert the component leads through the correct holes so they stick out on the side with the copper strips or circuit traces.

6 Place the solder next to the component lead.

7 Apply the tip of the iron so it melts the solder and heats the pad and the component lead.

8 Wait until the solder melts, pause for a second, and remove the iron.

Note: This example uses too much solder to make the process clear. Use as little solder as possible to make a strong joint.

9 Do not disturb the joint for a few seconds while the joint cools.

Note: The component remains hot for 10 seconds or more. Do not touch it.

A A successful joint looks like a tiny hill. The joint should be solid. The component should not move.

B If the remaining lead is too long, snip it to size with snips or the cutting edge on a pair of pliers.

TIPS

How do I know which components go where?
Beginner-level kits often include a help sheet or web page with information about component identification and placing. Intermediate and advanced kits often *silk screen* — print, usually with white lettering — component orientation on the board, with component references you can check off against a list.

Where can I learn more about circuit diagrams?
You can find all the details you need online. Search for "basic electronics." Basic circuits use 15-20 standard component types. You do not need to understand circuit design to read a circuit. Note that some components need to be oriented correctly. If you place them the wrong way around they do not work, and the circuit may not work either.

Create a Circuit on Stripboard

You can use stripboard for small custom electronic circuits. *Stripboard* is a thin plastic laminate board with a grid of holes joined by lines of copper strips. To use stripboard, insert component leads and pins into the holes and solder them to the strips. You often need to cut some of the strips to avoid a short circuit.

If you breadboard a circuit, you can use the breadboard component layout as a starting point for a stripboard layout. Creating a working stripboard layout requires a combination of care, attention to detail, common sense, and occasionally some trial and error.

Create a Circuit on Stripboard

① Breadboard your circuit.

Note: This very simple example uses the LED circuit from the section "Control an LED with a Button."

② Look at the layout. Note the power lines, position of the circuit components jumpers, and whether the circuit needs to use the break in the middle of the breadboard.

Note: You can make the layout clearer by rotating the breadboard so that the strips are horizontal to match the horizontal lines on the stripboard.

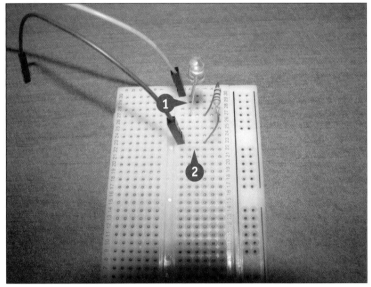

Ⓐ You can print out a stripboard guide and sketch the size and position of the components. Bend component leads and preplace the components to discover how many holes they cover.

Note: You can find free guides online. The number of holes and strips may not match your board. You can also use graph paper or even lined paper. Step **A** is optional but highly recommended.

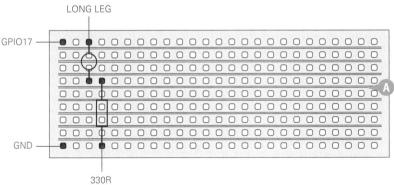

LONG LEG

GPIO17

GND

330R

294

3 Solder all the components to the stripboard.

Note: Start with the items that protrude the least from the top of the board. You can hold them in place with the weight of the board by turning it upside down, or with electrical tape, or with Blu-Tack.

Note: Use as little solder as possible so as not to join adjacent strips.

4 Cut the leads off the longer components.

5 Cut any tracks if you need to.

6 Connect and test your circuit.

The circuit should work correctly.

Note: If the circuit does not work, check for blobs of solder across strips, strips that should be cut but are not, components in the wrong places, components the wrong way around, or errors in the layout.

Note: A good first check is to make sure that power and other connections are correct. Use a digital multimeter (DMM) to test if the board is receiving the correct voltages.

TIPS

Is there an easy way to cut strips?
You can buy a special stripboard cutter tool. It looks and works somewhat like a sharpened screwdriver or drill bit. It costs a few dollars/pounds and is easy to find and buy online. You can also improvise a tool by embedding an old drill bit in the handle of an awl.

Is stripboard waterproof?
Stripboard is waterproof, as are most electronic components. But water is not an electrical insulator, so you must keep circuits dry to keep them working. One option is to set a circuit in a block of epoxy resin, which is available from hardware stores. Another is to add a waterproof case. Protection is defined by an IP (Ingress Protection) Code. IP67 is reasonably rainproof; IP68 can be submerged for long periods.

Understanding Further Options

You can use the skills you learned in this book to tackle more complex projects. Some possibilities include more complex sensors, video and audio expansion, a more powerful web server, and robotics. The Pi is only one example of a much wider world of single-board computers you can build into bigger projects.

Understanding Add-Ons

You can add various extras to your Pi, including small display panels with optional touch sensing, larger display screens, simple limited number/letter LCDs (liquid crystal displays), keypads and switch arrays, LED displays, various sensors, motors, and better audio among others.

Using Add-Ons

Although every add-on is different, most follow the same steps you learn in this book. You explore the options, connect them to the Pi's GPIO pins, install or build suitable software, often using someone else's "magic word" commands, and then customize the add-ons with your own code. You do not usually need advanced electronic design skills. But you do need to know basic Python and Linux.

```
GPIO.setmode(GPIO.BCM)
GPIO.setup(17, GPIO.OUT)
GPIO.setup(27, GPIO.IN)
while True:
    readButton = GPIO.input(27)
    GPIO.output(17, (not readButton))
    time.sleep(0.1)
```

Understanding Expansion Boards

You can connect individual components to your Pi by breadboarding them or soldering them onto stripboard. For convenience, you can also buy various pre-made expansion boards. Some boards include general features, such as a *prototyping area*, which is like a piece of stripboard that clips onto the Pi. Others add very specific extras, such as digital input and output pins, analog connectors that can measure or generate a varying voltage, *breakout boards* that make your Pi's pins more accessible with clear labels, and *buffers*, which protect your Pi's connections from damage.

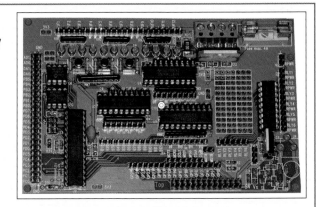

Understanding Arduino

The Arduino product range is a natural complement to the Pi. The range was designed as an affordable way to build systems around a computer chip that is even simpler and slower than the chip in the Pi. Arduino boards are available in a range of size, price, and performance options. You can extend the boards by plugging in *shields*, or expansion boards that slot on top of an Arduino to add a specific feature. Arduino boards have more electronic connection options than the Pi, and are supported by a wider range of free software and online tutorials. You can link a Pi and an Arduino together to get the best of both worlds.

Understanding C

The C language used with the Arduino is also available for free on the Pi. A full introduction to C is beyond the scope of an introductory book. In outline, you create software by writing code with an editor and passing it through a *compiler* tool called

```
//In c...
  main()
  {
      printf("Hello, world\n");
  }
```

cc. You typically build various sections of code separately, and link them together — also with cc — to create a finished binary. Because some projects have many files, you can use a tool called make, or an alternative called cmake, to manage the building and linking process.

Find Add-Ons

Adafruit Industries (www.adafruit.com) is one of the biggest suppliers of add-ons. Although based in the United States, you can find a list of international resellers on the website. Sparkfun (www.sparkfun.com) offers a wider range of components and options for constructors with some electronic design experience. In the United Kingdom, Ciseco (www.ciseco.co.uk), SK Pang (www.skpang.co.uk), and Cool Components (www.coolcomponents.co.uk) offer add-ons for the Pi and for other single-board computers.

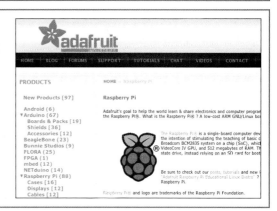

Index

Symbols and Numerics

A

B

Index

Index

Office

InDesign®

Facebook®

THE WAY YOU WANT TO LEARN.

HTML

Photoshop®

DigitalClassroom.com

Flexible, fast, and fun, DigitalClassroom.com lets you choose when, where, and how to learn new skills. This subscription-based online learning environment is accessible anytime from your desktop, laptop, tablet, or smartphone. It's easy, efficient learning — on *your* schedule.

- Learn web design and development, Office applications, and new technologies from more than 2,500 video tutorials, e-books, and lesson files
- Master software from Adobe, Apple, and Microsoft
- Interact with other students in forums and groups led by industry pros

Learn more! Sample DigitalClassroom.com for free, now!

We're social. Connect with us!

facebook.com/digitalclassroom
@digitalclassrm